© 2007 by SCALA Group, S.p.A., Firenze, su licenza E-ducation.it, Firenze

This 2007 edition published by Barnes & Noble, Inc. by arrangement with
SCALA Group, S.p.A.

Texts: Giulia Marrucchi, Riccardo Belcari
Project director: Cinzia Caiazzo
Editor-in-chief: Filippo Melli
Design: Gruppo Bandello Comunicazione
Graphics: Puntoeacapo srl
Translation: Johanna Kreiner, Jane Waller

ISBN-13: 978-0-7607-8887-5
ISBN-10: 0-7607-8887-1

Printed and bound in China

1 3 5 7 9 10 8 6 4 2

ART OF THE MIDDLE AGES

Giulia Marrucchi

Riccardo Belcari

BARNES & NOBLE

NEW YORK

TABLE OF CONTENTS

TABLE OF CONTENTS

TABLE **OF CONTENTS**

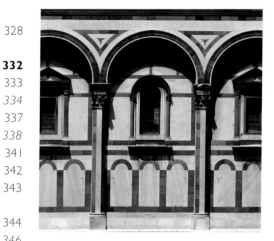

1. Paleochristian and Byzantine Art

In the year 313, when Constantine's edict conceded freedom of worship to Christians, the Church began to develop its own liturgy and to construct buildings for the gathering of the faithful. The new buildings did not propose new architectural schemes, but rather were developments of Roman structures, selected from those that were best adapted to the new requirements. The architectural models for churches were therefore not related to pagan temples but to the basilica, originally designed to house public assemblies, and the mausoleum with its centrally organized plan. The basilica was in fact designed to accommodate numerous worshipers in the distinct areas of the building: catechumens (converts prior to baptism) followed the rites from the quadriporticus, the faithful from the nave, the women from their special gallery (to the west), while the presbytery (to the east) was reserved for clergy. The centrally organized plan was used for mausoleums and baptisteries. Builders looked to Roman art for the technical and stylistic solutions as well: columns, capitals and architraves were often recovered directly from the ruins of Roman buildings, while the religious subject matter was the only aspect that distinguished the mosaics from other contemporary compositions.

2

3

1. Facing page: Barberini Ivory, detail of the emperor, early 6th century. Paris, Musée du Louvre.

2. *Doves drinking from a fountain*, 5th century. Ravenna, Mausoleum of Galla Placidia.

3. Sant'Apollinare in Classe, capital, mid-6th century. Ravenna.

FROM PAGAN ROME TO CHRISTIAN ROME: ARTISTIC MONUMENTS IN THE CITY OF PETER

The most famous basilicas were built in Rome immediately after the Edict of Constantine. This city had been witness to many martyrdoms and often the new religious buildings were located in the places where Christians had died. The ancient basilica of Saint Peter, for example, was built where Peter had been crucified during the persecutions under the emperor Nero. Begun in 324 and consecrated in 326 by Pope Sylvester, it was modified many times until Nicholas V, in the 15th century, began to consider a totally new building. The project of transformation did not begin until the papacy of Julius II who decided to demolish the ancient basilica at the beginning of the 16th century. The paleochristian church was a basilica with a central nave and two aisles on either side, separated by four lines of twenty-four columns bearing a straight architrave. The roof rested on wooden trusses, and there was a quadriporticus in front of the entrance for catechumens. Thanks to these new buildings Rome acquired a new importance in the Christian world and became the center of Christianity, although it gradually lost its role as political capital. The events of the 5th century accelerated the decline of the Rome, while raising other cities to imperial roles.

4

4. Giovan Battista Ricci da Novara, *Reconstruction of the interior of the ancient basilica of Saint Peter in Rome*, 16th century. Rome, Saint Peter, Sacristy.

THE IMAGES IN THE CATACOMBS

The ancient Christian cemeteries were underground galleries where the dead were laid to rest until the final resurrection. They were called catacombs from the local place name, ad catacumbas, which meant "near the hollow", of one of the first of these cemeteries: the catacombs of Saint Sebastian on the Appian Way. Situated along the main consular roads that led into the countryside outside of Rome, the catacombs were structured as a series of galleries on several levels, to make the best possible use of the space available. The loculi or burial niches were excavated in the walls of the passages, and were identified by symbols of the faith, inscriptions or images. An anchor, a fountain, a dove with an olive branch, a palm leaf or a crown, were all references to hope, solace, peace and the rewards of life after death. The symbols were often accompanied by paintings which expressed the hope of Salvation: the Good Shepherd who saved his sheep, Daniel who survived the lions, the three youths who survived the furnace in Babylonia, Noah who survived the flood. Other images refer to faith in the resurrection, such as Lazarus who intervened for the faithful or Christ who healed the blind and paralytics. The Madonna, the apostles, and the martyrs were depicted as they prayed for and assisted the community of the Church.

5

7

6

5. *Three men in the furnace,* 3rd century. Rome, Catacombs of Priscilla.

6. *The Good Shepherd,* 3rd century. Rome, Catacombs of Priscilla.

7. *Noah and the dove,* 2nd century. Rome, Catacombs of Saint Peter and Saint Marcellinus.

THE REPRESENTATION OF CHRIST

Between the 2nd and 5th centuries the Church elaborated the dogma of Christ from the gospels: Christ, who incorporates truly divine and human nature, is both God and man united in a unique person. He was sent to earth by his Father to save humanity from sin, and he was born to Mary, the Virgin descended from David. He lived and died on earth, and was resurrected to ascend to Heaven where he will reign for eternity. During the paleochristian era Christ was often depicted symbolically, as a fish (the Greek word *ichthus* is an acrostic of the expression "Jesus Christ son of God the Savior"), and through the images of other animals: the lamb, for example, sacrificed during the Hebrew observance of Passover referred to the sacrifice of Jesus, as did the mother pelican plucking at her breast to feed her young with her own blood. During the 4th and 5th centuries the iconographies of the principal themes of Christ's message were developed and were used until the Middle Ages to illustrate the concepts of doctrine: the image of the Good Shepherd, for example, represented the idea of God's love for mankind, while most of the other iconographies focused on the concept of Christ the conqueror who, garbed as a warrior, tramples the monsters described in Psalm 91. The image of the Savior seated among the apostles referred to the prophesies of Christ; the imperial iconography, where Christ is depicted frontally, enthroned between the apostles Peter and Paul with the cosmic symbols of his reign at his feet, represented his sovereign role. The same theme was further developed in the *Traditio legis*, which shows Christ handing a scroll to Paul, or in *Giving the Keys of the Kingdom to Saint Peter*, which the papal see used to affirm the dominant role of the Roman church. Sometimes the figure of Christ enthroned was surrounded by the apostles, who were charged by their Master to evangelize the world; in other examples the figure of

Christ is surrounded by an oval lozenge and is flanked by the four symbols of the Evangelists, known as *Maiestas Domini*, the most characteristic representation of the revelation of Christ to man. Later the same scheme was modified to include the symbols of the Passion: Christ is still enthroned, but his body is partially revealed to show the wounds in his hands and his side. According to the doctrines of the 12th century, it was precisely his suffering that bestowed the universal kingdom on Christ and qualified him to judge. At the same time, the image of the dead Christ began to dominate in the iconography of the Crucifixion, replacing the older formula of the living, triumphant Christ.

9

8

8. *Sarcophagus with Adoration of the Magi*, detail. Rome, Vatican Palaces, Pio Christian Museum.

9. *The Good Shepherd*, 3rd-4th century. Rome, Vatican Palaces, Pio Christian Museum.

THE CATACOMBS OF SAINT CALLISTUS

The complex of Saint Callistus, which includes various catacombs as well as churches, chapels, funeral monuments and mausoleums, is located at the center of the archeological area delineated by the Ancient Appia and Ardeatina roads and Vicolo delle Sette Chiese. The galleries, on four levels, are over 12 miles long and they are estimated to have provided a resting place for 500,000 burials. The name of this large Christian cemetery comes from that of the deacon Callistus (or Callixtus) who administered it during the pa-

pacy of Zephyrinus (199-217) and enlarged the existing structure, which had become the official burial place of the Roman church. Callistus himself then became pope (217-222). These catacombs remained ecclesiastical for a long time, as is evidenced by the numerous inscriptions which relate to church dignitaries buried there, together with public officials, artisans and traders. The prevalence of upper-class burials may help to explain the strong monumental aspect of the whole area, which includes many painted chambers, others decorated with stone inlays and mosaics, and chambers with skylights also decorated with paintings. In the open spaces of

10

11

10. Catacombs of Saint Callistus, crypt of the popes, late 2nd-early 3rd century. Rome.

11. Catacombs of Saint Callistus, *The Good Shepherd*, 3rd century. Rome.

the grid of galleries, there were richly decorated sarcophagi.

The complex consists of several nuclei that were connected during the 4th century: the oldest areas include Area I and the zones of Gaius and Eusebius; later the areas of pope Miltiades, Soteris, Liberiana and the so-called Labyrinth were added.

Area I includes two separate underground complexes that date from the end of the 2nd century. The Popes' Crypt, with the most ancient tombs of the popes, is here. Behind this, the crypt of Saint Cecilia, where all the martyr's relics were kept until they were transferred by Pope Paschal I to Santa Cecilia in Trastevere, was built in the 4th century. The chamber of Orpheus is just beyond the Popes' Crypt, where the mythical hero is depicted on the ceiling while he plays his lyre, seated on a large stone.

In another gallery there are five small chambers painted in the 3rd century, known as the "Sacraments" because the iconography was previously thought to represent them symbolically. Actually, some of the subjects are repeated in more than one chamber: the banquet scene appears in all five, the Jonah cycle in four, the Good Shepherd in two. In the area of Gaius and Eusebius, built in the 3rd century, there are many chambers with painted decorations, including those of the "pecorelle" (little sheep) with the Good Shepherd, others with scenes of Moses and the miracle of the loaves. Other chambers with painted decorations are to be found in the Miltiades zone, named for the last pope entombed there, including the one called "four seasons" in honor of the ceiling decoration with flowers and birds. The Soteris area, constructed circa 325-375, includes a central plan chamber and a gallery with a remarkable painting of the Adoration of the Magi, a theme that was later very widely used, with the Madonna and Child, and the Magi kings who offer their gifts.

12

20

12. Catacombs of Saint Callistus, *Fish and eucharistic bread,* **detail. Rome.**

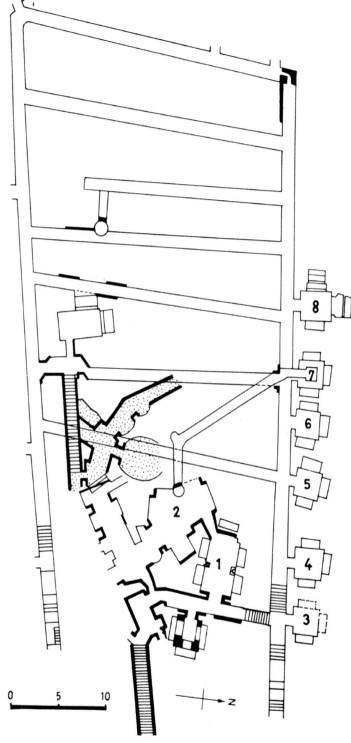

The decorations were mainly applied to the ceilings of the chambers, where they were developed with central symmetry: a central medallion is the starting point for rays that define different geometric areas which contain just as many different decorations and subjects.

In addition to the biblical subjects already mentioned, there are scenes and figures from daily life, with reference to commercial activities but also to the *fossores*, or grave-diggers, who were responsible for the burial of the dead and had acquired a role in the religious hierarchy. These officials are often represented in the catacomb wall paintings: in chamber A3 of the Sacraments, from the first half of the 3rd century, the grave-diggers appear at the sides of a rich decoration, with a central banquet scene surrounded by Jonah's Repose, Imposition of the Hands, and Abraham's Sacrifice. The inscriptions and graffiti are also a source of important historical evidence. An epigraph on a marble transenna, or screen, includes the first use of the expression "p(a)p(a)" or pope, referring to Pope Marcellinus (296-304). Marble slabs with inscriptions of Pope Damascus' elegies for saints and martyrs are a special case, in relation to the martyrs of this complex.

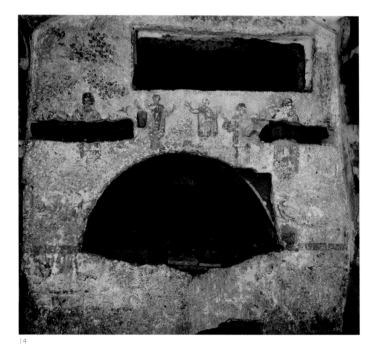

13. **Plan of the Catacombs of Saint Callistus** (from the *Encyclopedia of ancient art*, Rome 1959, vol. II, p. 418).

14. **Catacombs of Saint Callistus, chamber of the Five Saints, wall paintings of praying figures. Rome.**

These catacombs are located on the Via Salaria and may have been named for the owner and donor of the land where they were built. Under the protection offered by the emperor Constantine, the Church was finally able to access the resources it needed to continue its mission. This affected the catacombs as well: they were enlarged and new decorated spaces were added, as was true for the catacombs of Priscilla too during the first quarter century. The complex is composed of three areas: the Arenario nucleus, the "Greek chapel" nucleus, and the Acilii hypogeum complex. In the Arenario, used for group burials, the Old and New Testaments are evoked together in a single image: the Madonna and Child are depicted facing a third figure, thought to be a prophet (Isaiah perhaps). The painting has recently been dated to between 230 and 250. The Arenario also includes the "Velatio" chamber, decorated with numerous paintings depicting Biblical episodes, including Jonah and the Whale, Abraham's Sacrifice, and Three young Hebrews in the Furnace, dated to between 260 and 280. At the center of the ceiling there is a medallion with the Good Shepherd, between two couples of quails and peacocks: earthly birds on the one hand, heavenly birds on the other. The chamber is particularly well known for the image, in the lunette, of the deceased woman wearing a red robe and a veil, in the act of praying. The scene has been interpreted as *velatio virginis*, or the consecration of a virgin by the bishop. The decorations of the chamber reflect the iconography of everyday life and the new artistic trends inspired by the biblical tradition. The nucleus known as the "Greek chapel" or "crypto-portico", divided into zones A and B, owes its name to the presence of red inscriptions in Greek. The cycle of Susanna was depicted above

a painted wainscot that imitates slabs of marble. Cosmic themes, in a Christian interpretation, were depicted on the ceiling that is quite damaged. In the cooper's chamber, a realistic scene from daily life was depicted: a compact group of coopers transport a cask, a clear reference to the earthly activity of the deceased. The paintings in the catacomb chambers are accompanied by symbolic inscriptions included among the funeral inscriptions. The symbols are nothing more than iconographical references, although still quite evocative, such as the dove with an olive branch which alluded to the end of the universal Deluge; a fish, a ship or an anchor, which represented the theme of the journey of life.

15

16

17

15. Catacombs
of Priscilla, 1st floor
central gallery,
3rd century. Rome.

16. Chamber of the veiled
woman, lunette with
praying figure, 260-80.
Rome, Catacombs
of Priscilla.

17. Catacombs
of Priscilla, The coopers,
3rd century. Rome.

ARCHITECTURE AND MOSAICS IN THE BASILICA OF SAINT MARY MAJOR

The basilica of Saint Mary Major is one of the most grandiose historical documents of paleochristian architecture in Rome. It was built in the middle of the 5th century in the Suburra quarter, a common-place neighborhood, so the location of the church was more central than previous basilicas, which had been built in outlying areas by imperial orders to perpetuate the cult of the first Christian martyrs. It was the first church in Rome to be dedicated to the Virgin Mary. Inside a 17th century façade it conserves its original aspect, only slightly disturbed by the golden caisson ceiling and the two arches that interrupt the lateral colonnades at the transept, which was added in the 13th century together with the polygonal apse. It has a basilica plan with lateral colonnades; straight architraves, like those in the original Saint Peter, rest on Ionic capitals. Above the architrave pilasters rise to the ceiling, outlining mosaic panels and windows. Many decorations enrich the architecture of the building, focusing attention on the harmonious and grandiose forms of the central nave. The lighting is carefully studied to contribute to this effect: the central nave is illuminated by the

18

**18. Saint Mary Major,
central nave,
5th century. Rome.**

19. *Adoration of the Magi*,
detail of the mosaic on
the arch of triumph, first
half of the 5th century.
Rome, Saint Mary Major.

20. *Return of the
explorers*, mosaic of the
central nave, first half
of the 5th century.
Rome, Saint Mary Major.

21. *Crossing the Red Sea*,
mosaic of the central
nave, first half of the 5th
century. Rome,
Saint Mary Major.

light from the windows, while the lateral aisles remain in the shadows. The wall surfaces are enlivened by color and reflected light, thus reducing the perception of their solidity. The walls are decorated with rich cycles of mosaics from a vast iconographical repertory which united stories from the Old and New Testaments and others from apocryphal gospels. The episodes from the Childhood of Christ are depicted on the arch of triumph, one after another, in long overlapping strips. A gem-studded throne stands at the center, surrounded by Peter and Paul and the four symbols of the evangelists: a crown and a cross appear on the cushion, and represent the divinity which is present but invisible.

The story begins from the upper left with the scene of the Annunciation: the Virgin is seated on a throne and is surrounded by angels in the temple where, according to apocryphal texts, she had been nourished since her childhood, while the announcing angel is still flying toward her against a sky of red clouds. The next scene on the same side is the Adoration of the Magi, who present their gifts to the Christ Child seated on a rich throne and flanked by angels, the Madonna

and a mysterious female figure who may personify the Church. On the other side of the arch, the scene of Presentation in the temple is depicted against the background of a colonnade, with the scene of the angel appearing to Joseph in a dream to one side. The prophetic revelation induced Joseph to flee to Egypt, where the family was offered hospitality by a prince, as illustrated in the scene below. In the space below, the Magi kings are received by Herod, who orders the Massacre of the Innocents. At the base of the arch, the cities of Bethlehem and Jerusalem are depicted with gem-studded walls, like the descriptions in the apocalyptic visions. The entire cycle, with the rich vestments, the luminous gold backgrounds, the compositions which show the biblical personages seated on precious thrones flanked by processions of angels, is particularly rich and emphatic. The episodes depicted along the nave, from the lives of Abraham, Jacob, Moses and Joshua, are quite different: in these scenes the figures are defined in three dimensions and are depicted in natural environments, against green fields and blue skies, where they move freely and interact with one another as illustrated by vivacious gestures and glances.

22

**22. Saint Mary Major,
arch of triumph, first half
of the 5th century.
Rome.**

ABRAHAM AND THE ANGELS

**First half of the 5th century
Rome, Saint Mary Major**

SUBJECT

The representation of *Abraham and the Angels* includes two distinct moments of the biblical story that are developed in two spaces against a single background, only slightly disturbed by the varied proportions of the figures.

The figures in the upper space, which illustrates the prologue of the episode, appear smaller and more distant: Abraham runs toward the angels, silhouetted against the fiery sky like a vision.

In the lower space the patriarch is depicted twice in the same scene: on one side he gives orders to his wife who is preparing the repast in front of his house, decorated with a cross on the gable;

on the other side, he gracefully serves his three mysterious guests, who have announced the birth of a son.

COMPOSITION

The narration is divided into two spaces, against a single naturalistic background.

The mosaicist did not find it necessary to separate the scenes with decorative or architectural frames: some elements, such as the branch of the tree and the roof of the house, actually invade the upper space, without disturbing the organic whole of the space.

The space of each scene is rigorously constructed. In the lower space it is even outlined and defined by the sloping planes of two tables which guide the lines of perspective in the composition. In this way a real, inhabited space is created, in which the figures move freely and are distributed in the depth of the scene.

Despite the artifice of the composition, necessary for clarity of narration, the mosaic has a naturalistic character which is evident in the expanse of the green fields, in the limpid and luminous sky with scattered clouds, in the solid volumes of the figures that cast long shadows on the ground.

THE BASILICA OF SAINT SABINA

The church was built on the Aventine hill during the first half of the 5th century by the Illyrian priest Peter, on the site where the matron Sabina's house originally stood. It was restored to its original appearance at the beginning of this century after radical renovation was undertaken: the caisson ceiling was removed, which restored its ancient interior proportions; the clerestory windows of the central nave and apse were re-opened, which restored light and color to the interior of the church. Now reached through a 15th century portico, Saint Sabina has a basilica plan with three aisles separated by colonnades; the capitals were recovered from an earlier building, probably of the 2nd century. A series of arches spring from the colonnades, leading the eye of the worshiper directly to the apse, and separate the extremely high, long and wide central nave from the lateral aisles. This effect is heightened by a carefully studied use of the light which floods in through the high arched windows to illuminate the central hall and the refined decorations of the pendentives where chalices, patens and symbols of Christ were represented with marble inlays. The stylistic uniformity, the elegant proportions, the rich decorations, the careful selection and disposition of antique materials, all make this an exceptional building. The sober beauty of its forms represents the classical rebirth promoted by the popes of the 5th century, when the grandeur of the imperial Roman capital was a constant source of esthetic and ideological inspiration. The new Rome of the papacy came forward as an heir to the ancient city, and was full of grandiose building projects that were intended to elevate the city to its bygone splendor.

23

**23. Saint Sabina, apse,
5th century. Rome.**

24

25

24. Saint Sabina, capitals
and marble inlays,
5th century. Rome.

25. Saint Sabina, central
nave, 5th century. Rome.

THE WOODEN DOOR

The door of the basilica of Saint Sabina is a rare example of wooden sculpture from the early centuries of Christian art. It originally included twenty-eight rectangular panels of different sizes, illustrating episodes from the Old and New Testaments. Carved in cypress wood during the first half of the 5th century, the panels are surrounded by a double frame. The internal frame quietly accompanies the smooth edges of the panels with vegetal motif decorations, while the external frame presents a more exuberant, perforated decoration of grape vines. In the eighteen surviving scenes, it is clear that two workshops with distinct stylistic languages were involved. The first workshop, which produced the scene of *Elijah and the Chariot of Fire*, had a refined, naturalistic style. The figures, with their lengthened proportions and soft contours, are inserted into an airy composition characterized by naturalistic details such as the outline of a tree and the cliff where a lizard is fleeing. The narration depends on the clear gestures of the participants: the miracle takes form in the commanding presence of the angel, who leans toward Elijah to grasp his mantle, while two peasants withdraw in fear. The second workshop divides the spaces to separate the narration of separate incidents: a single panel includes the Healing of the blind, the Miracle of the loaves and the fish, the Wedding at Cana, with stocky figures who make uncertain gestures in spaces with uncertain perspective construction.

This work illustrates the fact that by the 5th century, along side the artisans of the classical tradition, there were less refined artists who introduced the medieval style.

26   27   28

26. *Elijah taken up to Heaven*, detail of the wooden door, about 422-32. Rome, Saint Sabina.

27. *Triumph of the Christian Empire*, detail of the wooden door, about 422-32. Rome, Saint Sabina.

28. *The mission of Moses*, detail of the wooden door, about 422-32. Rome, Saint Sabina.

29. Facing page: Wooden doors, about 422-32. Rome, Saint Sabina.

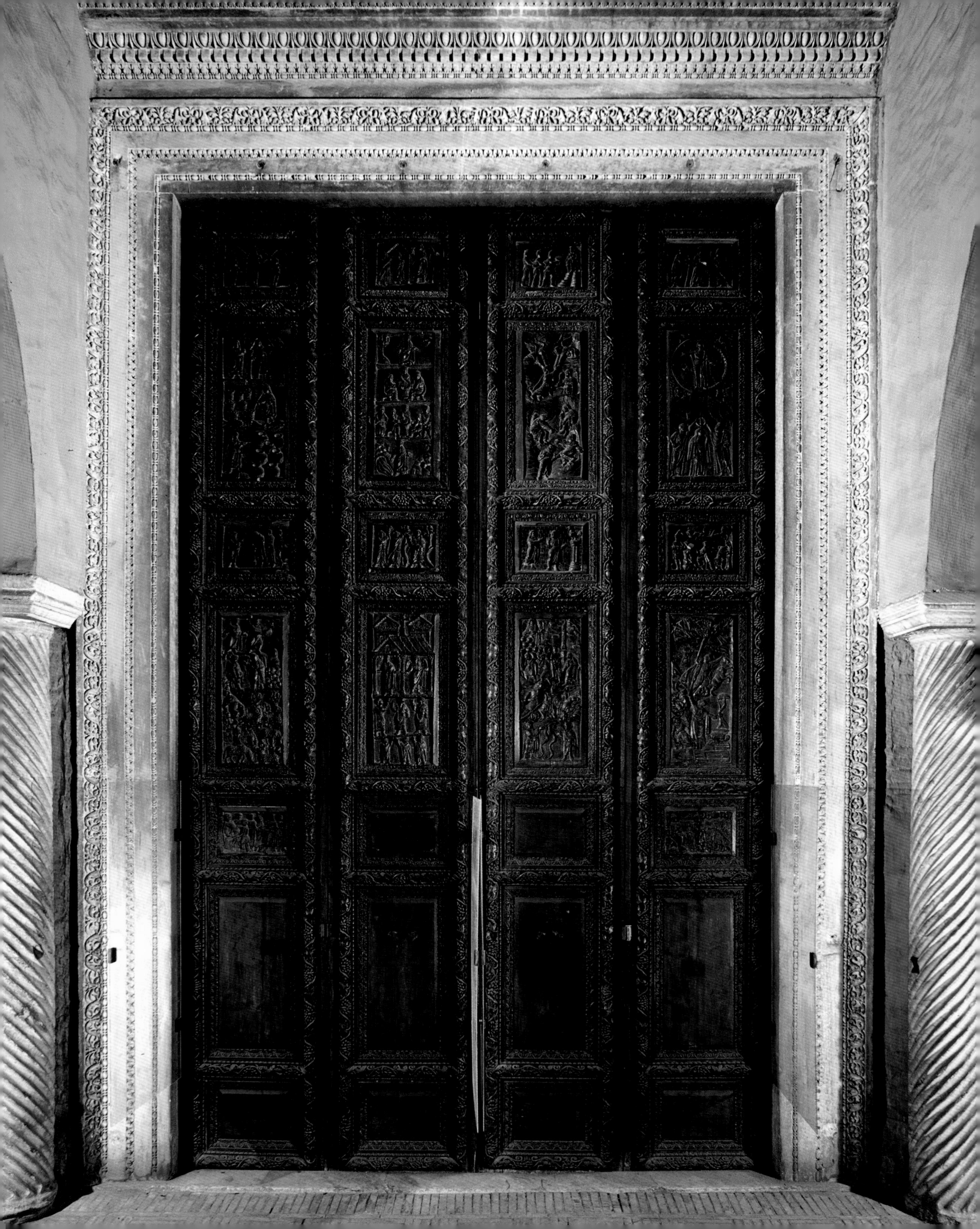

THE MAUSOLEUM OF SAINT CONSTANCE

Among the buildings that represent the inheritance of the Christian world from the classical world, Saint Constance is one of the most important examples. The church reproduced the scheme of the great imperial mausoleums with its circular plan, mosaic decorations and the circular corridor surrounding the central space where the sarcophagus of the saint is located. However the ancient architectural scheme was charged with new significance, through the play of light that was interpreted as a symbol of divine grace. Flowing in through the large clerestories above the drum and through the opening at the center of the dome, daylight illuminates the central space of the building. The space is surrounded by a double row of columns with Corinthian capitals (and a fragment of straight architrave) which define the border of the shadowy circular corridor with its barrel vault completely covered with mosaic decorations. Here there are a series of separate panels

30

30. Mausoleum of Saint Constance, façade, 4th century. Rome.

**31. Mausoleum of Saint
Constance, interior,
4th century. Rome.**

with various decorations, similar to precious textiles, separated by frames of vegetal elements and ribbons: designs of crosses and stars, braids surrounding medallions, faces and winged figures, animals and birds, bundles of grain, branches with flowers and fruit, peacocks and other amazing birds, all set off against stark white backgrounds. The figurative repertory evidently harked back to classical iconography but often acquired a new symbolic significance. The theme of the grape harvest, for example, was frequently depicted in ancient art along with the other agricultural events that marked the calendar, but now referred to the wine of the Eucharist and the sacrifice of Christ, the salvation of mankind. The image itself was not modified however: the grapevines cover the entire vault while birds continue to pluck at the bunches being gathered by the young harvesters. Others lead the loaded wagons to the vats where a few putti are vigorously treading on the grapes.

32

**32. *Portrait of Constantine,*
detail of the ceiling
mosaic, 4th century.
Rome, Mausoleum
of Saint Constance.**

33

34

33. *The blessing of Christ,*
mosaic in the lunette
of the apse, 4th century.
Rome, Mausoleum
of Saint Constance.

34. *The grape harvest,*
detail of the ceiling
mosaic, 4th century
Rome, Mausoleum
of Saint Constance.

The sarcophagus of princess Constance, daughter of the emperor Constantine, currently exhibited in the Vatican Museums, was originally located in the Mausoleum of Saint Constance. The form and the material, which are different from those produced in Rome, suggest to scholars that it was fabricated in the Orient about the middle of the 4th century and then transported to Rome. Porphyry was considered an extremely precious material, and was usually used only in Imperial commissions, which could also justify the employment of foreign craftsmen. The decoration is based on the usual theme of the grape harvest. Alluding as it did to the wine of the Eucharist, the theme was often associated with funeral monuments. Under a festoon sustained by human masks, the curled sprays of vines were sculpted in high relief to frame the illustrated scenes. Plump little putti are busy gathering bunches of grapes that are later pressed in enormous vats, while the scenes also include figures of animals such as peacocks and rams.

35

35. *Sarcophagus of Constantina*, detail of the putti harvesting grapes, mid-4th century. Rome, Vatican Palaces, Pio Christian Museum.

36. *Sarcophagus of
Constantina*, mid-4th century.
Rome, Vatican Palaces,
Pio Christian Museum.

SARCOPHAGUS OF GIUNIO BASSO
3rd or 4th century
Rome, Vatican Grotto in the Basilica of Saint Peter

The sarcophagus prepared for the prefect of Rome, Giunio Basso, like that for Constantina, included classical elements interpreted according to the new Christian symbolism.

The epigraph inscribed on the upper cornice of the sarcophagus indicates the name of the person buried inside and the year of his death, 359. Some scholars date the fabrication of the sarcophagus to this year, others date it earlier on the basis of the solid volumes of the figures and the clear conception of their space.

Episodes from the Old and New Testaments are illustrated on the front, in a sequence based on symbolic correspondence and composition rather than chronological order.

Christ occupies a central position in both orders: in the upper scenes he is seated on a throne, with the cosmos at his feet, symbolizing the universality of his reign, and Peter and Paul at his sides; in the lower scenes he is depicted as he entered Jerusalem riding on a mule.

The lateral faces have symmetrical compositions: the arrest of Peter corresponds to the arrest of Christ;

two figures have been added to the traditional representation of Daniel in the lion's den, to match the distribution of the elements in the corresponding panel on the other side, where Adam and Eve stand at the sides of the tree of knowledge.

COMPOSITION

The sculptor has constricted the relief of the scenes into a framework of architectural elements. The episodes are organized in two orders, separated by columns with Corinthian and composite capitals, which separate deep cavities where the figures in high relief move with ease.

The architectural grid is softened by rich decoration, which swathes the column shaft with sprays of vegetation or fluting, and finishes the straight architrave of the upper order with a cornice.

The carving is particularly elaborate in the lower order where the niches are finished alternately with arches and gables, and some animal figures are inserted in the triangular spaces above the columns.

The scenes at the edges of the sarcophagus are also based on symmetry: the figure of Job seated on the dunghill corresponds, on the other end, to Pilate,

while the *Sacrifice of Isaac* contrasts with the *Arrest of Paul*.

MILAN CAPITAL CITY AND THE BASILICA OF SAN LORENZO

At the end of the 4th century, after the death of Emperor Theodosius, the empire was definitively divided into the Eastern Empire with capital in Constantinople, and the Western Empire. The Western capital was transferred to Milan due to the decay of Rome, and Milan enjoyed a period of great artistic splendor and building fervor that culminated with the construction of the Basilica of San Lorenzo. The building represented a turning point in the history of paleochristian architecture. It was located not far from the residence of the emperor, and was the first large church with a central plan. It functioned as the church of the palace, and it was therefore taken as a model for a long series of imperial churches built later everywhere in Europe.

The basilica of Milan, had a great front quadriporticus built mostly with columns recovered from the ruins of pagan buildings, and the building itself had a square plan with impressive angle towers.

On each of the four sides, four great semicircular chapels extend beyond the perimeter of the building, dilating the internal space which was originally covered by a great dome.

37

38

**37. Basilica
of San Lorenzo Maggiore,
exterior, late 4th-early 5th
century. Milan.**

**38. Basilica
of San Lorenzo Maggiore,
interior, late 4th-early 5th
century. Milan.**

ART OF THE 5TH CENTURY IN RAVENNA

In the year 402 the emperor Honorius abandoned Milan and transferred the capital of the empire to Ravenna, a small city with a port on the Adriatic Sea, naturally protected by the surrounding marshes. Until the year 476, when the Western empire fell, the Adriatic city led the weak empire, lacerated by internal struggles and the attacks of the barbarians. Ravenna was provided with the new architecture that was appropriate for its new role. The extraordinary artistic flowering left traces such as the Orthodox Baptistery and the Mausoleum of Galla Placidia. Honorius' sister was also responsible for the construction of the church of Saint John the Evangelist. Divided into three aisles by two colonnades, it includes elements that became typical of the basilicas of Ravenna, in the form of the apse, and the truncated pyramidal impost block (or dosseret block) set above the capitals of the columns. The mosaic decorations illustrate the trend away from the concrete and realistic vision of the world that came from Western sources, to a more abstract artistic language that originated in the Orient, more adapted to the new symbolic requirements of Christianity.

39

40

39. Saint John the Evangelist, interior, about 430. Ravenna.

40. *Saint Lawrence*, detail of a lunette mosaic, 5th century. Ravenna, Mausoleum of Galla Placidia.

THE MAUSOLEUM OF GALLA PLACIDIA

Tradition has linked the name of Galla Placidia, Emperor Honorius' sister, who was regent between 425 and 450 in the name of her son Valentinian, and who fervently continued the patronage of the arts initiated in Rome by her father Theodosius I, with the construction of this building. The building, now below current ground level, has a cross form plan, with barrel vaults over the four transepts and a dome at the center.

On the exterior the dome is enclosed in a square tower that rises above the lateral wings, each crowned by a gable with a heavy cornice. The external appearance of the building is characterized by the geometric division of the masses, emphasized by the sober brick surface, slightly enlivened by a series of blind arches.

The architectural characteristics of the interior of the small cross form oratory are literally transfigured by the brilliant mosaic decorations, that were installed above high marble paneling on the walls. The light that filters timidly through the alabaster panels of the windows illuminates the great gold cross that occupies the center of the dome, against a blue sky where the stars are aligned in concentric circles and the symbols of the evangelists float among the clouds.

41

41. Mausoleum of Galla Placidia, exterior, 5th century. Ravenna.

42. Facing page: Mausoleum of Galla Placidia, interior, 5th century. Ravenna.

The cross, symbol of the death and resurrection of Christ, is acclaimed by the apostles who occupy the lunettes below, swathed in their candid tunics, underneath giant shell-like canopies which augment their dignity. Among them Saint Peter may be recognized by the key he holds in his hand, and Saint Paul with his long face, pointed beard and bald head.

The lunettes at the ends of the main wing of the building have more complex decorations, where the mosaicist attempted to recreate a more naturalistic atmosphere and gave the image the appearance of narrating a story. Christ appears in the role of Good Shepherd above the entry, his divinity manifested in the golden tunic, his purple mantel, his halo and the cross he carries in place of the curved staff of the shepherd. His body moves freely in the surrounding space, and is the focal point of the composition, gathering the groups of sheep, which expressly do not respect any rigid symmetry.

The treatment of their fleece, and likewise the treatment of the rocky landscape with its occasional tufts of grass, reveal the artist's intention to mimic reality. The same characteristics are to be found in the opposite lunette, where Saint Lawrence walks briskly and freely toward the gridiron of his martyrdom, faced in the name of the Gospel, the four books of which appear in the open closet.

43

43. *The Good Shepherd*,
lunette mosaic,
5th century. Ravenna,
Mausoleum of Galla
Placidia.

THE ORTHODOX BAPTISTERY

The Baptistery of Saint John at the Spring was built next to the ancient cathedral which was destroyed in the 5th century. Today its proportions are quite different because the ground level has risen significantly. The building is known by a variety of other names: it is called Neonian in honor of its founder, Bishop Neone; it is also known as the Orthodox baptistery in honor of those who followed the official doctrine of the Church and to distinguish it from the Arian baptistery, that of the heretics who denied the divine nature of Christ according to the doctrine of Arius.

As in the case of the Mausoleum of Galla Placidia, the interior of the building with its rich decorations of marble and mosaics, contrasts starkly with the simple and linear forms of the exterior. The external walls of the baptistery are constructed in simple brickwork, with limited decorative elements of blind arches and pilasters in low relief on the upper part of the drum. Below the large windows that are centered on each side of the octagon, there are four projecting apses alternated with four doors, today almost completely below ground level.

The octagonal hall is almost entirely covered with polychrome decorations: marble inlays and stuccos are combined for the dou-

44

45

44. Orthodox Baptistery, interior, mid-5th century. Ravenna.

45. Orthodox Baptistery, exterior, mid-5th century. Ravenna.

46

ble order of the blind arches of the walls, and culminate in the brilliant mosaic decorations of the dome. Built with a system of clay tubes that greatly reduced the weight of the dome, the interior surface of the dome itself is divided into three concentric zones. The ideological and actual center of the composition represents the Baptism of Christ: the nude figure of Jesus is depicted against a gold background, half immersed in the waters of the Jordan River, personified by the elderly bearded man to his right. On the other side, Saint John stands on the rocky shore.

A slow, solemn procession of the twelve apostles is depicted in the order below the central disk, which has been subjected to many restorations; the apostles are separated by golden candlesticks with floral motifs and are accompanied by drapes which form a festoon behind each apostle's head. The mosaicist developed the faces like portraits, and alternated the colors of the tunics and cloaks to add rhythm to the composition. In the lowest section eight candelabra separate eight sections, subdivided by architectural elements into an apse flanked by two porticos, containing altars, thrones and gardens. These include a representation of the heavenly Jerusalem, to which the gardens of paradise refer, the

47

46. Cupola mosaic,
detail with lectern,
mid-5th century.
Ravenna, Orthodox
Baptistery.

47. Orthodox Baptistery,
interior, detail of marble
inlays, mid-5th century.
Ravenna.

48. Cupola mosaic with
the Baptism of Christ,
mid-5th century.
Ravenna, Orthodox
Baptistery.

empty thrones for the elect, the throne of Christ under the sign of a cushion and a cross.

A stucco decoration at the height of the windows of the baptistery seems to reproduce a tromp-l'oeil image of the women's gallery of the early Christian churches.

Each side of the octagon is divided into three niches by marble columns with Ionic capitals. Small stucco shrines, with a shell at the center of the semicircular or triangular pediment are inserted in the lateral arches.

These frame rigidly frontal masculine figures holding open books and closed scrolls; for this reason they have been identified as representations of the prophets of the Old Testament. With the exception of the hands and the faces, characterized by wide-open eyes, the bodies appear quite flat; in fact the folds of their garments, rather than developing volume, cover the surface with thin engraving.

Originally, this effect was undoubtedly diminished by the polychrome finishing which was an integral part of this type of sculpture: the stuccos were modeled to be colored, which made up for the lack of relief.

49

50

49. Stucco tabernacle with a figure of a prophet, mid-5th century. Ravenna, Orthodox Baptistery.

50. Cupola mosaic, detail of Saint Peter, mid-5th century. Ravenna, Orthodox Baptistery.

THE CAPITAL OF THE EXARCHATE: ART IN RAVENNA DURING THE 6TH CENTURY

The artistic flowering of Ravenna began, as we have seen, in 402 when Honorius transferred the capital of the Western Empire to the city and continued through the reign of Theodoric the Ostrogoth (494-526), until the city was conquered by the Byzantine general Belisarius. During the reign of the barbarians, the city maintained the Roman artistic tradition, based on local artisans and probably supported by the sovereign himself: Sant'Apollinare Nuovo repeated the basilica scheme of Saint John the Evangelist and the mosaics

51

51. A high façade remains where the Goths royal palace once stood: although it was probably constructed at the end of the exarchate, it is traditionally believed to be a part of Theodoric's Palace. Scholars believe that the façade, with arches on columns that frame the two central openings shrouded in shadows, is actually the narthex (or western porch for women) of the ancient church of San Salvatore ai Calchi.

illustrate the search for a new abstract language which characterized the decoration of the Arian baptistery as well.

The Mausoleum of Theodoric is based on the techniques and the monumental character of imperial Roman architecture, except for the pincer motif frieze on the cornice, a typical design of Gothic gold work.

When Ravenna became capital of the exarchate, in the middle of the 6th century, it was strongly influenced by Byzantine culture. Relations between the two cities were so close that in many cases Ravenna imported marbles and sculptures directly from the court of Constantinople, and even whole composition drawings and specialized artisans.

During those years the city developed a typical artistic language that represented a very harmonious synthesis of the Byzantine oriental tradition and the Roman tradition of the West, so evident in the exceptional polychrome of the mosaics, the symbolism of the compositions and the central plan of San Vitale.

52

53

54

52. *Portrait of Justinian,* second half of the 6th century. Ravenna, Sant'Apollinare Nuovo.

53. *Twelve Apostles Sarcophagus,* mid-6th century. Ravenna, Sant'Apollinare in Classe.

THE MAUSOLEUM OF THEODORIC

The reign of Theodoric, who succeeded his father in 470-471, lasted until his death in 526, and was characterized by a policy of renovation and reconstruction of many urban and rural structures, which was the source of his fame as the epitome of the builder king.

This fame was not a tradition after the fact: Theodoric was praised in life and death for this quality by authors such as Ennodius, Isidorus of Seville and Paul the Deacon. The most important construction commissioned by Theodoric was the royal mausoleum built in a Gothic burial area.

The construction is unique in its genre, but is part of a long series of late antiquity funeral buildings with a central plan. The lower floor has a decagonal plan, while the upper floor has a smaller circular plan, on which the monolithic dome rests.

This is decorated with the so-called pincer motif of German origin,

54. Mausoleum
of Theodoric, early 6th
century. Ravenna.

often used in gold work and other forms of art. The differences between the two parts of the building have given rise to various theories, including changes of plans, of design and of architect, as well as the hypothesis that the building was not completed and was later spoiled. However, various historical sources would tend to support the idea that the building is the result of a single project where different traditions meet, judging by the methods of construction and the decorative repertory. The two floors of the construction have also been interpreted as having different functions, the one as the space where the porphyry sarcophagus would be housed, the other as a commemorative chamber. From a technical point of view, the use of the large square blocks of limestone from Istria, instead of the brickwork which characterized all of Theodoric's commissions in Ravenna, gives cause for reflection. The limestone monolith which covers the building and was positioned between 522 and 526 has long inspired curiosity due to its dimensions (diameter 36 feet, weight 440 tons), its geographical origin and the means of transport. The stone is similar to the blocks used to construct the mausoleum and could come from the quarry of Grožnjan, in the Buzet region on the Istria peninsula, or from the Kras plateau near Trieste, areas that have similar geological characteristics. Around the edge of the dome there are twelve projecting brackets, evidently necessary to maneuver the monolith during positioning and placement because of the openings. It is likely that foreign artisans were brought to Ravenna to build the

mausoleum, Syrians perhaps, who are documented to have worked in Jerusalem, Antioch and even in Constantinople. They were capable of working with enormous slabs of stone, which were often used in contemporary buildings in Syria and Asia Minor, but were not known in the West where the most commonly used material was brick. The presence of an architect by the name of Aloisius at the service of Theodoric, of Syrian origin according to some scholars, is indeed documented.

55

56

55. Mausoleum of Theodoric, interior of the dome, early 6th century. Ravenna.

56. Mausoleum of Theodoric, detail of the cornice, early 6th century. Ravenna.

SANT'APOLLINARE NUOVO

The basilica, originally dedicated to the Savior, was built at the end of the 5th century during the reign of Theodoric, and was partially redecorated in the following century under Byzantine rule. Its plan was like that of the Roman basilicas during the era of Constantine but it had other local characteristics which distinguished the architecture of Ravenna. The basilica ends with a single apse, which is semicircular on the interior and polygonal on the exterior, flanked by two rectangular service chambers. The exterior walls are very simple in both the brickwork and the decoration with blind arches. The interior, on the other hand, has a very elegant style. It is divided into three aisles by two colonnades of Greek marble; the impost blocks set above the Corinthian capitals as the base for the arches accentuate the architectural forms and lend a special energy to the space.

57

57. Sant'Apollinare
Nuovo, interior,
late 5th-early 6th century.
Ravenna.

MOSAIC DECORATIONS BETWEEN THEODORIC AND JUSTINIAN

The mosaic decorations of the church of Sant'Apollinare Nuovo, organized in three orders along the lateral walls, were partially renewed during the era of Justinian (the middle order). The original mosaics, applied during the reign of Theodoric, include the scenes from the life of Christ, alternated with architectural elements, in the top order; the figures of men in the middle order and the terminal scenes of the lowest order, with Christ and the Madonna enthroned and surrounded by angels, the port of Classe and Theodoric's palace. The mosaics of this period indicate that the mosaicists were still bound to the late Roman tradition: the figures have a certain plasticity and move freely in their space, but unrealistic gold backgrounds have substituted blue skies, limiting the solidity of the volumes of the objects. In the episodes from the Gospels, the gold backgrounds are combined with summary architectural and naturalistic elements that still attempt to represent a real space, while the lively gestures and expressions make an important contribution to the efficacy of the narration. In the frontal hieratic images of Christ and the Madonna that terminate the procession, the tone is more solemn, projecting them beyond the human experience into the sphere of divinity. At the other end of the procession reality

58

59

58. *Theodoric's Palace,*
late 5th-early 6th century.
Ravenna, Sant'Apollinare
Nuovo.

59. *Port of Classe,*
late 5th-early 6th century.
Ravenna, Sant'Apollinare
Nuovo.

60. Facing page:
Samaritan at the well,
late 5th-early 6th century.
Ravenna, Sant'Apollinare
Nuovo.

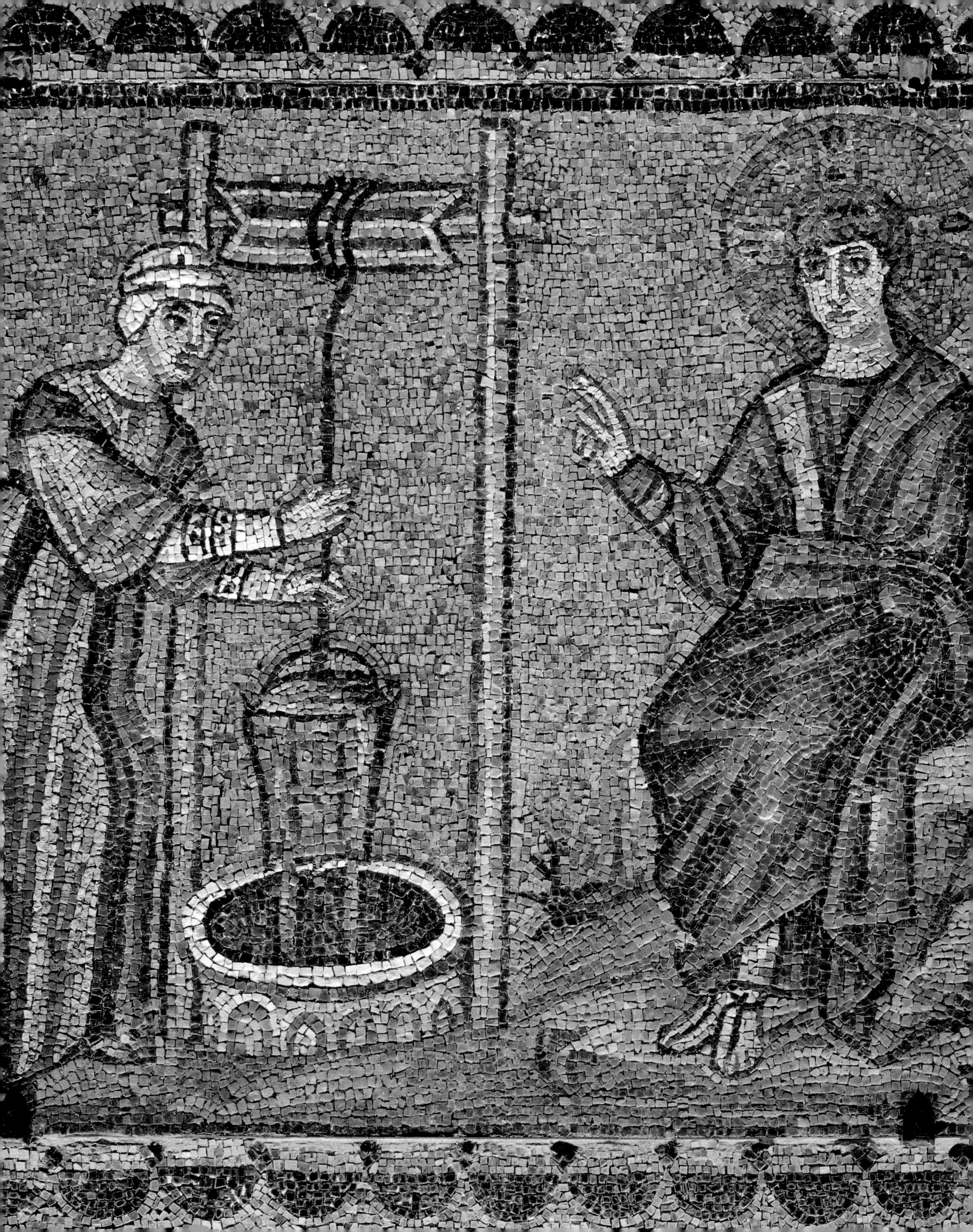

is the protagonist of the scenes: Classe and Ravenna are described in great detail, while the plane where the buildings stand is tipped up to make them all visible above the walls and towers and Theodoric's palace. The latter gives us an image of the royal palace, a courtyard with a portico whose wings, for the purposes of representation, are all aligned on a single plane. In the 6th century curtains substituted the inhabitants, but traces of them remain in the hands resting on some of the columns. During the same period, when the church was reconciled with the catholic cult, the decorations of the lower order were also renewed, substituting the dignitaries of the Ostrogoth court of the original procession with martyrs and saints. On one side there is a procession of virgins with votive gifts in their veiled hands, separated by meager palms, following the Magi kings. The faces are all alike and inexpressive, the bodies flat and static, while great attention was dedicated to expressing the dazzling beauty of the precious designs of the textiles, the jewels and diadems, represented in gold against gold. On the other side, Saint Martin leads the procession of martyrs who are silhouetted in their white tunics against the gold background. A timid effort to vary the figures was made in the drapery of the garments, but the lifeless expression of the faces would seem to have been imposed.

61

62

63

64

61. *Jesus before Pilate,* late 5th-early 6th century. Ravenna, Sant'Apollinare Nuovo.

62. *The loaves and the fish,* late 5th-early 6th century. Ravenna, Sant'Apollinare Nuovo.

63. *The last supper,* late 5th-early 6th century. Ravenna, Sant'Apollinare Nuovo.

64. *Christ in majesty with four angels,* late 5th-early 6th century. Ravenna, Sant'Apollinare Nuovo.

65

66

67

61

65. *Procession of the virgins*, detail, second half of the 6th century. Ravenna, Sant'Apollinare Nuovo.

66. *Prophet*, detail, late 5th-early 6th century. Ravenna, Sant'Apollinare Nuovo.

67. *Procession of the martyrs*, detail, second half of the 6th century. Ravenna, Sant'Apollinare Nuovo.

SAN VITALE

The outstanding monument from the golden era of Ravenna, after the conquest by the Emperor of the East, Justinian, is certainly the Basilica of San Vitale. Construction began in 525 under the auspices of the bishop Ecclesius, just back from a mission to Constantinople with Pope John I. The particular octagonal plan of the church probably reflects the influence of the architecture of the imperial capital. The exterior of the building, characterized by a projecting apse flanked by two wings, is two stories high, each of which corresponds to one of two concentric octagons of the plan. The lower level traces the perimeter of the building and covers the aisle that surrounds the central hall and the women's gallery above, while the upper level traces the perimeter of the drum and dome above. The dome is based on eight wedge-shaped pillars at the heart of the centrally organized spaces. The pillars frame ample semicircular apses, defined by a double order of columns and arches which in turn delimit the surrounding ambulatory. The compact volumes perceived outside the building are completely transformed by the complex scenery of the interior bearing elements and the play of light and shadow, which make the mosaics glow and reduce the perception of wall mass or weight. The splendid decorations, which arrived ready to be set into place directly from the sculptural workshops of the Eastern capital, vie with the mosaics in mitigating the sense of mass of the heavy bearing walls and pillars. Touched by the play of light, every architectural element seems to come alive; the perforated vegetal motif of the capitals and the screens gives them the consistency of lace. The capitals no longer refer to classical orders but have taken on new forms: some are pyramidal, others have a wavy outline, full of chiaroscuro, as if they were swelling. The decorative elements are stylized and set out symmetrically in low relief with engraved details. The original mosaics are still visible in the presbytery.

68

68. San Vitale, exterior, mid-6th century. Ravenna.

69

70

71

69. *Jeremiah*, detail,
mid-6th century.
Ravenna, San Vitale.

70. *Saint Mark the
Evangelist*, detail,
mid-6th century.
Ravenna, San Vitale.

71. San Vitale, interior,
mid-6th century.
Ravenna.

72

Garlands of leaves and fruit divide the vault of the presbytery into four sections where a vine of gold-spotted acanthus twines around the little animals and birds that inhabit the space. The mystical Lamb is depicted at the center, sustained by four angels with arms raised. The decorations of the lower panels, like those of the vault, allude to the sacrifice of Christ: in addition to the figures of the evangelists, identified by their symbols, and episodes from the life of Moses, other figures include Abraham, on one side receiving the angels who come to announce the birth of a son, on the other side as he prepares to sacrifice his son. The hierarchical representation in the apse vault, with its golden aura, contrasts strongly with the naturalistic representations of the mosaics described above. Christ the Savior appears at the center as a beardless youth who offers the crown of martyrdom to San Vitale, while bishop Ecclesius holds a model of the church and two angels add to the solemnity of the scene. Underneath the celestial court, the imperial court is also gathered in a celestial setting, and each individual figure is rendered as a portrait: on one side the Emperor Justinian with his advisors, on the other side the Empress Theodora with her handmaidens who participate in the celebration of the Eucharist, each carrying a paten and a chalice.

73

72. *Sacrifices of Abel and Melchizedec,* detail of Abel, mid-6th century. Ravenna, San Vitale.

73. *Court of Justinian,* mid-6th century. Ravenna, San Vitale.

74. Facing page: *Moses on Mount Sinai,* mid-6th century. Ravenna, San Vitale.

MOS

THEODORA'S COURT
mid-6th century
Ravenna, San Vitale

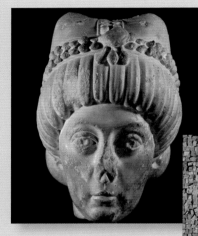

Theodora's head, 6th century. Milan, Castello Sforzesco, Museo dell'Arte Antica.

Scholars recognize the features of her face as an authentic portrait of Theodora, whose strong personality is also evident in the intense expression of the figure.

This realism is combined with the extreme stylization of the figures, which are static silhouettes against the golden background. Every details serves to illustrate the dignity of the imperial procession: accompanied by a numerous group of richly dressed handmaidens and servants,

Theodora wears a heavy, dark and shiny mantle, and precious jewelry with set stones and pearl pendants.

SUBJECT

Even though she never visited Ravenna, the wife of Emperor Justinian was depicted inside the church of San Vitale, as a participant in the celebration of the Eucharist, carrying the chalice of wine toward the altar.

the procession winds through a luxurious space, furnished with rich draperies and elaborate architectural structures.

COMPOSITION

The composition is framed by architectural elements that add richness to the scene without creating any illusion of space. Depicted in a single plane, they represent a flat setting for the scene.

Although the first servant opens the curtain with one hand, alluding to the procession moving across the room, the figures seem to be immobile, simple outlines that do not have any real volume. Weightless, they seem to float above the floor, one next to the other, so their feet overlap in some cases.

The niche behind the empress makes her figure monumental, separating her from the surrounding reality.

SCULPTURAL DECORATIONS

The so-called basket type capitals were used in the church of San Vitale for the fourteen columns that divide the central space from the ambulatory on the ground floor (capitals with lotus leaves, the impost block above with Justinian's monogram), and also for the women's gallery above where the impost block is again engraved with a monogram. The capitals depend on the chronology of the church, estimated to be 525-550, and were imported from Constantinople. The shafts of the columns in the presbytery, at ground level and the gallery above, are monoliths of Proconnesian marble from the quarries on the island of Marmara, prepared in Constantinople as was usual during this period. Most of the columns have marks of origin. One of the marks, with the letters iota and omega (Ioannou), appears eighteen times in San Vitale and has also been identified in the Basilica of Euphrasius in Porec, in the church of Saint John at Ephesus, and in Hagia Sophia in Constantinople. The capitals used in the two triple-arch apses also have the impost block above and are similar in form to the truncated pyramidal blocks used in

the ambulatory. Each face of the block is trapezoidal, framed around the edges, with a deep drilled decoration of acanthus leaves and other vegetation. These stylized branches form five circles united by a circular element formed by a braid of double ribbon. The circles are placed at the center of each face of the capital, to form a cross. Traces of red and gold pigment are still visible on the background and vegetation. The impost blocks of Proconnesian marble are of the usual truncated pyramidal form.

The side facing the presbytery is decorated with shorn lambs facing a ribbed Latin cross, each with a fore-paw raised. Behind the lambs there are two stylized trees. On the back side, facing the ambulatory, there are two peacocks facing each other as they drink from a two-handled jar. There are traces of color here too: the tree is green, the pupils, the paws of the lambs and the cross are golden. The repeated motifs are quite common, also on sarcophagi. Unlike the other impost blocks in the church these don't have any marks of origin, even if it is likely that they too came from Constantinople and were sent to Ravenna together with the other sculptural decorations during the first half of the 6th century.

75

76

75. San Vitale, view of the ambulatory, mid-6th century. Ravenna.

76. Triple arched opening on the right, about 525-550. Ravenna, San Vitale.

**77. San Vitale, capital,
mid-6th century.
Ravenna.**

The basilica was built in the 6th century near the ancient fortified port of Classe to house the relics of Sant'Apollinaris which were later transferred inside the walls of Ravenna. Originally it was only a short distance from the sea; today it stands alone in the countryside because the waterline has continued to recede. The basilica, with a nave and two aisles separated by arches that spring from two colonnades, includes the typical elements of the Ravenna style: impost blocks, swathed in flourishes of rich foliage, are in place above the Corinthian capitals; the two service rooms at the end of the side aisles flank the polygonal apse; a system of arches define the lateral wall surfaces. While nothing remains of the marble panels that decorated the walls, recovered in part by Alberti for use in the construction of the Malatesta temple, the original mosaic decorations have

survived in the presbytery. The date of the mosaics on the triumphal arch, where the image of Christ is surrounded by the symbols of the Evangelists, lambs in file and the archangels Michael and Gabriel, is still subject to debate, while the decoration of the half-dome of the apse is certainly contemporary to the period of construction of the church. A great jeweled cross suspended against a starry sky dominates the composition; it is flanked by the busts of Moses and Elijah and three sheep, identified as the apostles Peter, James and John.

Thus the transfiguration of Christ is represented in a symbolic manner, set against the background of a field of flowers, where Saint Apollinaris and some sheep (the number suggests that they represent the apostles), are present at the miraculous event.

The entire scene has been stylized and abstracted, so that each element is just a flat colored outline, a decorative element in a symmetrical composition.

78

**78. Mosaics of the arch
of triumph, detail
with Christ. Ravenna,
Sant'Apollinare in Classe.**

79

80

81

ART OF THE MIDDLE AGES

**79. Mosaics of the arch
of triumph, detail
with Saint Luke. Ravenna,
Sant'Apollinare in Classe.**

**80. Sant'Apollinare
in Classe, apse,
mid-6th century. Ravenna.**

**81. Sant'Apollinare
in Classe, façade,
mid-6th century. Ravenna.**

The throne was probably carved in Constantinople in the middle of the 6th century. Justinian donated the throne to Massimiano, the Bishop of Ravenna, who had been particularly deferential to imperial policies. Today it is conserved in the Archiepiscopal Museum of Ravenna. It is shaped like an easy chair: it has a semicircular seat surrounded by armrests and a high rounded back. The wooden structure, now replaced by synthetic material, is covered with rectangular ivory panels framed by cornice bands of rich vegetal motifs; sheets of parchment substitute the missing panels. The variety of formal compositional elements of the sculpted panels indicate that various artisans contributed to the fabrication; the differences have been ascribed to different places of origin. The front panels, with the four evangelists flanking John the Baptist who carries the sacrificial lamb (symbol of the Redemption of Christ), resemble works from Constantinople: the figures are situated against a background of architecture, in a niche with a shell canopy, and have long, elegant forms further developed by the soft, accommodating folds of their garments, from which the robustly modeled heads emerge. The figures in the panels on the back of the throne have more stocky proportions, where scenes from the childhood and miracles of Christ are depicted, as do the figures on the armrests where the panels illustrate stories of Joseph. The former, which recall Syrian examples, are in low relief inside measured spaces; the latter, with their agitated compositions, had their origin in Alexandria.

82

83

82-83. *Throne of Massimiano,* mid-6th century. Ravenna, Archiepiscopal Museum.

84-85. Facing page: *Throne of Massimiano,* detail of Joseph and his brothers. On the following pages: detail of the front, with the four evangelists flanking John the Baptist, mid-6th century. Ravenna, Archiepiscopal Museum.

During the reign of Justinian (527-565), sculptural workshops in Ravenna produced various types of liturgical furnishings, sarcophagi and capitals of precious marble. Techniques included softly contoured low relief, that was sculpted by removing material from the background plane, and excellent chiaroscuro effects with deep drill work. Some of the decorative schemes, especially animals face to face, were reproduced in the different types of sculpture. On a fragment of a slab for the sarcophagus of Ecclesius the Bishop, at the time of his death in 532 or 534, two pairs of animals are face to face at the sides of a jeweled cross. At the front of the scene there are two small deer, behind them two larger peacocks and at the back of the scene two palm trees. Here again the mirrored animal motif, that was so popular in the sculpture of Ravenna and, in general, during the reign of Justinian, appears. On this slab however the composition is renewed, with four animals and the trees. The style of the fragment is similar to other decorative elements, such as the altar frontal in San Vitale, with particular reference to the low relief and refined details, and to the impost blocks of the same church. Among other liturgical furnishings there is a slab re-worked as an altar, again in San Vitale, with two lambs facing a Latin cross, underneath a crown or a lamp.

The representation of lambs is confirmed not only on the sarcophagi of Ravenna, such as the one known by this name in the church of Sant'Apollinare in Classe, but also on the impost blocks of the lower passageway of the presbytery in San Vitale. The relief is flat, without any suggestion of fleece around the soft contours of the animals. The slabs have been dated to the Justinian era and some scholars believe they were made in Constantinople.

**I. Sarcophagus
of the lambs,
5th-6th century. Ravenna,
Sant'Apollinare in Classe.**

In 539 Justinian conquered Istria (Croatia), a region with strong ties to both Constantinople and Ravenna, which enjoyed a period of great artistic activity. An important Christian cultural center was built in the mid 6th century by the Bishop Euphrasius at Porec, a city on the west coast of the Istrian peninsula. A legible inscription in the semi dome of the central apse refers to that event, and seems to suggest that a previous religious building had stood there.

The most recent archeological research indicates that the new basilica commissioned by Euphrasius made use of the perimeter walls of an earlier building, except for the eastern wall because the length was inferior (about 115 feet). Eighteen columns with various types of capitals and polished impost blocks with the bishop's monogram divide the building into three aisles, that finish with three semicircular apses. The perforated capitals, similar to many examples in Ravenna, include a variety of composite styles: some derive from the Corinthian type with acanthus leaves, others are decorated with palms, still others are divided into two fields with eagles on the upper part. The columns are again of Proconnesian marble from Marmara, which supplied many building sites during the era of Justinian; most of the precious marbles came from Constantinople.

Traces of the original decorations remain on the underside of

86

87

86. Basilica of Euphrasius, apse, mid-6th century. Porec.

87. Basilica of Euphrasius, capital, mid-6th century. Porec.

ART OF THE MIDDLE AGES

the arches of the north colonnade where there are geometric designs, animals and plants of stucco, and the pavement of the aisle on the right. The railing that separates the presbytery has been reconstructed using slabs of marble with various motifs referring to Christ (monogram, cross, doves and deer facing a jar). Part of the liturgical furnishings are later, as is the case of the ciborium made by Venetian artisans in 1277, where the capitals with two fields were perhaps recovered, possibly in reference to the ciborium of the 6th century. In the apse, with the bishop's throne at the center, a series of marble inlay panels are decorated with geometric designs. A stucco cornice separates the marble panels from the mosaic decorations of the semi dome, where the Madonna and Child

are depicted among the angels, saints and other figures including Euphrasius, who holds a model of the building, and may have been responsible for the iconographic program.

These mosaics are similar to those of San Vitale in Ravenna, while those on the triumphal arch, representing Christ and the twelve apostles, were for the most part redone.

The baptistery is on the same axis as the basilica, separated by a square atrium, and was also commissioned by Bishop Euphrasius. The complex also includes, on the north side of the atrium, the bishop's palace. It was a single project, with the ambition of affirming the autonomy of the Porec seat, an ambition which led to extreme consequences with the schism of Aquileia in 557.

88

88. Basilica of Euphrasius, central nave, mid-6th century. Porec.

CONSTANTINOPLE AND IMPERIAL ARCHITECTURE: THE BASILICA OF HAGIA SOPHIA

The Eastern Roman Empire was born in 330 when Constantine transferred the imperial capital from Rome to Byzantium, and came to an end in 1453 when conquered by the Turks. During this period of time Constantinople developed its own identity, thanks to the cultural activities promoted by the various emperors, and the new stylistic language of Byzantine art was very highly esteemed in the countries of the Western world. One of the greatest expressions of the new Byzantine culture was the church of Hagia Sophia, founded

at the time of Constantine. Destroyed by a fire during a popular uprising, it was rebuilt by Justinian in 532 as tangible sign of imperial munificence. The church has a rectangular plan and it is divided into three aisles by a double order of arches, but the structure definitely appears to be centrally organized as a consequence of the great dome. Mounted on four great corner pillars and flanked by two semi domes, it dominates a single vast space where all structural elements have been eliminated. As a consequence the central nave is isolated from the side aisles, which are developed on several levels and are punctuated by columns and pilasters. The lighting also exalts this solution, illuminating the central area and leaving the side aisles in shadow. Flowing in through the windows at the base of

89

89. Hagia Sophia, exterior, 6th century. Istanbul.

the dome, a myriad of shafts design rays along the walls or cross at different heights, reducing the material impression of the wall mass. On the inside the architectural structure of the basilica of Hagia Sophia is transformed by the brilliant mosaics, restored and liberated from the oil paintings that had masked them from the middle of the 19th century when the church functioned as a mosque. The chromatic and luminous qualities of the mosaics unify a decorative program that was actually carried out in different epochs. In the narthex and on the underside of the arches there are still some vague traces of the aniconic decorations of the 6th century, schemes elaborated at the time of Justinian, characterized by geometric and floral designs, stars and whorls of acanthus stretched out on a gold background. The first figurative mosaics date to the 9th century. The *Enthroned Madonna and Child with two angels* in the apse is a work of great ability, in the pictorial quality of the forms, distributed with an appreciable sense of space, and in the varied distribution

91

90. Facing page:
Christ in majesty, 1034-42. Istanbul, Hagia Sophia.

91. Hagia Sophia, interior, 6th century. Istanbul.

of the tesserae, which are adapted to the image and achieve great sweetness in the faces thanks to the inclusion of natural stones.

The later cycles reflect the developments of painting in Constantinople: *Emperor Leo VI prostrate at the feet of Christ Enthroned* on the lunette above the door of the narthex; the *Fathers of the Church* on the northern gable of the nave; the *Enthroned Madonna and Child with emperors Constantine and Justinian* (10-11th centuries) on the lunette above a door to the narthex.

The same symmetrical composition also appears in *Christ enthroned between Constantine IX and Empress Zoe* (1034-42), in the *Madonna and Child between John II Comnen and Irene* (1122), and in the *Deesis* mosaic of the south gallery (mid 13th century).

The work recovered ancient iconographic types in the organic harmony of the forms, the humanity of the faces, the naturalism of the draperies, the refined colors and transparencies. The decorations of the pulpits, the capitals, the screens and the cornices of Hagia Sophia go far beyond the canon of sculpture in classical architecture where the forms were used only to evidence the structural function of the various elements. The repertory of the forms from previous eras was ignored or profoundly modified: the acanthus leaves adhered to the shaft so that the plastic distinction of the capitals was progressively reduced, while well-defined geometric and vegetal compositions were drawn out along the back plane or were transformed into perforated sculpture distinguished by its chiaroscuro effect. Ethereal decorative schemes expanded to cover capitals, cornices and walls like arabesques, contributing together with the mosaics to the weightless transformation of the architecture.

92

93

92. *Christ enthroned between Constantine IX and the Empress Zoe,* detail of Constantine IX, 1034-42. Istanbul, Hagia Sophia.

93. *Deesis* mosaic of the south gallery, detail of Christ, mid-13th century. Istanbul, Hagia Sophia.

**94. Capital. Istanbul,
Hagia Sophia.**

THE SANCTUARY OF SAN SIMEON THE STYLITE AT QAL'AT SEM'ÂN

The area of northern Syria delimited by the cities of Apamea, Antioch and Aleppo, is a mountainous region known by the name of Belus. It had long been under Hellenic influence, and benefited from extraordinary development during the first centuries of the Christian era. This lasted until the conquest by the Arabs in 636 when the economic system that sustained the wealth of the whole area dissolved.

Among the many churches that were constructed starting in the 4th century, an important center of pilgrimage was built at Qalat

Siman between 480 and 490 around the pillar of San Simeon the elder, perhaps commissioned and funded by Emperor Zenon.

Simeon the Stylite was a follower of an extremely dedicated form of religious life that characterized early ascetic monasticism from the 5th century. This consisted of living on the top of a pillar, exposed to the weather. However, the practitioners were not isolated, but admired and venerated in life by pilgrims and cared for by monastic communities.

The impressive complex dedicated to San Simeon Stylite the Elder is composed of four basilicas, aligned on the main axes, that surround a central octagonal building. The basilicas to the south and west have a narthex, while the basilica to the east has three

95

**95. Basilica
of San Simeon,
baptistery, 480-90.
Qal'at Sem'ân.**

96

97

96. Basilica
of San Simeon,
the column of San Simeon.
Qal'at Sem'ân.

97. Basilica
of San Simeon, lateral
quadrangle, 480-90.
Qal'at Sem'ân.

98
          99

projecting semicircular apses. The complex, centered on the column where the ascetic spent part of his life, was walled and included two other churches in addition to the main building, a square baptistery, service buildings and accommodation for pilgrims. The entrance was through a monumental portal to the southern basilica.

The model of the cross-form martyrium based on a centrally organized plan (here octagonal) covered by a dome was typical of architects from Constantinople, and is also recognizable in the church of Saint John the Evangelist at Ephesus. The same narthex and projecting apses are also to be found in other buildings commissioned by the imperial court. Some of these architects from Constantinople also worked in the Syrian monastery at Qartamin.

The octagon at Qalat Siman, based on arches on all sides, had a dome of lightweight materials, presumably of wood. This is an example of the intermingling of local techniques with foreign construction methods that came from the center of power.

Architectural decorations at Qalat Siman are limited to the capitals, mostly imitations of Corinthians, with the wind-blown foliage that also appears in other churches of the Belus area. In some cases the lower part of the spiny acanthus leaf capitals also depict shields with Latin crosses and geometric motifs. In both cases, the decorative elements reveal negative triangles of perforation that required notable drill work.

In the 10th century the monastery was incorporated inside an imposing Byzantine fortification with twenty-seven towers.

**98. Basilica
of San Simeon,
octagonal structure.
Qal'at Sem'ân.**

**99. Plan of the San
Simeon complex
(from the *Touring guide
to Syria*, p. 106).**

This term refers to the period of Egyptian history between the 4th century and the middle of the 7th, up to the Arab domination. At that time Christian Egyptians were known as Copts and monasticism was widely diffused. During this period this movement emerged and focused on asceticism in the desert, where the first buildings for monastic life were constructed. From the middle of the 4th century monasteries formed an almost uninterrupted chain along the edge of the desert on both banks of the Nile. It was their activity which almost completely converted Egypt to Christianity in the following century. There are not many traces left of the earliest architecture. More important examples are to be found with reference to the 5th and 6th centuries in urban contexts, the most important of which is the episcopal church of Hermopolis, a large three-aisle basilica, incorporated in a larger complex. Urban religious buildings were richly decorated with sculpture, while the monastery churches

I

II

I. *Madonna and Child with saints*, detail, 5th-7th century. Cairo, Coptic Museum.

II. Saint Catherine's Monastery, 6th century.

III

were generally without this type of plastic enrichment. Where present, sculpture was primarily limited to architectural decoration, especially relief work. The iconographic themes referred to antiquity until the Christian symbols and subjects appeared at Oxyrhyncus and Ahnas. The use of Christian themes expanded later, between the 5th and 8th centuries, as demonstrated by the sculptural materials from Bawit. The changes are most evident in the capitals, produced in great variety. The level of workmanship is very high, like that from Constantinople. The stone was carved as if it were wood, as can be seen in the basket capitals, many of which are divided into two zones with different decorative motifs. Most of the decorations are vegetal motifs such as acanthus, vines or wind-blown foliage, occasionally they also include symbols that refer to Christ such as the cross and even animals. The Coptic wall paintings in Egypt are among the rare examples from this period still existing in the Middle East. The monasteries of Saqqarah and Bawit were endowed with many of these paintings; they can be dated approximately to between the 5th and 7th centuries, although their liturgical functions are not yet known. Most of these paintings were located in the apses, where Christ in Majesty is often surrounded by the symbols of the four evangelists and appears above a lower order where the Virgin and Child with the Apostles was represented, as in the case of the monastery of Apollo at Bawit. The iconography of the apse and the individual decorative solutions used reappeared later in Romanic art in Europe. The textiles of the Copts are particularly well-known.

Numerous fragments of Coptic textiles, from different places and epochs, are conserved in various places. Some come from funeral contexts and were cloths used to cover or garb the deceased; others come from garments, head coverings, curtains, cushions, and refer to various social classes. Technically, most of the Coptic textiles seem to be similar to tapestry, made on vertical looms where the warp threads were completely covered by the weft. The repertory of decorations was conserved over a very long period and included, in addition to those derived from Greek and Roman art, the innovations that came from contacts with the Sasanians, the Byzantines and the Arabs: thus it included mythological personages and stories, pastoral and hunting scenes, Christian themes such as the Good Shepherd, and scenes from the Old Testament.

Symbolic representations such as the cross, birds, angels and saints, were very frequent. The history of Coptic art was brusquely interrupted in the 7th century by the Muslim conquest.

IV

III. *Christian with a saint*,
5th-7th century. Paris,
Musée du Louvre.

IV. Capital divided
into two zones, with rams
and birds, 6th century.
Cairo, Coptic Museum.

V. Coptic textile. Paris,
Musée du Louvre.

2. Art in Medieval Palaces and Monasteries

For many years scholars believed that the invasions of the barbarians had interrupted all cultural and artistic activities, so the Middle Ages were considered, and called, the Dark Ages. Today the true importance of this period of history is recognized. The barbarians developed new techniques and new esthetics, that rejected classical canons of beauty and proportions in favor of a more symbolic and stimulating visual language that was more fantastic and imaginary, geometric and colorful. Carolingian art includes buildings, renovation of monasteries, pictorial cycles, illuminated manuscripts and luxury items. This phenomenon is generally identified as the Carolingian renovation.

Charlemagne himself played a central role in initiating this process, which was carried on by his sons Louis the Pious and Charles the Bald. The internecine struggles in the empire and the new invasions of Normans, Saracens and Huns, limited patronage. After a period of poorer quality, and reduced quantities of artistic production, a new moment of splendor accompanied the Ottonian court in the second half of the 10th century.

2

3

1. Facing page: *Ruodprecht, Gertrude Psalter, A saint*, 10th century. Cividale del Friuli, Cathedral.

2. Doors of Saint Bernward, detail of *The labors of the forefathers*. Hildesheim, Saint Michael.

3. *A hen with her chicks*. Monza, Cathedral Treasury. The work, traditionally considered a gift from Queen Theolinda to the Basilica of Monza, is usually dated to the 7th century.

THE LOMBARDS

Recently the definition of Lombardic art has broadened to become a historical reference rather than an ethnical one. Today, in fact, it refers to all of the artistic activities from the middle of the 6th century, when the Lombards crossed the Alps, conquered northern Italy and established their flourishing reign that fell only in 774 to the armies of Charlemagne.

The new political system broke all bonds with the ancient world. The objects that were undoubtedly made by the Lombards, especially arms and jewelry found in the tombs, have many characteristics in common with the goldwork of all the barbarians: the brilliant colors combine enamels, precious stones and vitreous paste, and make up for the simplicity of the geometric and interlace decorations. The culture of the invaders also influenced the local sculptors, who produced only architectural decorations with few exceptions.

The surfaces were covered with decorative designs and symbols, with a flat, low relief technique that created sharp contours in the foreground against the sunken back plane. When the intention was figurative, the composition was uncertain and the flat, stocky figures float in their space. However, the frescoes of Castelseprio and the temple of Cividale also confirm that this period of history was capable of producing works of great quality, where the ancient tradition appears to be extremely vital.

4

4. *Altar frontal of Sigwald,*
**8th century. Cividale del
Friuli, Christian Museum
of the Cathedral.**

5

6

7

5. *Peace of Duke Orso,*
mid 8th century.
Cividale del Friuli,
Archeological Museum.

6. *The Desiderio cross
of Galla Placidia,*
end 8th-early 9th centuries.
Brescia, Civic Museum
of the Christian Era.

7. *Crown of Theodolinda,*
about 600. Monza,
Cathedral Treasury.

THE LOMBARD TEMPLE OF CIVIDALE

The temple is one of the most interesting and best-preserved artifacts of Lombardic architecture. Erected in the most safely defended part of the city, where the residence of the king's steward was also located, it originally served as the palace chapel and was annexed to the adjacent convent of Santa Maria in Valle only later. The building has a raised western hall, covered by a spacious cross-vault, and the presbytery to the east on a lower level, divided into three narrow aisles by double columns. The columns carry a straight architrave from which the three barrel vaults spring directly. While the masonry seems rather coarse and includes stones of varying dimensions, the structure of the presbytery is more refined: next to spoliatory Roman material,

there are also bases, columns and capitals made expressly for the temple. The structure is further ennobled by rich wall decorations that some scholars date to a later period. Marble facings, stucco ornaments and paintings adorn the walls under the vaults that were originally decorated with mosaics. The decorative stucco panel above the entrance is extraordinarily well preserved. Between two horizontal cornices of star-like flowers, six regal female figures stand at the sides of a niche. They are elegantly proportioned and solidly modeled; the faces are sculpted like portraits and gestures are natural, all characteristics that were hard to find in contemporary sculpture. The same fresh and natural style is to be found on the surround of the arch below, where plump bunches of grapes hang from the twisted vine.

8

9

8. Lombard temple, interior view of the rood-screen, 8th century. Cividale del Friuli, Santa Maria in Valle.

9. Lombard temple, interior view, 8th century. Cividale del Friuli, Santa Maria in Valle.

10. Facing page: Lombard temple, detail of stucco relief panel above the entry door, 8th century. Cividale del Friuli.

THE ALTAR OF THE DUKE OF RATCHIS

Another emblematic work of Lombardic origin in the city of Cividale is the stone altar of the Duke of Ratchis. The altar can be dated precisely, thanks to the inscription on the upper border, which affirms that it was donated to the church of Saint John by the Duke of Ratchis, who bore this title from 737 to 744 when he succeeded Luitprand as king of the Lombards. The altar is a rectangular parallelepiped made of limestone from Istria, the sculpted scenes are all framed with decorated cornices. On the front panel a beardless Christ appears on a lozenge carried by four angels, under the hand of God and surrounded by adoring cherubs. On the opposite side the confessional window is flanked by two jeweled crosses. the two end panels are illustrated with episodes from the life of Christ: on the left, in the *Visitation*, Mary embraces her cousin Elisabeth; on the right, Mary is enthroned and holds the Child for the adoration of the Magi kings. The flat, simplified forms and the thin, shallow grooves of the draperies annul the volume of the figures, a typical stylistic characteristic of medieval sculpture. The human body appears to be deformed and awkward: the limbs are unrealistically long, the figures seem to float in the air, their great eyes wide open in their inexpressive faces.

11. *Altar of the Duke of Ratchis, Visitation,* **737-44. Cividale del Friuli, Christian Museum of the Cathedral.**

12. *Altar of the Duke of Ratchis, Christ in majesty,* **737-44. Cividale del Friuli, Christian Museum of the Cathedral.**

13. *Altar of the Duke of
Ratchis, Adoration of the
Magi,* 737-44. Cividale del
Friuli, Christian Museum
of the Cathedral.

FRONTLET OF A HELMET WITH THE TRIUMPH OF AGILULF

7th century
Florence, Bargello Museum

SUBJECT

The Lombard king is represented in a scene of triumph, like the Roman emperors, on the frontlet of the helmet. Agilulf sits on his throne, surrounded by winged victories and his court.

The figure of the king, who has a long beard, is rigid and squarely faces the observer while he blesses with the right hand and holds his sword in the left.

Two warriors who wear barbarian armor, conical helmets with plumes and carry round embossed shields assist him.

Despite the coarse forms, and the monstrous facial expressions, the artist attempted to create the full volumes of the figures and achieved an unusual plasticity in the scenes, which include minute, naturalistic details of the costumes of his fellow citizens.

The victories lead the procession of the vanquished who render honor to the conqueror: behind the supplicants who bow down with their hands stretched out, two squires carry the crowns, that are the symbols of the recently acquired authority over the defeated peoples, to their king.

COMPOSITION

The scene is organized symmetrically, the procession of supplicants and squires appears on both sides of the Lombard king.

The coordinated alignment of the figures in the foreground and the absence of any indication of a support under their feet, makes them seem to float weightlessly in their space. The slightly staggered position of the figures does not depend on the desire to create a sense of depth, but rather accompanies the outline of the frontlet so that the whole surface is decorated uniformly.

THE MEROVINGIANS

The Merovingian dynasty had ruled over Gaul from the time of Clovis, who conquered it at the end of the 5th century, until 751 when after the deposition of Childeric III, Pepin the Short began the Carolingian dynasty.

Merovingian rule had not truncated the late Roman civilization: the Franks quickly assimilated the culture of the local populations, absorbing their institutions and customs. The continuity of artistic traditions was not interrupted, although the artists did naturally incorporate the taste of the barbarian aristocracy that commissioned the works and buildings needed to show their prestige. The gold smiths, in particular, incorporated the innovative elements of decoration, especially the geometric designs and the colored style that incorporated glass paste, enamel and precious stones.

In the field of architecture the late imperial buildings were an important point of reference but the wall decorations acquired an original aspect.

The qualitative level of sculpture was maintained by the workshops in Aachen, specialized in the production of capitals.

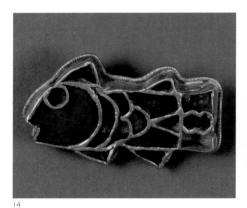

14

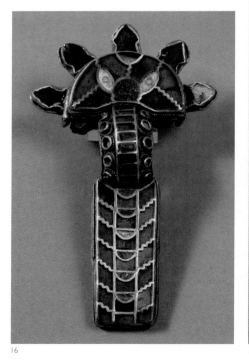

16

15

14. Fish-shaped fibula,
6th century. Florence,
Archeological Museum.

15. Eagle-shaped fibula,
about 500. Nuremberg,
Germanisches
Nationalmuseum.

16. Stirrup-shaped fibula,
6th century. Florence,
Bargello Museum.

THE BAPTISTERY OF POITIERS

The building was constructed on the ruins of a paleochristian baptistery of the 4th century that had an octagonal font at the center of a square hall. Its appearance, however, can be dated primarily to the 7th century, when it was transformed into a church with a cruciform plan. The perimetric walls were rebuilt with long stones and bricks, while the plan was enlivened by the additions of apses: the eastern apse had a polygonal outline, while the apses at the sides of the nave, today semicircular, were originally square. The construction thus comprises a group of impressive architectural elements, crowned by triangular pediments, bordered below by tall pilasters, almost absorbed into the wall surface.

The rudeness of the forms is somewhat mitigated by the minute

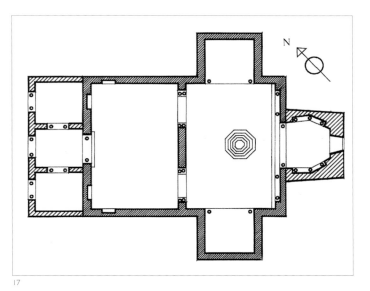

17

18

17. Plan of the baptistery of Poitiers (from M. Durliat, *Des barbares à l'an Mil*, 1985).

18. Baptistery of Poitiers, exterior, 7th century.

decoration that covers the wall surface, which combines bricks and small blocks of stone.

The wall surface is also animated by the chromatic effects of brackets, detailed gables, panels sculpted in low relief, pilasters topped by capitals with tiny vegetal motifs.

The internal decoration was characterized by the arches that spring from the columns and capitals produced in the workshops of Aachen.

19

19. Baptistery of Poitiers, detail of the southern façade, 7th century.

THE CRYPT OF JOUARRE

Founded at the beginning of the 7th century by Adon, Jouarre was one of the seven abbeys in the valley of the Marne, a consequence of the monastic mission of the Irish Saint Columbanus. Among the buildings of the monastery, rebuilt more than once, the crypt of the basilica of Saint Paul near the cemetery is an outstanding monument of pre-Carolingian art. A burial place of privilege, it was built by bishop Agilbert who, about the year 670, had retired to the convent where his sister Theochilda was mother superior, and here he was subsequently buried. Originally the crypt was behind the apse of the church on the same level. The crypt is divided into three aisles by a double line of marble columns; the cross-vaults, erected in the 12th century, spring directly from the capitals and substitute the original ceiling which was either barrel vaults or perhaps flat. The aristocratic function of this monument is evident from the richness of the forms, where the workmanship of specialized artisans is combined with the use of materials that were not local. The columns are all ancient, accurately selected for dimension and form, while the capitals seem to have been sculpted especially for the crypt. Some are Corinthian, others are composite, but all of them have been attributed to 7th century workshops in the mountains of the Pyrenees. They were transported from the workshops to the site by sea and then up the Seine and Marne rivers. The dominating influence of the ancient traditions is also evident in the masonry of the western wall, decorated in the 8th century with a screen of *opus reticulatum*.

20

20. View of the crypt, 7th century. Jouarre, Saint-Paul.

The populations that historians have so disparagingly defined as barbarians achieved extremely refined results in the field of jewelry. This art form was more adapt than others to the semi-nomadic life that the warrior tribes conducted. The custom of burying the dead with their arms and jewels, symbols of their social standing, has also contributed to the conservation of these artifacts. In addition to a great variety of fibulae, pins and buckles, there are also pendants, necklaces and crowns. The artisans were experts in of all techniques - from embossing to filigree, from granulation to perforation – but seemed to prefer inlays above all other techniques: it creates an animated surface with its cavities and settings for precious stones and glass paste, and the vivid colors. The decorative repertory was primarily ornamental and also influenced contemporary sculpture. Later, under Charlemagne, jewelry production was used to produce religious and ceremonial objects. In fact, the surviving works of the 9th and 10th centuries come mostly from cathedral treasuries, where they were donated by the emperors and members of the nobility. In any case, imperial orders prevented the dead from being buried with their jewels, and permitted only noble and royal burials to include a personal ornament of a certain importance. Among these the jewel that legend says belonged to the emperor himself is an exceptional example: between two enormous sapphires, relics of the Virgin's hair and a fragment of the True Cross are conserved. When the Ottonians renewed their relations with Byzantium, jewels acquired a new delicacy and technical virtuosity, particularly evident in the examples found in the underground chambers at Mainz. They are traditionally believed to have been worn by the empress Gisela on the day of her marriage to Conrad II. In France, on the other hand, economic difficulties following the Norman invasion and the introduction of a new style of garment, characterized by a double tunic with long sleeves and a high collar, limited the production of jewels. The artifacts from this period are primarily rings and belts with elaborate buckles. The rings, judging by the romantic and magical phrases inscribed on them, were either engagement rings or gifts between intimate friends. Alongside of crowns, diadems and ceremonial jewels, the production included primarily collars, clips and round pins with decorative figures at the center, made with enamels and precious stones. The latter were often insignia of an order, a corporation or an association.

I. Gold buckle.
Florence, Bargello
Museum.

II. Fibulae. Cologne,
Romano-Germanic
Museum.

Gold was considered the material manifestation of divine light and this was the reason why it was used to create all objects that had any relation to the sphere of the sacred. A high level of specialization was required to master the complex techniques: goldsmiths were often authentic artists and their works occupied the top position in the hierarchy of the arts. In the prime of the Middle Ages goldwork was influenced by the style of the barbarian populations, which favored colored, ornamental designs. The Carolingian production is almost completely lost, its importance is known through literary sources and very few examples, while from the Ottonian period there are many more works, produced in the schools that grew up near the principal abbeys. Later sacred goldwork adopted new styles and materials. The goldsmiths then produced altarpieces and monumental reliquary cases, preferably in gilded copper.

III. Gold cross, 7th century. Cividale del Friuli, Christian Museum.

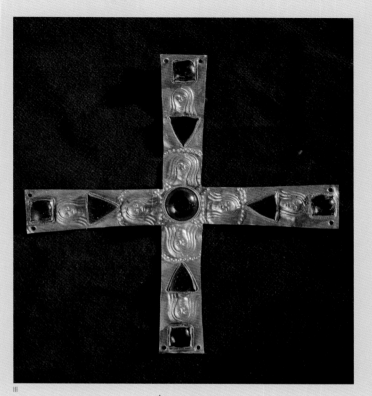

III

IV. THE IRON CROWN
Monza, Cathedral Treasury

The "iron crown" takes its name from the thin sheet of iron that lines the crown, which legend says was obtained from a nail from the cross of Christ. The refined workmanship, with set gems, and embossed and enameled stylized flowers, has led some to doubt the traditional date for the period of production in the 9th century, in favor of a late Roman origin. Donated to the basilica of San Giovanni di Monza by Theodolinda, the first Catholic Lombardic queen, it was used to crown the kings of Italy from Berengario I (888) to Napoleon I (1805).

IV

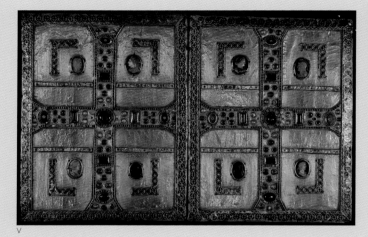

V

V. GOLD COVER OF THE MISSAL OF THEODOLINDA
Monza, Cathedral Treasury

Donated by Pope Gregory the Great to the Lombardic queen Theodolinda in 603 for the baptism of her son, the missal cover is divided by the arms of a large, gemmed cross, decorated with antique cameos and precious stones, and bordered by a frame of glass paste. The colored style of the barbarian gold work was here combined with a symmetrical composition, balanced and not overly complex, suggesting that it had been made in Rome.

VI

VI-VII. COVER OF THE MISSAL OF ARIBERT
Milano, Cathedral Treasury

Forming the top of a liturgical chest for the missal, the cover is organized around the figure of Christ on the cross which is surrounded by minute enamelwork scenes illustrating a vast iconographical program related to the themes of the Passion, framed by filigree ornaments and set stones. The work, dated to the middle of the 11th century and commissioned by Archbishop Aribert d'Intimiano, reveals many analogies with contemporary imperial production, in the refined workmanship, the motif of the halo with the cross, and the design of the folds of the loincloth.

VII

VIII. GOLD ALTARPIECE
Venice, Cathedral of Saint Mark

The altarpiece is composed of a Gothic style frame, decorated with perforated leaves, gems and tabernacles which, in the mid 14th century was used to mount 245 *cloisonné* enamels made during the previous two centuries illustrating scenes from the lives of Christ and Saint Mark, in addition to prophets, angels and apostles. The enamels that form the lower part, accompanied by Latin inscriptions, probably came from the altarpiece of the Basilica of Saint Mark made in 1105, while the enamels from the top, from the spoils of the looting of Constantinople a few years earlier, were added during the renovation in 1209.

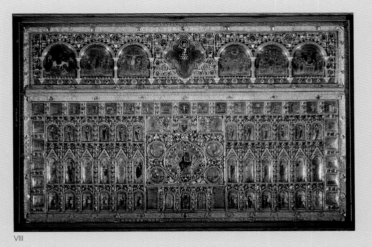

VIII

IX-X. RELIQUARY OF THE HOLY CORPORAL
Orvieto, Cathedral

The reliquary, made in 1347 by the Sienese Ugolino di Vieri and his assistants, represents one of the masterpieces of Gothic goldwork. Structured like the façade of a cathedral, there are three doors divided into enameled panels representing episodes from the life of Christ and the miracle of the corporal: in 1264 in the town of Bolsena, during a Mass celebrated by a Boer priest who did not believe in the miracle of the Eucharist, the linen cloth was soaked with the blood of the host. The goldsmith had a real talent for telling his story and was also well informed about Sienese painting of the same period.

IX

X

THE VISIGOTHS IN SPAIN

In Spain the era of the barbarian invasions was marked by the arrival of the Visigoths, a Gothic tribe that sustained an extraordinary artistic development at the same time as other areas of Europe were in full decline. The Visigoths interrupted the contacts of the Iberian peninsula with the Latin world, strengthened the contacts with Africa and produced forms of original beauty.

During the 7th century architecture took on special characteristics and a fascinating variety of designs. Small churches were built with a short, wide plan and a rectangular apse, where the fine masonry technique still represented an inheritance from the Romans. The

21

21. San Julián de los Prados, façade, 812-42. Oviedo.

22. Facing page: Votive crown of the Visigoth king Reccesuinth, 649-72 Madrid. Archeological Museum.

stones were large and uniform, cut with sharp edges, and such fine joints that they seem to be without mortar.

Toledo, the new capital of the kingdom, was probably the center of diffusion of this style of architecture that was also distinguished by the exceptionally rich sculptural decorations that included elements from a great variety of sources, ancient and Byzantine, Syrian, Egyptian and others from the north of Africa.

The types of capitals illustrate this eclectic taste: while Gaul remained faithful to marble capitals, made in the workshops of Aachen, that recalled classical styles, Spain made fanciful stone capitals. Not even the invasion of the Arabs, in 711, interrupted this tradition, as may be seen in the churches of the Asturias of the 9th and 10th centuries: their forms descend directly from the churches built two centuries previously.

23

24

23. San Miguel de Lillo, exterior, about 842-50. Oviedo. San Miguel is an example of an pre-Romanic Asturian building.

24. Monastery of Santa Maria, 7th century. Quintanilla de Vinas (Burgos).

SAN PEDRO DE LA NAVE

This monastic church built in the mid 7th century has a cruciform plan and is extremely interesting although quite small. The masonry of the walls and the vaults is finely done; the smooth straight surfaces clearly define the solid and empty volumes of the space, enriched by the finely worked stone capitals.

The church is divided into three aisles by pilasters that, delimiting small spaces, made it possible to cover the space with a vault. This culminates in the central cross vault, which springs from four columns. As in ancient architecture, the columns are not incorporated into the wall but have been applied to it. Sculpted capitals with a very high abacus top the columns. Two biblical scenes appear framed by the rigid leaves that cover the corner angles: *Daniel in the lion's den* and the *Sacrifice of Isaac*. The sculptor has deepened the flat background plane in order to sculpt the foreground figures with light and detailed carving that also aims to create the volumes of the faces.

25

26

25. San Pedro de la Nave, interior, mid-7th century. Zamora.

26. San Pedro de la Nave, exterior, mid-7th century. Zamora.

SANTA MARIA DE NARANCO

The palace of Naranco, commissioned and built by king Ramiro in the mid 9th century, was the only royal construction that did not pertain to the sacred to be built during the monarchy of the Asturias. It was transformed into a church only in the 11th century, when it was dedicated to the Madonna.

A two story building, it is distinguished by the perfection of the proportions, the fine workmanship of the masonry and the decorative sculptures. Each floor is organized in a central hall flanked by two lateral chambers, covered by a barrel vault of tufa stone with transversal arches. The arch appears in several places in the building: a trio of arches defines the porticos on the short sides, echoed in the triple-light window above, and also appears in the blind arches along the walls of the main hall on the top floor. Here the interior wall surface is animated by the spiral decoration of the column shafts and the Corinthian or truncate pyramidal capitals, where human and animal inspired forms populate the spaces divided by ribbon bands.

27

28

27. Santa Maria de Naranco, view of the portico, mid-9th century. Oviedo.

28. Santa Maria de Naranco, façade, mid-9th century. Oviedo.

29. Facing page: Santa Maria de Naranco, interior, mid-9th century. Oviedo.

IRISH MONASTIC CENTERS

After the introduction of Christianity to Ireland in 431, according to the will of Pope Celestine I and the missionary work of men like Palladius and Saint Patrick, the monasteries played a central role in the promotion of the arts, especially in production of illuminated manuscripts, metal working and masonry.

For a long time monastic architecture was characterized by wood construction, that included complex structures, as narrated in the writings of the Venerable Bede. During the 8th century the first simple stone buildings began to appear. The monastic settlements were generally small areas surrounded by circular walls; inside

30

31

30. Gallarus Oratory, 8th-10th centuries. Dingle Peninsula.

31. Lindisfarne Priory, Holy Island.

32. Facing page: Monastery of Clonmacnoise.

33

there were modestly proportioned buildings and high circular bell-towers (*cloigtech*) for the bells that regulated the daily cycle of the monastic life.

There are also a few constructions built of stone slabs with the dry stone wall technique, on sites related to the presence of hermits and difficult to date, such as the Gallarus Oratory on the Dingle peninsula (Munster). The building, which is quite small and without ornament, can be dated approximately to between the 8th and 10th centuries. The typical roof type of the wood cabins (*clochàn*) was adapted to the rectangular plan of the stone building.

The most important monasteries were Glendalough, Monasterboice and Clonmacnoise. Monasterboice is one of the oldest Irish monasteries, founded by Saint Buite (†521), a disciple of Saint Patrick. Glendalough was founded in the second half of the 6th century by Saint Kevin (498-618 circa) who was the abbot there for many years.

The monastic complex of Clonmacnoise was founded in 545 by Saint Ciarán near the Shannon River, the most important north-south waterway of the island.

During the Middle Ages it became one of the most important centers of artistic production of the island, with an important *scriptorium* and capable artisans to work metal and stone.

**33. Monastery
of Glendalough, second
half of the 6th century.**

INSULAR MANUSCRIPTS

The oldest illuminated manuscripts produced in the Irish *scriptoria* date to the early 7th century. They introduced the Insular script, a semi-uncial Latin script that has a decorative value of its own, to which geometric and zoomorphic ornaments, derived from the most precious metal work objects, were added.

In the *Book of Durrow*, the most important insular manuscript of the period (written toward the end of the 7th century), the ornamental repertory includes the interlaced frames that were typical of the northern islands. The chromatic palette is limited but well distributed in the magnificently executed designs.

The book also includes the solution of a page dedicated to the portrait of the evangelist, derived from Late-antique Mediterranean models.

Another of these manuscripts, the *Book of Lindisfarne*, written by the scribe Eadfrith, the bishop who died in 721, is considered one of the most superb expressions of the insular manuscript tradition during the first millennium. The codex, conserved in the British Library of London, includes both the interlace motifs and a series of new elements derived from Mediterranean models including the tables of the Canons and the portraits of the evangelists, captured in the act of writing.

In the *Book of Echternach*, another gospel book, the stylized decorations again derive from metalwork. The only full page illustrations are the portraits of the four evangelists, but the balance between the interlace motifs of the frames, the stylized figures, the pose of the lion of Saint Mark, all contribute to make this one of the finest examples of medieval manuscript art.

The *Book of Kells* is the most famous medieval manuscript prior the Carolingian era. It was made in the mid 8th century, probably on the island of Iona (one of the Hebrides off the coast of Scotland), and only later taken to Kells where it was kept in the Church of Saint Colombanus for many years. It is a codex of the Four Gospels, with

34

35

34. *Book of Kells, Canon Table*, mid-8th century. Dublin, Trinity College.

35. *Book of Kells, Portrait of John the Evangelist*, mid-8th century. Dublin, Trinity College.

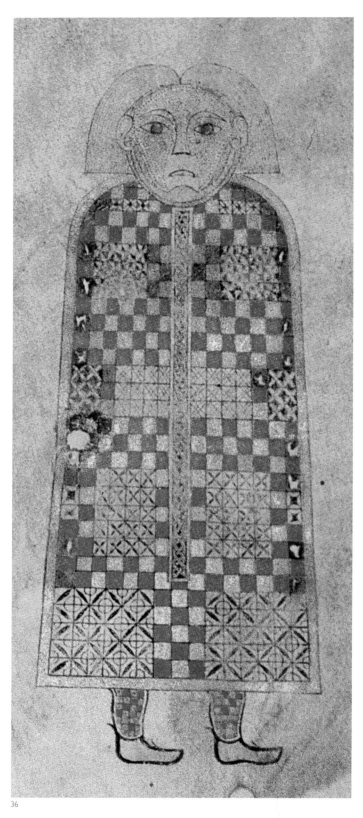

symbols and portraits of the evangelists. Today the beginning of the codex is missing. The team of illuminators and scribes who collaborated to produce the 340 leaves of parchment that make up the codex used the skins of about 170 calves. It opens with an image of the four Evangelists and continues with the tables of the Canons, which indicate the correspondence between the gospels and the Latin Vulgate bible, according to the system created by Eusebius in 330 and approved by Jerome in the 4th century. In the *Book of Kells* the tables of the Canons are positioned within an architecture transformed into simple geometric shapes, completely covered with the interlace designs of Celtic origin. With the exception of the portraits of the evangelists, there are only a few other full page images in the *Book of Kells*, some of which face the so-called carpet pages, pages with no text or figures dedicated to pure ornament. This codex also includes the oldest known image of the Madonna and Child (f. 7v) in a Western illuminated manuscript.

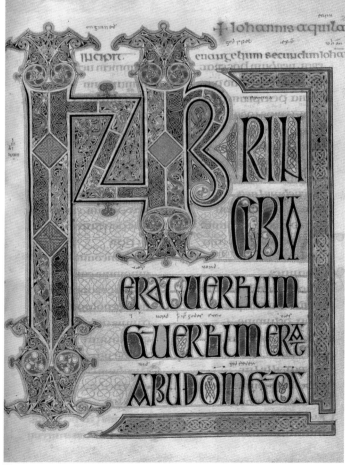

36

37

36. *Book of Durrow, Matthew the Evangelist,* end of the 7th century. Dublin, Trinity College.

37. L*Book of Lindisfarne,* illuminated page of the Gospel of Saint John, 710-21. London, British Library.

CROSSES OF IRELAND

The high crosses of Ireland are among the most interesting artifacts of the island and are intimately identified with the island itself. They are to be found everywhere, especially in the vicinity of the most important centers of worship and are very numerous near the monastic sites.

Presumably, the crosses were erected to identify sacred lands or to protect adjacent buildings.

The production of these important signposts depended on the availability of large monoliths and the knowledge of how to work them, from the cutting of the stone to the carving of the details, and how to mount them on the great bases that were planted on the ground. A

38

**38. Cross of Muiredach,
about 920. Monasterboice.**

39

high cross is composed of a base, a monolithic shaft that terminates with the horizontal arms of the cross, sometimes joined by a circle for practical motives, and is often topped by an element like a reliquary. Another variety, the so-called ogham-stones, are monolithic stone slabs with inscriptions. In most cases sandstone was used.

The decorative repertory includes both abstract designs and Christian subjects drawn from the Sacred Scriptures. The former derive from metal work; with regard to the latter, in a number of cases it has been possible to identify a single workshop source. These are the crosses, with scenes from the Old and New Testaments, located in the central and eastern parts of the island at Durrow, Kells, Clonmacnoise and Monasterboice. The principal motive for erecting the great monoliths was undoubtedly

39. North Cross, 9th-10th centuries. Clonmacnoise.

the representation of the cross, but there are some examples with the abstract interlace designs that also appear in the illuminated manuscripts and enjoyed such a long period of diffusion. The best known examples are the crosses of Clonmacnoise and Monasterboice, some of which present scenes of the Passion of Christ, and the Moone High Cross, with stories from the Old and New Testaments.

At Clonmacnoise, at the center of the island where the important monastic complex was founded in 545, the *South Cross* is decorated with panels of interlace motif, while the *Cross of the Scriptures*, probably from the early 10th century, presents scenes from the New Testament related to the Crucifixion.

The *Cross of Muiredach* at Monasterboice, crafted in about 920, is decorated with scenes from the Bible and the Gospels, and is one of the most important masterpieces of stone in medieval Europe. On the eastern side the scenes include *Adam and Eve*, *Cain slaying Abel*, *David and Goliath*, *Adoration of the Magi*, and at the center of the cross, the *Final judgment and weighing of the souls*. On the western side the scenes represent the *Passion of Christ*, and at the center, the *Crucifixion* and *Resurrection*. At Moone, one of the tallest crosses is decorated with biblical scenes, each surrounded by a smooth flat frame, put into relief by the deepened background plane, creating a tight orderly composition. The high crosses, which a recent census numbered at over two hundred examples, date to the Late Middle Ages, between the 9th and 10th centuries. Some of their iconographic characteristics are comparable to those of Northumberland, while the presence of some subjects indicate contacts with Rome and Italy. In some cases there are inscriptions with the names of abbots and kings who commissioned the works, confirming their prestigious origins.

40

41

40. Cross of the Scriptures, early 10th century. Clonmacnoise.

41. Moone High Cross, 9th century.

42

42. Moone High Cross, *Sacrifice of Isaac* **and** *Daniel in the lions' den,* **9th century.**

43. Facing page: Moone High Cross, *Temptations of Saint Anthony,* **9th century.**

BENEDICTINE MONASTERIES DURING THE LATE MIDDLE AGES

The diffusion of the rule of Saint Benedict and the construction of the numerous monastic complexes is attributable to the will of Charlemagne himself. In Italy, for example, the future emperor took a personal interest in the Abbey of Farfa, located in a strategic position between Rome, the Lombard duchy of Spoleto and Cassino. In 817 the Benedictine rule was imposed on all Carolingian monastic orders. The most famous monasteries of Italy were Bobbio, Novalesa, Nonantola and San Vincenzo al Volturno.

Many of these monasteries were founded following important donations of vast lands, for the purpose of reinforcing instead of dispersing family estates; additional prosperity was guaranteed by royal donations. As centers of construction activities and refined artisan workshops, these monasteries played an important role of mediation between politics and culture and were often the nucleus of new towns. The monastery of Bobbio was founded about 613 by the Irish Saint Colombanus at the center of a forest, but not far from the main road connecting Piacenza and the Po valley with the Ligurian sea, through the Apennine mountains. Due to lack of archeological research the

plan and extension of the monastery during the Late Middle Ages are not known, however numerous decorative elements of stone have survived that reveal a high level of workmanship; the production of illuminated manuscripts in the *scriptorium* of the complex was also quite refined. San Pietro della Novalese was the most important monastery in the Piedmont area, along the road from Val di Susa to Moncenisio and on to France. The monastery was founded in 726 and was endowed with many lands. A 12th century book, the *Chronicon Novaliense*, supplies precious information which has been integrated by the results of many archeological investigations of the monastery complex. Among the abbots of the Novalesa abbey, Saint Eldrad deserves to be remembered: he was already venerated in the 12th century when a fresco cycle was dedicated to his life in the 9th century oratory, also dedicated to him. Nonantola, located in a strategic position along the road that connected the Piedmont and Po valleys with the city of Modena and Tuscany, was founded about the middle of the 8th century. This monastery also was endowed with vast lands and it had one of the most important scriptoria during the Late Middle Ages in northern Italy. Finally, San Vincenzo al Volturno presides over an important area at the border of the empire. It was founded at the end of the 7th century and the beginning of the 8th by three monks from

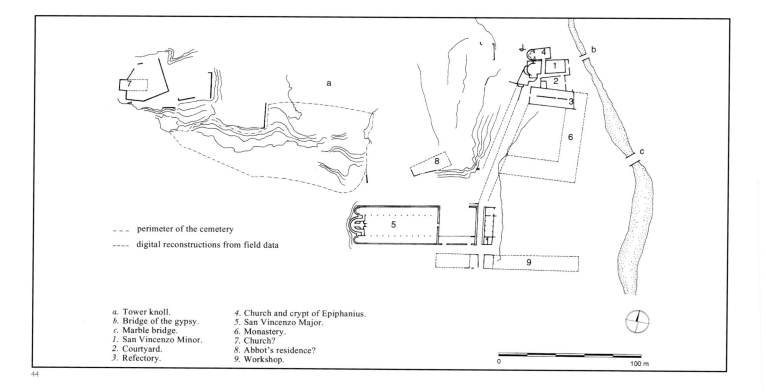

perimeter of the cemetery

digital reconstructions from field data

a. Tower knoll.
b. Bridge of the gypsy.
c. Marble bridge.
1. San Vincenzo Minor.
2. Courtyard.
3. Refectory.
4. Church and crypt of Epiphanius.
5. San Vincenzo Major.
6. Monastery.
7. Church?
8. Abbot's residence?
9. Workshop.

44

44. Plan of the excavations at San Vincenzo al Volturno (from *Enciclopedia dell'Arte Medioevale*, Rome 1999, vol. X, p. 318).

Farfa, and the monastery remained linked to the Lombardic patronage. The first community was not successful, but later another successful foundation was made under Carolingian auspices. This was the period of economic growth, expansion of the complex and construction of the great church of San Vincenzo Maggiore, and the presence of highly specialized workshops for glass and enamels. Until the 1980's, before the archeological excavations were begun, of the imposing complex only the frescoed crypt was known.

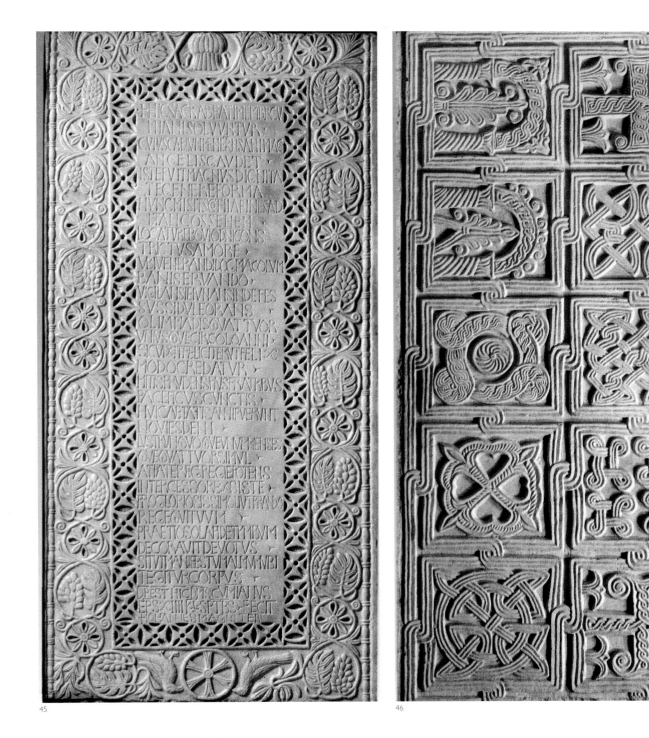

45

46

45. Magister Iohannes, Sepulchral slab of bishop Cumian, front, 8th century. Bobbio, Museum of the Abbey of San Colombano.

46. Back of the Cumian slab, recovered and sculpted as part of the presbyterial parapet. Bobbio, Museum of the Abbey of San Colombano.

PLAN OF THE ABBEY OF SAINT GALL

The Benedictine monastery, located in the Swiss canton of the same name, owes its name to Gall, an Irish disciple of Saint Colombanus, who founded it in 614.

During the Carolingian era it was one of the leading monastic centers, the site of important cultural and artistic moments. The famous plan was found in the abbey and is now preserved in the Staadtbibliotek Vadiana di San Gallo. Drawn on a total of five parchments sewn together, and accompanied by sketches and precise captions in red ink that identify the numerous buildings and spaces, the plan is a very precious and revealing document about what a monastic settlement was like during the Carolingian period. Not really a project or a survey, it represents a sort of ideal model sent to Abbot Gosbert before the year 829. The entire complex is centered around the square cloister with its covered walkway. The abbey-church with its double apse and the abbot's residence are located to the north.

The quarters for the monks (cells and refectory) were located to the south, to the west were workshops, orchards and vegetable gardens, and quarters for servants. Inside the main rooms the basic furnishings are also indicated schematically. The captions also include details about the varieties of legumes and fruit that were cultivated.

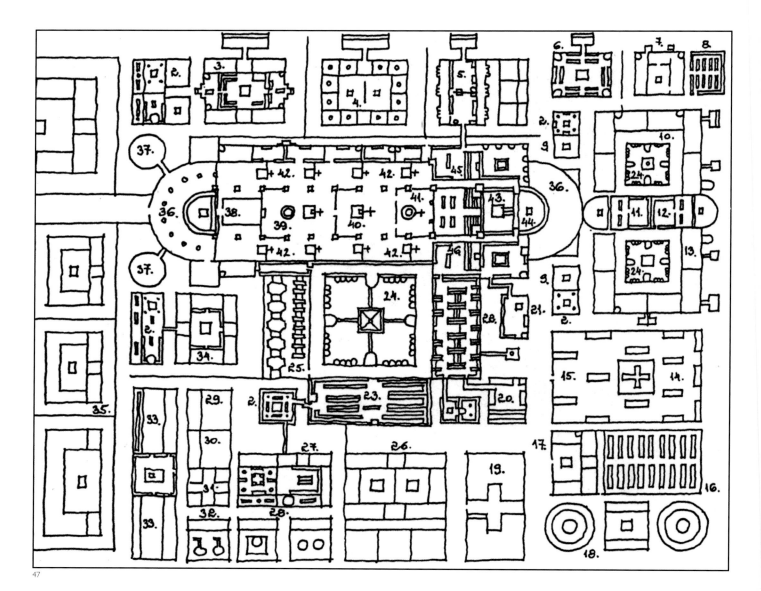

47

47. Sketch of the plan of the abbey of Saint Gall.

48. Facing page: _Psalterium aureum,_ second half of the 9th century. Saint Gall, Stiftsbibliothek.

RENAISSANCE OF THE CAROLINGIAN EMPIRE

Between the 8th and 9th centuries Charlemagne imposed a decisive turn of events on Europe by building a vast empire that explicitly harked back to that of ancient Rome: the Holy Roman Empire. Looking back to models of Rome under Constantine, the sovereign of the Franks presented himself as the legitimate heir of Constantine and, contemporaneously, emphasized his bond to the Church. This intention is clear in every work of art of this period, identified as the "Carolingian Renaissance" by scholars. This definition depends on the systematic references to ancient art imposed by the emperor, especially in the schools of the great abbeys of this period. In Aachen the emperor built a new residence, worthy of his new political role and a tangible expression of his cultural program.

The orientation of the palace chapel conditioned the disposition of all the other parts of the palace, which was an island to itself in the surrounding urban context of Roman origin. On one side the imperial complex bordered on the city, on the other it finished with the throne room, a basilica still partially standing which had three apses, and flat arches decorating the exterior walls. A stone corridor connected these buildings and divided the interior court of the palace from the exterior, where there were wooden buildings for the members of the court.

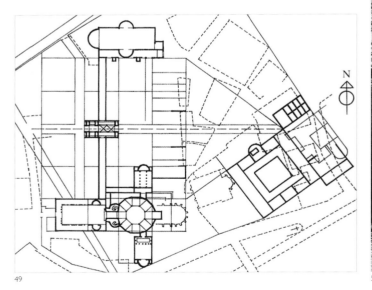

49

50

49. Plan of the imperial palace in Aachen (from M. Durliat, *Des barbares à l'an Mil*, 1985).

50. Abbey of Corvey, façade, 873-85. The façade of the abbey, framed by two square towers, illustrates the particular development of the western wing, called *Westwerk*, **a typical and widely diffused characteristic of the Ottonian era.**

51. *Donor*, 9th century.
Malles Venosta,
San Benedetto.

52

53

Einhard, the scholarly biographer of Charlemagne, names the "marvelous" basilica built in honor of the Virgin at the end of the 8th century as one of the most important constructions built by the emperor. The great architectural achievement was also endowed with precious materials and furnishings: in addition to the solid bronze doors and parapets, made in local foundries with excellent results for the period, columns and slabs of ancient marbles were brought from Ravenna and Rome to adorn the church.

The building inherited its basic structure from antiquity, the central plan of San Lorenzo in Milan and the church of San Vitale in Ravenna. Precise proportions conferred harmony to the whole construction, which focused on the central octagon, surrounded by aisles on two levels, under the dome. The architectural elements

52. Palatine Chapel, interior, 790-800. Aachen.

53. Palatine Chapel, gallery with the throne of Charlemagne, 790-800. Aachen.

grow narrower as they rise, a visual confirmation of their structural value. The lower level, under a projecting cornice, consists of eight arches that spring from solid pillars that carry the slender columns of the loggia above.

The entry, behind a quadriporticus as in the paleochristian basilicas, forms a projecting block between the two stair towers. The imperial loggia is located on the upper level, above the entry, and was connected directly to the palace through a multistory gallery: here the emperor greeted the acclamation of his subjects and followed Mass from his throne that faced the apse.

54

54. Palatine Chapel, interior, detail of the bronze parapet and the marble facing, 790-800. Aachen.

EQUESTRIAN STATUETTE OF CHARLEMAGNE
about 860-870
Paris, Musée du Louvre

SUBJECT

The bronze statuette, despite its small size, recalls classical equestrian statues of antiquity, which reflects a clear political message. This iconography clearly identifies the significance of the personage, identified as Charlemagne by some scholars, as one of his successors by others.

The scepter (lost) and the crown allude to his royalty, while the sword and the horse, which were recast during the Renaissance, refer explicitly to his role as a warrior.

This work, together with the screens and doors of the Palatine Chapel of Aachen indicate the refined capability of the Carolingian foundries, which found unending inspiration in the ancient sources.

COMPOSITION

Referring to statues such as Mark Aurelius in Campidoglio, this work returns to the ancient Roman model of free-standing sculpture.

Marco Aurelio, 161-181 A.D. Rome, Piazza del Campidoglio.

Like the ancient emperors, the Carolingian sovereign sits astride his charger albeit somewhat stiffly, without the exuberant attitude of his ancient prototypes. Despite the full volume of the figure, completed by heavy drapery, the limbs are still, the gaze fixed afar: the figure seems isolated and does not interact with the surrounding space.

CAROLINGIAN MONUMENTS IN EUROPE: GATEHOUSE OF THE ABBEY OF LORSCH AND THE CHURCH OF SAINT JOHN IN MÜSTAIR

Charlemagne constructed many important buildings all over western Europe to consolidate his role as the new emperor and also to control ever wider territories. The Gatehouse is the only remaining monumental element of the Carolingian Abbey of Lorsch, built at the end of the 8th century and later destroyed. As revealed by the archeological excavations, the Gatehouse stood in the court in front of the abbey-church and constituted the grandiose entrance despite its small dimensions. On the ground floor it has an open portico on pillars, the upper floor is a single rectangular hall with a fresco cycle representing a classical loggia. The references to ancient art are also to be found in the exterior decoration of the building, composed of two orders.

Semicolumns surmounted by composite capitals sustain an architrave with vegetal motifs, which sustains ten slender fluted pilasters crowned by pointed gables. The use of the building, apparently a guest-house for the Carolingian emperors during their visits to the monastery, led the architects to make use of the ancient tradition from which the new sovereigns claimed to descend directly. This influence is also evident in the ornamental repertory and in the plan of the Gatehouse that harks back to the form of the Roman triumphal arches. However the ancient model seems to have been somewhat misinterpreted in the architectural orders, which have lost their original structural significance, and also in the polychrome of the stones cut into squares, lozenges and polygonal shapes which disguise the true mass of the masonry. During the period in which the Abbey of Lorsch was being built, Charlemagne also founded the Abbey-church of Müstair, another component of the imperial policy to control the alpine passes with a

55

56

55. Abbey of Lorsch, gatehouse, end of the 8th century.

56. Abbey of Lorsch, capital of the gatehouse, end of the 8th century.

network of monasteries. During the Gothic period the original hall of the church was divided into three aisles by two colonnades, and vaults substituted the original wood truss roof. The hall also has a rich and well-organized fresco cycle that has been heavily damaged by poor restorations. These restorations are responsible for the brown-ochre tonality visible today and the removal of the gold highlights that usually added luminosity to the scenes. The narration has great rhythm, based on solid and balanced compositions and a meditated distribution of the figures, often framed by complex architectural backgrounds. The monumental scene of the Final Judgment on the inner face of the front façade is balanced by the triumph depicted in the main apse, where a gemmed cross represents the glory of Christ, and episodes from the Old and New Testaments are aligned along the walls within frames of garlands and ribbons. The scenes are ordered by subject rather than by chronology: clearly the episodes that were prior to the birth of Christ

are interpreted as prophetic allusions to the events narrated in the Gospels. According to the canons of composition that were already used at Castelseprio and later recovered in Ottonian painting, the illustrated narration continued through a series of panels so that the painting becomes a means of education and moral elevation.

57

58

57. *Scene from the life of Christ.* Müstair, Convent of Saint John.

58. *Statue of Charlemagne,* detail, 12th century. Müstair, Convent of Saint John.

GOLD ALTAR-PIECE

Vuolvinio, about 850
Milan, Sant'Ambrogio

SUBJECT

The altarpiece of Sant'Ambrogio represents one of the most astonishing accomplishments of Carolingian goldwork. The form recalls that of ancient sarcophagi so it seems to be a sort of ideal tomb of the saint whose body does actually appear in the lower compartment and can also be viewed from the back by opening two doors. Episodes from the Gospels surround the central image, on the front, where Christ is seated at the center of the cross, surrounded by the symbols of the Evangelists and the Apostles who participate in the revelation of Christ to humanity. The elongated, trembling figures fill each panel with agitated gestures, which contribute to the brilliant effect of the luminous surface.

The embossed relief is simpler and more monumental on the rear panels where the figures emerge from the flat background plane. The patron and the author of the precious altarpiece are portrayed on the center panel, surrounded by scenes from the life of Saint Ambrose and underneath the winged figures of the archangels Michael and Gabriel.

The bishop of Milan, Angilbert, and the artist Vuolvinio, accompanied by the inscriptions which identify them, kneel before Saint Ambrose who crowns and blesses them for the importance of their role.

COMPOSITION

The entire structure is composed of embossed and chiseled panels of gold plate and gilt silver plate, enclosed in enameled frames decorated with gems and precious stones.

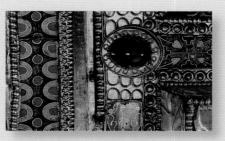

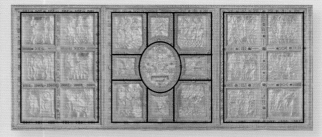

The front side, which faces the assembly of the worshipers in church, is divided into three parts: the central part contains a large cross and the figures are disposed around it.

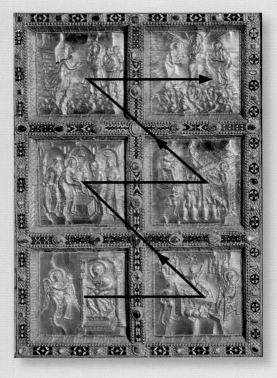

The rear side, which could be viewed and admired only by the priests or those who approached the tomb of the saint, is also divided into three parts. The confessional doors occupy the central part, decorated with four circular panels and small elegant heads of enamel.

The two side elements are divided into six panels where the narration of the Gospel proceeds from left to right and from the bottom to the top.

UBI PEDE A RO...S C...NI...CAT DOLENTI

...LLEN...MADSE VIDE T V NC EN....E

...IOCTAVO DIE ORDINATUR E P...

...SVENI...ANE DORMIENS TV RON...VR...T

...LEXAMAPV PVERIOS C...OCLEVI...A...RO...

...BROSI SEMILATE FFACTI GVF..T...

S. PICES VMME PATER FAMVLOM ISERERE BEN

The technique of enameling, which goes back to antiquity, consists of applying glass paste to metal sheet. It is therefore linked to the production cycles of glass and jewelry and is divided into two distinct activities: preparation of the components and, later, application to the metal supports. The diffusion of this technique would seem to originate in Byzantium, reaching its height from the 11th century on. During the Middle Ages a number of enameling procedures were known and practiced: *cloisonné*, *champlevé*, *de plique*, translucent. Much of the information available about enameling techniques comes from the treatise *De diversis artibus*, written by Theophilus in the 12th century. The author described the various phases in great detail, from the preparation of the metal sheet to the final polishing; he also affirms that one of the basic materials, the glass, was obtained by melting down ancient mosaic tesserae. Finally, he listed the objects most adapted to the technique, beginning with golden chalices.

The raw materials for preparing the enamel are a mixture of silicates including soda and potash with silica and lead oxide, red lead and the coloring matter, usually metallic oxides as for glass. The glass paste obtained was then crushed, ground, sifted, and then fired at various temperatures, in any case not less than 1300° F. The word enamel itself derives from a Germanic root which refers to the critical phase of production, the smelting of the raw materials. The final steps of production, cooling and polishing, were quite delicate because the final result had to be flawless. The metal support was prepared separately and there were several techniques for applying the enamel: it could be applied with cold adhesives, or with the more elaborate techniques of *cloisonné* and *champlevé*.

The *cloisonné* enamel was generally applied to gold sheet, occasionally to silver. The design was traced on the sheet with very thin and narrow vertical strips of metal to form the areas (that Theophilus called *corriolae*) where the glass paste was subsequently deposited.

One of the first objects made in *cloisonné* enamel during the High Middle Ages was the cross of Pope Paschal I (817-824) for the *Sancta Sanctorum*, the papal chapel in the Lateran. From that moment the technique was very widely diffused in Europe and many extremely refined, precious examples have survived. On the famous altarpiece of Sant'Ambrogio, made between 833 and 840, there are more than 1000 *cloisonné* enamels, by this time considered as important as the precious stones, cameos, pearls and coral, with which they

I. Reliquary Statue
of Sainte-Foy,
9th-10th centuries.
Conques, Church
of Sainte-Foy.

were associated. This technique characterized the production of the 11th century and into the 12th, appearing in famous objects such as the reliquary of Sainte-Foy of Conques. The champlevé enamel technique, developed principally during the 12th and 13th centuries, was made with copper or bronze instead of gold or silver. The areas to be enameled were outlined by raising (*en champlevé*) the metal of the support with a burin. Scratches on the supporting sheet improved the adhesion of the enamel. Between the second half of the 12th century and the 13th century this technique reached its apogee in the regions of the Moselle and the central Rhine area. Nicolas De Verdun, the goldsmith, was particularly well-known for his production of this type of enamel. The term *de plique* refers to enamels of the first type, where only gold sheet was used. For the translucent enamels, on the other hand, the most commonly used metal was silver, engraved with decorative and figurative designs later covered with several layers of enamel. The amount applied affected the intensity of the color. During the 12th and 13th centuries, enameling was used primarily for liturgical ornaments and fittings such as chalices, crosses, ciboria, and reliquaries, in addition to portable altars and the covers of sacred books. However, there are also cases of enamels being used in domestic fittings of great value and even on tombstones.

II

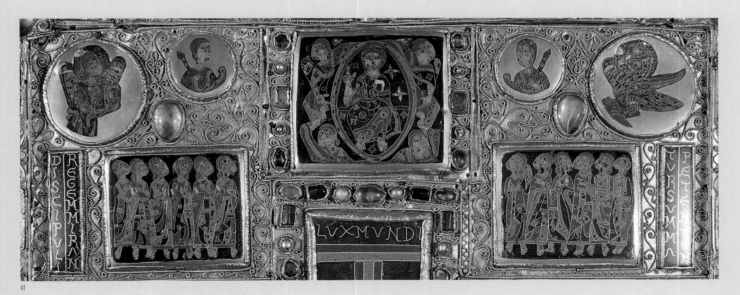

III

II. *Iron crown*, detail, 9th century. Monza, Cathedral Treasury.

III. Cover of the *Missal of Ariberto*, detail, second half of the 11th century. Milan, Cathedral Treasury.

ART OF THE MIDDLE AGES

Many examples of liturgical decorations and fittings from the Late Middle Ages have come down to us, especially those from the end of the 8th century through the first half of the 9th. Some are elements of balusters and screens for the choirs and presbyteries, others are elements of ciboria, altars, burial slabs and so forth, which share an ornamental repertory that was the most widely diffused in Carolingian Europe, where these objects were distributed as a consequence of the new liturgical requirements: the interlace patterns of ribbons and cords of one of more strands were associated with spirals, and also occasionally with vegetal elements, rarely with zoomorphic figures, in both cases highly stylized.

Studies of the numerous examples of sculpted stones with interlace motifs, registered between Rome and the north of Italy, have led to the hypothesis that a distinctive style originated in the Rhaetian Alps. Similar to the situation in the Pyrenees, where the sculpture distributed in Gaul originated, this style was exported from Val

59

60

61

59. Ciborium, 8th-9th centuries. Sovana (Grosseto), Santa Maria Maggiore.

60. Pilaster decorated with a braid motif, 9th century. Pisa, Cathedral.

61. Pilaster or panel of the presbyterial screen, 9th century. Nin, Croatia.

62

Venosta and the Engadin district (where there are still famous examples) to the rest of Italy.

The most interesting of these furnishings with the interlace designs are the pilasters and the screens that separated the altar from the congregation, or delimited the space for the monks, present in the monastic churches and in cathedrals. The pilaster strips were attached to the masonry pilasters with a system of interlocking joints or metal cramps. A limited number of ciboria in good condition are still extant, although not free of tampering, as well as an ample number of fragments. The basic model consists of a shrine composed of columns with capitals (often monolithic), which carry the arches that sustain the covering of heavy stone slabs.

The material is usually local and may include stone elements recovered from ancient buildings, especially those of marble. Occasionally there are traces of polychromy and it may be that these furnishings, like other elements of medieval sculpture, were sometimes colored. Many of these slabs were later recovered to use the undecorated face for other uses, such as pavements, but they were also included in the masonry of later buildings as a symbol of continuity with the past.

The important aspect is that the repertory of interlace designs appears in a surprisingly homogeneous manner in countries quite far apart, which demonstrates not only the existence of a formal repertory, but also the diffusion of technical and stylistic solutions. The areas of Europe where they are concentrated are northern Italy and Rome, the Swiss cantons, France, Austria, southern Germany, Istria and Dalmatia, where some of the best examples are to be found. Elsewhere they may have been imitations or the work of traveling artisans.

The first works of this type date to the end of the 8th century, most refer to the first quarter of the 9th century, but they continued to be made for the rest of the century and even later, when there was a revival of the basic motif, the interlace designs, between the 11th and 12th centuries in some regions.

62. Decorative slab from the basilica of Roselle, signed Magister Iohannes, 8th-9th centuries. Roselle (Grosseto), Podere Serpaio.

THE FLABELLUM OF TOURNUS

9th century
Florence, Bargello Museum

SUBJECT

The fan known as the flabellum of Tournus, made of finely pleated parchment with the handle and case of ivory and bone, is one of the most important artifacts of Carolingian art. It had a liturgical function, because it was used to free the altar of insects during the celebration of the Eucharist, and is now preserved in the Bargello Museum of Florence, where it was donated by the French antiquarian in 1888.

It is composed of three separate parts: the handle, the case, and the fan itself. The ivories have a uniform style and therefore come from the same workshop, but the whole object was undoubtedly created at one time with exceptionally fine workmanship. The probable relations with the following of Charles the Bald, together with the presence of antique stylistic elements support the hypothesis that it may have been made near the imperial court and then later offered to the monks in the abbey of Tournus.

COMPOSITION

The handle is made of elements of bone, separated by green-colored joints. On one of the joints it is possible to read the dedication: + JOHEL ME SCAE FECIT IN HONORE MARIAE (Johel made me in honor of Saint Mary). The handle elements are decorated with a rich repertory of vegetal and animal designs. The handle finishes with a small capital with the figures of Saint Peter, Saint Philibert, Saint Mary and Saint Paul (in substitution of the original figure of Saint Agnes).

The fan itself is made of a long, pleated strip of parchment, fastened at the base. The decoration is organized in three concentric tiers. The painter used a variety of colors, among which green and red predominate. The outermost strip of decoration presents a vivacious interlace based on animal and vegetal motifs, while the central strip also includes figures of saints. The inscriptions allude to the liturgical use of the fan, with an explicit request to chase away the flies and to give relief from the heat, and also confirm the dedication to the Virgin and to Saint Philibert.

The fan case was made by uniting small ivory panels, decorated with flower sprays, vines, animals and birds, as well as small panels with bucolic scenes from the Eclogues by Virgil.

In the medieval world of art, ivory was used with special attention. On the one hand, ivory might be seen as a category of sculpture, because it was often used in the form of panels sculpted in low relief or statuettes. On the other hand it was quite close to the realm of luxury. During the Middle Ages ivory was considered a very precious material, considering how difficult to obtain it was. Therefore it was reserved for the production of important objects, the attributes of temporal and spiritual power, such as the imperial throne or the bishop's throne, scepters and crosiers, consular and imperial writing tablets. However most of the surviving ivories were made for religious purposes and include the bindings of liturgical manuscripts, writing tablets, tabernacles, liturgical panels and devotional statuettes.

I. *Nuptial casket*. Rome, Palazzo Venezia.

II. THE BARBERINI IVORY
Paris, Musée du Louvre

This ivory, originally part of a writing tablet dated to the beginning of the 6th century, is divided into five panels. On the central panel the emperor (identified as Anastasius I by some, as Justinian by others) is portrayed in a triumph over the barbarians. The personification of the earth appears amid the hoofs of the charger, to symbolize the extension of the emperor's dominion. In the small panel to one side a Roman general pays homage to him by offering a statuette of Victory. On the lower panel Shiites and Indians offer their tributes, while the top panel portrays Christ in the act of blessing him.

III. ALTAR FRONTAL WITH SCENES FROM THE LIFE OF CHRIST
Salerno, Museo Diocesano

The panels and decorative fragments of the altar frontal, which may have been part of a throne or a reliquary, demonstrate the quality of ivory carving in the 12th century in the workshops of Salerno, where they created a synthesis between the Byzantine models and those of Western Romanesque art. Decorative frames with animal and vegetal motifs surrounded the fifty-four panels in low relief with scenes from the Old and New Testaments, where the figures are sculpted with classical proportions and a talent for narration.

IV. CRUCIFIX
Madrid, Archeological Museum

The crucifix was offered to the Cathedral of Léon by King Ferdinand I and Queen Sancha in 1063. This work illustrates how artists in Spain adapted techniques and decorative elements from Islam to religious Christian art, especially in the ivories carved in special workshops. The cross appears to be decorated with Mozarabic elements: on the back, fantastic animals appear among the leaves; on the front and along the borders, there are twisted human figures that represent, on one side, the fall of the damned, and on the other side, the resurrection of the dead.

IV

V. GIOVANNI PISANO, MADONNA AND CHILD
Pisa, Museo dell'Opera del Duomo

The statuette was made between 1298 and 1299, as documents report, for the major altar of the cathedral where it stood in a tabernacle between two angels with golden wings. Giovanni Pisano took advantage of the natural curve of the ivory in the inclination of the mother who leans back to sustain the weight of her son. The iconography, diffused by French sculpture, copied the draperies, the folds and the position of the Child, to express the dynamic tension of the bodies and the solidity of the volumes, rather than any intention to create mannered elegance.

V

MANUSCRIPT ILLUMINATION AT THE COURT OF CHARLEMAGNE

An evaluation of Carolingian painting, almost completely lost, would not be possible without the illuminated manuscripts produced in the *scriptoria* of the court which made an important contribution to European culture of this period.

Charlemagne's political ambition, to create a class of educated men, both lay and religious, to administer the different aspects of his reign, included the necessity to make a major cultural reform, entrusted to the care of famous men close to the court such as Alcuin of York. The importance assigned to the study of classical authors led to the increased production of books. The reformation of writing and the vast production of illuminated manuscripts must therefore be interpreted in the light of this ambitious cultural and political program.

When he returned from a visit to Rome in 781, Charlemagne commissioned a gospel book from Godescalco. The codex, now known by the name of the artist, was made in only two years in the palatine school in Aachen. It included the portraits of the evangelists, pen in hand, in the act of writing while seated at their desks.

The posture and the gestures of the evangelists, and the presence of the fountain of life, an iconographic theme here introduced for the first time in Western art and often repeated thereafter, point

63

63. Missal of Godescalco,
Portraits of Saint Luke
and Saint Mark, **781-783.**
Paris, Bibliothèque
Nationale.

to Middle Eastern thematic origins. It may be that the role played by Einhard, the biographer of Charlemagne, contributed to the development of a school at the court.

Of the production of those years, all of outstanding quality, four books remain, all four are gospel books.

One of these, which had belonged to Charlemagne himself, was donated by his son Louis the Pious to the Saint-Médard of Soissons Monastery in 827.

The elaborately illuminated pages of the codex present animated scenes, architectural backgrounds and the renewal of themes such as the fountain of life, surrounded by exotic birds and animals. In this case, however, the reference to classical models is clear, as it is in the other gospel books of the group. In the Lorsch gospel book, now in the Vatican library, and in the Saint-Riquier gospel book, now in the municipal library of Abbeville, the full page portraits of the evangelists and the architectural backgrounds that recall ancient models also appear; in all examples the chromatic palette is limited. The theme of this group of codices was quite successful and was copied by Archbishop Ebbo about 823 when he commissioned the gospel book now at Epernay. Here the figures of the evangelists have lost the hieratic character of classical descent, and have become extremely vibrant, the same vitality distinguishes the little figures of carpenters and masons at work on the gables of the architectural structures that surround the tables of the canons.

64

65

153

64. *Missal of Saint Riquier, Portrait of Saint Matthew*, end 8th-early 9th century. Abbeville, Bibliothéque Municipale.

65. *Missal of Saint Médard of Soissons, The fountain of life*, end 8th-early 9th century. Paris, Bibliothéque Nationale.

THE OTTONIAN EMPIRE AND ART OF THE YEAR 1000

The adjective "Ottonian" refers to the period of history that goes from the middle of the 10th to the first decades of the 11th century, marked by the dominion of the sovereigns of Saxony who were also invested with the role of emperor of the Holy Roman Empire. In the Germanic regions, this period coincided with the flowering of the arts promoted by the emperors within the area of their courts. The artistic production was influenced by the Carolingian tradition combined with direct Byzantine influence, favored by the marriage of Otto II with the Byzantine princess Theophano. Ottonian ecclesiastical architecture continued the Carolin-

gian tradition of basilica plans enriched with the choirs and towers that took the form of the Westwerk. This multistorey element of the building, on the western side of the church, contributed to a rigorous definition of the space, as did the repetition of a square module elsewhere in the building. The constructions of this period contain the seeds of some innovative characteristics, such as a new concept of the wall, now animated by cornices and pilasters, that reveals affinities with the Romanesque sensibility. In the field of sculpture the production in the workshops of Hildesheim was outstanding. Due to the efforts of bishop Bernward, the technique of bronze-casting was recovered after many years of substitution by metal embossing, and the workshops were able to send liturgical items of fine quality all over Germany.

66

67

66. Cathedral of Saint Martin and Saint Stephan, view of the eastern arm of the cathedral. Mainz. Founded in 1081, the complex was rebuilt at the beginning of the 12th century. The dimensions of the Ottonian church were conserved. The stair towers date to the 11th century.

67. Font, 11th century. Hildesheim, Saint Michael.

68. Ciborium, detail of
Saint Ambrose between
saints Gervasio and
Protasio and two
Benedictine monks with a
model of the new
ciborium. Milan,

Saint Ambrose. The
ciborium of painted
stucco was erected
above the gold altar of
Vuolvinio in the 10th
century, and is evidence
of the vitality of the

workshops in Milan
during the Ottonian era
although they were better
known for ivory carvings.

**69-70. Ciborium, details of
*Sant'Ambrogio between
two devotees and Saint
Tecla between two
devotees*, 10th century.
Milan, Saint Ambrose.**

SAINT MICHAEL IN HILDESHEIM

Saint Michael in Hildesheim is the masterpiece of Ottonian architecture in Saxony. In this building the forms of the Carolingian vocabulary found their perfect expression, anticipating solutions that would be used later in the Romanesque churches of Saxony.

Bernward, tutor of the future emperor Otto III and bishop of the city, had founded the abbey which it served in 996. It has a triple aisle plan where pillars alternate with columns to separate the side aisles (one pillar every two columns) and it has two transepts. The eastern transept finishes with three apses, while the western transept rises above an ample crypt, on a level with the floor of the church, surrounded by an ambulatory. The whole building seems to be designed according to precise proportions, which are evident on the plan where the square module is repeated, and in the sober definition of the exterior volumes with smooth compact masonry.

The bronze doors also contributed to the majesty of its aspect. Today the doors are preserved in the cathedral of the city. The two leaves of the door, cast in solid bronze, are each divided into 8 rectangular panels where the figures in high relief move against the smooth background plane enlivened by sketchy indications of natural and architectural scenic elements.

The panels reveal a notable compositional ability in the distribution of the planes and the illusion of depth, so that the figures move freely in their space, with dramatic intensity.

The dedication of the artist also emerges from the iconographical confrontation between the episodes from Genesis on the left and scenes from the life of Christ on the right, to illustrate how the life and sacrifice of the Messiah led to the salvation of man after the original sin.

72

71. Facing page: *Column of Bernward*, detail, 11th century. Hildesheim, Saint Michael.

72. Saint Michael, exterior, 1010-33. Hildesheim.

73

75

73. Saint Michael, nave, 1010-33. Hildesheim.

74. *Doors of Saint Bernward*, detail of *Scenes of the life of Christ*, 1015. Hildesheim, Saint Michael.

75. Saint Michael, capital, 1010-33. Hildesheim.

74

76

77

76. Saint Michael,
baluster of the choir,
1010-33. Hildesheim.

77. *Doors of Saint
Bernward*, detail
of *Stories of Adam
and Eve*, 1015.
Hildesheim,
Saint Michael.

SAINT GEORGE IN OBERZELL

The church of Saint George in Oberzell was part of the network of shrines and chapels under the guidance of the Abbey of Reichenau. The abbot Otto III founded it at the beginning of the 10th century and the construction was probably related to the acquisition of the relic of the head of Saint George by the abbey. The church has a basilica plan, divided into three aisles, that ends with an elevated choir, above which another tower rises. Truncated pyramid capitals top the columns of the nave. The cycle of frescoes that decorate the church, despite the losses and tampering, constitutes one of the most magnificent decorative monuments of the Ottonian era. The fresco cycle is organized in two tiers above the corbels of the arches, where the busts of the abbots are depicted in a series of medallions. The two tiers are framed and divided by a meander motif painted over low relief. In the upper tier the figures of the apostles are depicted between the windows, while below scenes from the life of Christ exalt the miraculous episodes. The episodes on the north wall are *Casting out the demons in Gerasa*, *Healing the man with dropsy*, *Calming the storm*, *Healing the blind*, followed on the south wall by *Healing the lepers*, *Raising the dead son of the widow in Nain*, *Raising the daughter of Jairus*, *Healing the woman subject to bleeding* and *Raising of Lazarus*. The events are illustrated in such a clear manner that the episodes are immediately recognizable. The figure of Christ is placed clearly at the center of the scene and is depicted with clear, powerful gestures, surrounded by those who witness the miracle and seem to confirm the truth of the events. Even though much of the modeling of the figures has disappeared, carried away with a layer of plaster that had covered the frescoes, the chiaroscuro relief of the figures can still be appreciated, while traces of highlights and outlines suggest how they appeared originally. The backgrounds, on the other hand, are uniform and divided horizontally into bands of different colors, occasionally interrupted by architectural structures that in some cases become urban panoramas.

78

**78. Saint George, nave,
10th century.
Oberzell.**

79

80

79. *Jesus casting out the demons in Gerasa,* 10th century. Oberzell, Saint George.

80. *Resurrection of Lazarus,* 10th century. Oberzell, Saint George.

THE CATHEDRAL OF SPEYER

In 1024 Conrad II, founder of the new Salian dynasty, immediately following his election to the imperial throne, commissioned the construction of the cathedral of Speyer.

The church has a long triple aisle, closed by a large transept and a *Westwerk* with two towers. The flat covering of the central nave was substituted in 1080 by the cross vaults that still stand, which accentuate the ascensional expression of the structure. The semicolumns along the walls of the central aisle, that rise above the arches and the clerestory windows to sustain a series of arches, also contribute to this effect.

This system represented a significant innovation with respect to the Ottonian plan of the building. The walls were no longer conceived as flat surfaces, which had been used ever since the paleochristian era to display paintings and mosaics, but became a modeled surface characterized by projections and hollows, anticipating the Romanesque sensibility.

81

82

164

81. Cathedral of Speyer, east wing of the crypt, 11th century.

82. Cathedral of Speyer, exterior, 11th century.

83. Facing page: Cathedral of Speyer, view of the nave looking toward the altar, 11th century.

IVORY CARVING IN MILAN DURING THE OTTONIAN PERIOD

After the annexation of the kingdom of Italy, the emperor Otto I (936-973) consolidated his political power and promoted the development of the arts. After the conquest of Lombardy in 951, the Milan school of sculpture became quite important and was the source of the ivory altar frontal that the emperor donated to the cathedral of Magdeburg. The panels, which narrate stories from the New Testament, represent one of the first autonomous artistic expressions of Ottonian art.

Other important works in ivory are ascribed to the same group of carvers, including the aspersorium (or *situla*) of the archbishop Gotofredo of Milan who commissioned it, as noted in the inscription at the top.

The bucket served for the benediction with holy water. The figures of the Madonna and Child with two angels (who carry a thurible and a similar situla), and the four evangelists (Mark, John, Matthew and Luke) each in the act of writing at a desk and associated with his symbol, are portrayed in a framework of simple architectural structures.

A series of poetic inscriptions on the arches complete and integrate the figures. The object therefore includes both traditional and innovative elements, even with regard to the iconography, and it is related to the ivory panel with Christ enthroned, Emperor Otto II, Princess Theophano, and little Otto III, dated 983 and still preserved in the museum at Castello Sforzesco in Milan. Both objects reveal the same sensibility for proportions and spatial construction that derives from classical antiquity, in fact both the situla and the panel inscribed *otto imperator* may be the work of the same carver.

The importance and creativity of the ivory school are confirmed by the stylistic comparisons with the painted stuccos of the contemporary ciborium in Saint Ambrose in Milan, where the first two Otto's also appear with their wives.

The exceptional quality of the ivory school of Milan was continued on the other side of the Alps, where the modeling and refined expressiveness were further perfected, as in the case of the Madonna of Mainz, made in Trier perhaps. The ivory panel represents the Virgin and Child enthroned in a small shrine, with characteristics that prefigure the Romanesque style.

84

84. Aspersorium of Gotofredo, end of the 10th century. Milan, Cathedral Treasury.

85. Facing page: Trivulzio Panel, about 980. Milan, Sforzesco Castle, Collections of Applied Arts.

IHS XPS

SCS MAVRITIVS SCS MAVRITIVS

OTTO IMPERATOR

THE ABBEY OF REICHENAU AND OTTONIAN MANUSCRIPTS

The name of the Abbey of Reichenau is associated with an extraordinary series of illuminated manuscripts made during a period of over fifty years around the year 1000, that is, some of the most famous Ottonian manuscripts. However, the matter of this activity at Reichenau constitutes one of the most debated cases of medieval art history: on the one hand the opinion that doubts the existence of a *scriptorium*, on the other the conviction that the abbey on Lake Constance was the center of diffusion of Ottonian manuscript illumination. Even though historical documents of this period do not ever mention a *scriptorium*, it is likely that a group of extremely fine manuscripts were produced here during a period of about fifty years.

The books of Reichenau have been classified into three groups. The first takes its name from Eburnant, one of the scribes of the evangelical primer known as the *Gero Codex*, made about 970.

The second group is named after the scribe Ruodprecht, who portrayed himself offering the finished psalter (now in the museum of Cividale del Friuli) to Egbert, Archbishop of Trier, who had commissioned it about 983, while the abbey was rising to dominance. The manuscript is enriched with decorations including vegetal interlace, masks, dragons and birds. Egbert also commissioned the *Codex Egberti*, with lavish illuminations by numerous artists, including the most prestigious Ottonian painter known as the Master of *Registrum Gregorii*, who contributed six leaves to the codex. The third group is known by the name of the scribe Liuthar, author of the gospel book by the same name, now in the treasury of the cathedral in Aachen. Reichenau, through imperial patronage, reached the height of its achievements, conserving the memory of previous Carolingian and Late-antique models, but creating a new language. The new symbolic references, the innovation of the composition and the amplification of the polychromy that were achieved around the year 1000 are particularly evident in the Gospel Book of Otto III, now in the library in Munich.

86

87

86. *Psalter of Egberto,* the letter B, end of the 10th century. Cividale del Friuli, Archeological Museum.

87. Ruodprecht, *Gertrude Psalter: David,* end of the 10th century. Cividale del Friuli, Cathedral.

**88. Gospel Book of Otto III,
end 10th-early 11th centuries.
Munich, Bayerische
Staatsbibliothek.**

LATE MEDIEVAL PAINTING IN ITALY

In the field of painting, the Ottonian era had contrasting sources: one was tied to the Byzantine tradition and symbolism that came through the court, the other was a more popular and expressive interpretation of reality. The pictorial cycles of the 10th and 11th centuries reveal, at times, the refined manners of the tradition from Constantinople, which maintained the Hellenistic tradition of modeling and profundity of space while creating, at the same time, a solemn image of divinity and power through the abstraction of the forms and materials. In other examples the simpler and more popular solutions prevail, to create a living and moving image, the expression of a new "vulgar" pictorial language. These pictorial languages

89

89. *Victory of the angels over the dragon of the Apocalypse*, 1050-75. Civate, San Pietro al Monte.

90. Facing page: *Crucifixion*, 9th century. Rome, Santa Maria Antiqua.

were alternated and mixed in Rome where, however, the styles of early Christianity remained stronger. At the same time, the city received strong Byzantine influences, especially between the 7th and 8th centuries when there were a number of popes of Greek and Syrian origin, or during the iconoclast persecution (726-87) when many oriental artists fled to Italy. A local school of mosaicists was also active in Rome during this period: they decorated the semidomes of the apses of major churches with brightly colored hierarchical figures against gold backgrounds or blue skies.

91

91. *Christ with saints*, 9th century. Rome, Santa Cecilia in Trastevere.

SANTA MARIA FORIS PORTAS IN CASTELSEPRIO

The fresco cycle in Santa Maria foris Portas in Castelseprio, which represents the best example of Late Medieval painting, was discovered in 1944 under layers of whitewashing and later paintings. It decorates the eastern apse of a small single aisle church that had survived the destruction in the 12th century of Castelseprio, a town along the road from Milan to the lakes and alpine passes that had been fortified by the Lombards. It represents episodes from the childhood of Christ, as narrated in the Gospel of Luke and the apocryphal gospels, which was very common in Oriental iconography. The scenes are disposed as follows: above the window, a shield with Cristo Pantocrator; on both sides of the window the *Annunciation*, *Visitation*, *Ordeal of bitter waters*, *Joseph's dream*, *Journey to Bethlehem*; on the lower tier, the *Presentation in the temple*, *Nativity* and *Adoration of the Magi*. The narration is characterized by swift free brushstrokes, with a few touches of clear luminous colors. The figures are lively and active in their spaces defined by architectural elements or solid landscapes. The painter has captured the human element of the sacred story in depicting Mary's difficulty in rising from her resting place, the impetuous energy of the angel, the silent exchange of glances between Mary and Joseph as they depart for Bethlehem. The fresco cycle seems to revive the Hellenistic pictorial tradition, with a much surer hand than to be found elsewhere in medieval painting. Scholars have explained the exceptional quality of these paintings with several hypotheses. The date of this cycle is thus still uncertain, some argue for the 6th, others for the 10th century, but it does seem almost certain that it should be attributed to an artist of Oriental origin, from a location where the classical tradition had continued almost without interruption.

92

92. *Journey to Bethlehem*,
detail. Castelseprio, Santa
Maria foris Portas.

93

93. *Presentation in the
temple.* Castelseprio,
Santa Maria foris Portas.

94. Facing page: *Joseph's
Dream.* Castelseprio,
Santa Maria foris Portas.

THE FRESCOES OF SAN VINCENZO AL VOLTURNO

The frescoes that decorate the cruciform crypt of the Monastery at San Vincenzo al Volturno were painted for Abbot Epiphanius (826-43), who is also portrayed in the cycle.

The entire cycle is dominated by the figure of Christ, seated on a star-studded globe at the center of the vault to signify his role as Lord of Creation. On the walls there are figures of angels and saints, episodes from the life of Christ, scenes of martyrdom of Saint Lawrence and Saint Stephan. The semidome of the apse is occupied by the image of the Madonna with an ample halo, and she also appears in the *Annunciation* on the facing wall.

The decorative program, that scholars have linked to the writings of the theologian and abbot Ambrose Autperto, seems to dedicate particular attention to the Virgin, her maternity, the assumption and her heavenly regality. This particular iconography is related to some examples in Rome, the origin of which is also associated with Byzantine influence on the composition as a whole and the single details.

Oriental sources also influenced the expressions and gestures of the figures, set against colored backgrounds, where the painter has created a certain illusion of spatial depth by scaling the figures. In some scenes the tone is dramatic, as in the provincial currents of Byzantine art. In the *Crucifixion*, for example, the Madonna seems to rush toward her son, while Saint John withdraws, his hand on his cheek expressing his dismay and grief. Christ, instead, is immobile, with eyes wide open, the conqueror of death.

95

96

97

95. *Angel,* about 830. Monastery of San Vincenzo al Volturno, Crypt of Epiphanius.

96. *Crucifixion with Abbot Epiphanius kneeling* in the foreground, about 830. Monastery of San Vincenzo al Volturno, Crypt of Epiphanius.

97. *Martyrdom of Saint Lawrence,* about 830. Monastery of San Vincenzo al Volturno, Crypt of Epiphanius.

98. Facing page: *The Virgin with a Saint,* about 830. Monastery of San Vincenzo al Volturno, Crypt of Epiphanius.

THE DECORATION OF SANT'ANGELO IN FORMIS

At the end of the 11th century the Abbot of Montecassino, Desiderio, a passionate restorer of antique culture, brought a group of painters and mosaicists from Constantinople to decorate the Benedictine abbey: at the same time they had a strong influence on local culture. Sant'Angelo in Formis, for example, illustrates the artistic renovation that touched the whole region after these events. The frescoes of the church, which had been built by Desiderio himself, indicate how much the local artisans had absorbed from the influence of Byzantine painting. The Abbot of Montecassino is portrayed in the apse, in the act of offering a model of the church to Christ, who is surrounded by the evangelical symbols. The decorations of the nave narrate stories from the Old and New Testaments, clearly for didactic purposes. The Old Testament stories are located in the aisles, while the evangelical episodes are set out in chronological order along three tiers on the walls of the central nave.

The cycle concludes emblematically with the *Last Judgment* on the western wall. The local artists freely interpreted the Byzantine forms to create a vivacious and flowing narration. They use the iconographical schemes, the types of figures, the draperies with the shadows and highlights of the oriental masters, but violent color contrasts, fully modeled forms, and the addition of movement and expression distinguish their work.

99

100

99. Cassinese school, frescos of the apse, detail of Abbot Desiderio with a model of the church, 11th century. Capua, Sant'Angelo in Formis.

100. Cassinese school, *Cain slays Abel*, 11th century. Capua, Sant'Angelo in Formis.

101

102

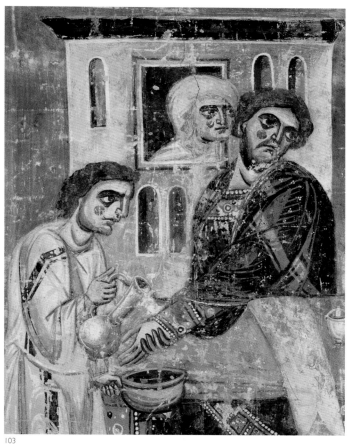

103

101. Cassinese school,
The Last Judgement,
11th century. Capua,
Sant'Angelo in Formis.

102. Cassinese school,
Gideon and the angel,
11th century. Capua,
Sant'Angelo in Formis.

103. Cassinese school,
Jesus before Pilate, detail
of Pilate, 11th century.
Capua, Sant'Angelo in
Formis.

105

104. Facing page: Sant'Angelo in Formis, interior, 11th century. Capua.

105. Cassinese school, *Crucifixion*, 11th century, Capua, Sant'Angelo in Formis.

THE FRESCOES OF SAN CLEMENTE IN ROME

The lower basilica of San Clemente, which was the primitive church dating to the end of the 4th century, was decorated with important frescoes on many occasions.

Notable, among others, are those to the left of the entrance, from the middle of the 9th century, which represent small panels with the *Crucifixion*, *Maries at the sepulcher*, *Descent to limbo*, and the *Wedding at Cana*.

The *Ascension* is in a better state of conservation. The figure of the Madonna, in a gesture of prayer, is placed against a background of ample areas of dark red and blue, surrounded by the apostles and the Savior inside a lozenge born by four angels.

The latter are depicted as they agitate their arms, cover their faces, blink their eyes, and so forth, revealing surprise, fear and emotional involvement. The figures are outlined and are well modeled despite the simplified color scheme. The frescoes along the left wall of the central nave date to the 11th century and narrate the legends of San Clemente and Saint Alexander. In this case the compositions are divided by slender architectural details, filled with small figures.

The narration has a more realistic tone, which includes details of embroidered textiles and precious objects, against the red backgrounds and fresh colors that recall ancient painting. The inscriptions along the lower margin, that refer the phrases pronounced by the protagonists of the scenes, also supply a very precious indication of the popular language in use at that time.

106

107

106. *Miracle of the Black Sea*, 11th century. Rome, San Clemente.

107. *Translation of the corpse of Saint Clement to Rome*, 11th century. Rome, San Clemente.

108

109

108. *Legend of Saint
Alexander,* 11th century.
Rome, San Clemente.

109. *Miracle of Sisinius,*
11th century. Rome, San
Clemente.

3. Cluny and the Romanesque Period in Europe

n 910 William III of Aquitaine founded the Abbey of Cluny in Bourgogne, a turning point in the religious and artistic history of the Middle Ages in Western Europe.

The new abbey brought about the revision of the Benedictine rule and, within a short space of time, created a wide network of subordinate Cluniac houses, becoming one of the richest and most powerful monasteries in Christendom. The tight legal and cultural structure of the Benedictine order has led some scholars to hypothesize about the existence of a Cluniac art, the outcome of centrally-planned guidelines, with well-defined characteristics, particularly in the field of architecture.

Such hypotheses cannot be treated as gospel, but it is likely that the liturgical needs of the order gave rise to a necessity to find new architectural solutions. In the course of time these would have been reused and adapted to buildings in different geographical areas, in the period in which Romanesque architecture was acquiring its particular characteristics.

2

3

185

1. Facing page: Abbey of Sainte-Madeleine, capital with mystic mill, about 1120-50. Vézelay.

2. Abbey of Sainte-Foy, capital with builders, 12th century. Conques.

3. Durham Cathedral, view of nave, 1093-1133.

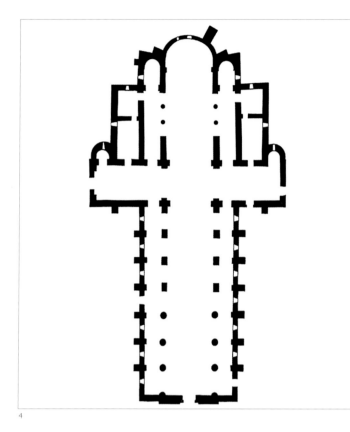

A NEW SPIRITUAL CENTER IN THE WEST: THE ABBEY OF CLUNY

In the space of less than a hundred years the mother church of the Cluniac order was rebuilt as many as three times to accommodate the needs of the growing monastery and the community of monks who inhabited it. In the first place the new rule had political implications. The order was no longer under the jurisdiction of the bishops and feudatories but directly responsible to the Pope, nor were the monks obliged to dedicate part of their time to manual and intellectual activities, as ordained by Saint Benedict four centuries previously ("ora et labora"). Prayer thus became the sole occupation of the Cluniac community, and the celebration of the liturgical office a fundamental part of monastic life. In his chronicle, Raoul Glaber describes the pomp and solemnity of these rites, which filled the entire day with no interruptions. The Cluniac revision thus also had immediate repercussions on the architecture of the mother church, which adopted solutions of a splendid and complex nature. Although nothing remains of the first Cluny church which was consecrated in 927, the excavations carried out in the past century have led to the recovery of the blueprint of the second building which was sited at the North-East corner of the

4. Blueprint of Cluny II
(from M. Durliat, *L'art
roman*, 1982).

5. Reconstruction of Cluny
II (from L. Grodecki,
F. Mutherich, J. Taralon,
F. Wormald, *The century
of the Year 1000*, 1974).

present-day cloister and built between 948 and 981, at the time of the Abbot Mayeul. All of 120 feet in length, the dimensions of the church of Cluny II were remarkable for the time: the longitudinal part was divided into three aisles with seven bays and ended in a narrow transept, with an expanded choir beyond. This was divided into three large aisles with two rectangular areas beside them and six apses facing them. In about the year 1000 a three-bayed (Galilean) narthex with an atrium in front of it was added on to the façade and the choir and dormitory were built.

All that remains even of the third church, which was founded in 1088 and destroyed at the time of the French Revolution, is part of the southern transept, with an octagonal bell tower.

Contemporary sources record that it was famed throughout Europe for the grand style of its architectural forms and the splendid sculp-

6

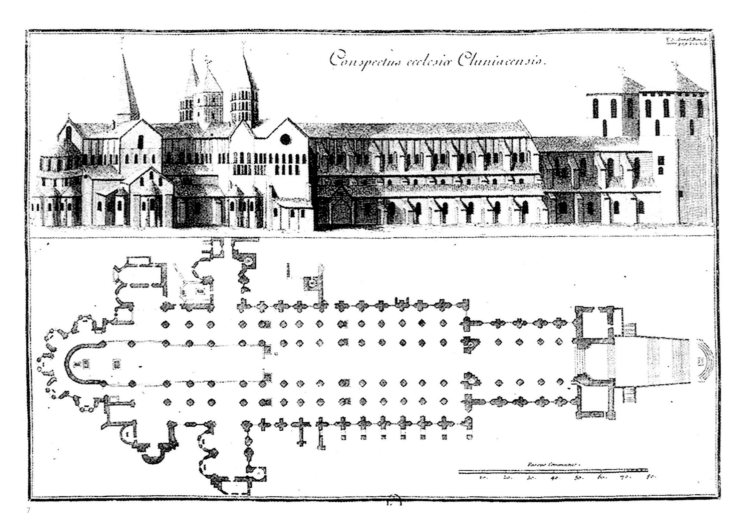

Conspectus ecclesiæ Cluniacensis.

7

6. Capital with four rivers of Paradise, early 12th century. Cluny, Musée du Farinier.

7. Blueprint and section of Cluny III (from Mabillon, *Annales ordinis benedicti*, 1713).

tural, pictorial and mosaic decoration with which it is adorned. Being 560 feet long and of monumental proportions, Cluny III was the largest church in Christendom. The complex blueprint shows how exceptional it was with its five aisles, double transept, choir with an ambulatory and five radial chapels, and five towers. A colonnaded three-aisled atrium was attached to the façade, which was flanked by two towers. The complex is distinguished throughout by its soaring structures. The walls of the nave were divided into three tiers with arcades, a blind triforium and windows, above which vaulting (probably barrel), rose to a dizzy height. The capitals from the ambulatory, which are now kept in the fourteenth century flour store which has been turned into a museum, bear witness to the richness of the original sculptural decoration. The surviving capitals are large and display a remarkable mastery of sculptural technique characterized by supple and delicate relief and delicate and elegant decorative rhythms. Their iconographic content is vast and is thought by some to illustrate the content of the epistle of Saint Pierre Damian in which the lives of the abbey's monks were eulogized. The eight tones of Gregorian plainchant, the seasons, the theological and cardinal virtues, original sin and the rivers of Paradise are depicted. Some capitals bear Biblical scenes such as the *Sins of the Forefathers* and *Sacrifice of Isaac* while others are in the Corinthian style.

8

8. View of octagonal tower (Clocher de l'Eau Bénite) above southern transept of ancient abbey church, 1088-1130. Cluny.

The monk had a foremost role in Medieval society, being at the top of the hierarchical system of the three ordines in the *ecclesiastical culture*: men of prayer (*oratores*), men of war (*bellatores*) and men of field work (*laboratores*). The monastic profession was regarded as the supreme expression of an authentic Christianity and the gateway to Paradise. The first monks distinguished themselves from the beginning of the Christian era: after the death of the apostles they withdrew to places untouched by the confusion of the world where they could follow the evangelical precepts in solitude. The spirit of self-sacrifice they shared with the first Christians set them apart. This entailed renouncing marriage and any kind of private property, and the propensity for a solitary and ascetic life. Later on, certain individuals took the initiative of adopting a rule and establishing a hierarchical system within communities. The monastic foundations became separate, self-sufficient worlds which were centers of work, prayer and culture.

From the mid 7th century onwards, many groups of monks adopted the rule of Saint Benedict through the support of the Church of Rome and the initiative of the Carolingians. In fact the monastic foundations enjoyed privileged relations with sovereigns and the nobility, who supported them with offerings and donations of property and land in exchange for prayers.

In the complex and beleaguered political system of the time, the foremost aim of this practice was to confer on the land an economic and administrative organization, which the monks were in a better position than others to guarantee.

This, however, resulted in the subordination of the monasteries to an external power – the bishop or the lord – and the consequent decline of monastic discipline. Reform was called for and most were in favor of "monastic liberty". The case of Cluny was exemplary. In the space of little more than a century, hundreds of monasteries were attached to the general abbot and under the direct tutelage of the Pope. The development of the Cluniac order was not an isolated case: from Saint Victoire in Marseilles to Vallombrosa, from Camaldoli to Citeaux, from Saint-Bénigne of Dijon to Hirsau, the 11th to the 12th century saw a proliferation of stable congregations gathered round a single main center.

Contemporaneously, a new religious type was emerging from the solitude of the cloister. Like Saint Francis they dedicated themselves to prayer and the *cura animarum*, lived as the poor and offered up their lives as an authentic evangelical testimony.

I. *Ottone Visconti welcomed by the people of Milan,* end 13th-early XIV century.

II. Buonamico Buffalmacco, *Stories of the anchorites,* detail, about 1325-50. Pisa, Camposanto.

III. After Paolo Uccello, *Scenes from hermit life,* about 1480. Firenze, Galleria dell'Accademia.

THE INFLUENCES OF CLUNIAC ARCHITECTURE IN EUROPE

It is probable that the architectural forms of Cluny II exerted a degree of influence on the surrounding regions but, given the "archeological" state of the rest of the abbey, this can only be proved at planimetric level. In particular, scholars have attributed to the model of Cluny II the complex presbyterial layout of several churches whose construction was often sponsored as part of the transfer of a monastic community into the jurisdiction of the Bourgogne abbey.

In many cases this involved a superficial similarity when, due to the demands of the liturgy, the need arose for the creation of supplementary spaces containing an altar around which all the monks could celebrate the daily mass. The Swiss church of Romainmôtier is one of the first examples of a church built on the Cluniac model. Having transferred to the jurisdiction of Cluny in 928, it was completely rebuilt between 1005 and 1030. Its architectural form is so similar to the mother building that scholars try to reconstruct the appearance of the lost abbey through Romainmôtier. Powerful monolithic pillars divide the length of the church into two aisles and a nave which end in a dwarf transept and Benedictine choir with three apses and a dome on squinches. The original wooden roof was replaced by the present vaulting in the mid 11th century, while a narthex with several floors, similar to the Galilean one in Cluny, was later attached to the façade

9

**9. Abbey of Romainmôtier,
nave towards entrance,
1005-30.**

of the church. The external decoration, on the contrary, reflects the "Lombard" Romanesque style with its rhythm of pilaster strips and blind arching and a crown of small cusped arches.

A few years after Romainmôtier, Santa Maria di Ripoll, the abbey of the most famous monastery in Catalonia and one of the most significant examples of early Romanesque art in Spain, was built. The building is divided into five aisles and reflects the influence of Cluny II in the complex design of the presbytery area. It has a large protruding transept, seven cemicircular apses and a lantern over the crossing. There is a simple single opening into the side apses, while the central one is more richly decorated with double arcading and small blind arches in the upper crowning part. These elements, together with the

10

11

10. Abbey of Santa Maria, Ripoll, first half of 11th century.

11. Abbey of Romainmôtier, nave towards altar, 1005-30

gallery which runs round the top of the arms of the transept and the crowning part of the octagonal lantern, bear witness to the "Lombard" Romanesque style having had repercussions as far as Spain, possibly through traveling craftsmen.

The spread of Cluniac models in France is proven by the Abbey of Notre-Dame in La Charité-sur-Loire which, after the donation of Geoffrey de Champallement, Bishop of Auxerre, became one of the five daughter-houses directed by the Bourgogne Abbey of Cluny. The primitive church, built between 1080 and 1090, was divided into five

aisles and ended in seven apses arranged in regular fashion beyond the transept according to the most widely used scheme in Cluniac architecture.

Later, when in about 1120 the choir of Cluny III was finished, the presbyterial area of Notre-Dame was modified according to the new model provided by the mother house. The three central apses were broken up and in their place an ambulatory with five radial chapels was inserted, while cusped arcading, with a false matroneum and three-light windows above, was inserted into the nave. The monastery

12

12. Abbey of Santa Maria,
Ripoll, apse, first half
of 11th century.

of San Salvatore a Capodiponte in the Province of Brescia represents one of the most important stages of Cluniac penetration into Italy at the end of the 11th century.

Recorded in a list which Hughes, Abbot of Cluny, had drawn up in 1095, it includes an almost intact church whose form reflects the innovations introduced by this monastic order. Having formerly had a narthex which was in time dismantled, it is divided into three aisles which end in a transept. The latter does not project beyond the perimeter walls and is surmounted by an elliptical dome, which is covered externally by a high octagonal lantern. In front of the three apses wide bays covered by groin-vaulting lend fluidity to the shape of the presbytery as is the case in many Cluniac churches.

From the outside the building gives an impression of volumetric solidity enlivened by pilaster strips and half columns which culminate in a denticulated frieze on the sides and in a crowning of cusped arches in the apse. The lantern towers above everything, the mullioned windows with two lights in every side lending impetus and lightness to the whole structure.

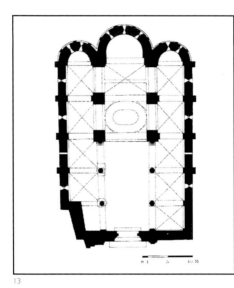

13

14

15

13. Blueprint, Abbey of San Salvatore, Capodiponte (from M. Durliat, *L'art roman*, 1982).

14. Abbey of Notre-Dame, La Charité-sur-Loire, apse, 12th century.

15. San Salvatore, Capodiponte, apse, end of 11-12th century.

In the course of the 11th century there was an increase in pilgrimage throughout the Western world, thanks to safer roads and the development of urban centers. For medieval man it represented a penitential and expiatory act, besides being the most effective way of ensuring the protection of God and the saints. During the long journey through faraway countries, the faithful would often also engage in an inner journey which brought spiritual growth. These itineraries had three types of destination. Besides those of the Holy Land and places which were hallowed in connection with the earthly life of Jesus, there were those connected with the appearance of the Archangel Michael (Monte Sant'Angelo in Gargano, Le Puy in Auvergne, Mont-Saint-Michel in Normandy, Sacra di San Michele in Val di Susa). However most of these journeys led to sanctuaries which evolved from places where tombs or relics of saints were kept. In Jerusalem for example, the tomb of Christ was worshipped, in Rome the tombs of the apostles Peter and Paul, and, after the discovery of the body of the apostle James, the faithful flocked towards the sanctuary of Compostela in Galicia. Here, on the Atlantic beaches, it became customary to collect a shell which was worn as a badge on the collar or wide-brimmed hat as proof of the completed pilgrimage. Later on the shell became the symbol of all pilgrims.

I. Pisanello, *Crest of the Pellegrini family*, 1437-38. Verona, Sant'Anastasia, Cappella dei Pellegrini.

II. THE PORTAL OF THE PORTICO DE LA GLORIA
Santiago de Compostela

According to legend the sanctuary was built in the place in which the Bishop Teodemiro miraculously found the burial place of the apostle James, having been guided by a star (the origin of the name *campus stellae*). Worship of the saint's tomb increased in particular during the long period of the *Reconquista*, the campaign against the moors in Spain, and reached startling proportions in the 11th century when it became the final point along a road punctuated with hospitals and hostels for the faithful.

III. RELIEFS OF THE CATHEDRAL FAÇADE
Fidenza

The story of Borgo San Donnino, the present day Fidenza, is connected to the worship of the relics of the eponymous saint whose life is illustrated in detail in the long carved frieze of the cathedral façade . This is why the town became an important place for pilgrims to stop at on their way to Rome along the Via Francigena. An example of this is documented in the relief which portrays a moment from the journey of two families of pilgrims, one rich and one poor, when some angels urge them to enter the cathedral.

III

IV. VOLTO SANTO
Lucca, Cathedral of San Martino

The crucifix represents Christ triumphing over death with open eyes and no evidence of wounds. As legend has it, Nicodemus, wishing to record for posterity the Savior's features, carved them in walnut wood with the aid of divine grace. After being hidden until the 8th century it was miraculously brought by sea from Jersualem to Luni from where it was taken to Lucca. It was the object of intense worship through the centuries and was visited by pilgrims from all over Italy and Europe, enabling the city to benefit from belonging to the pilgrimage routes to Rome.

IV

V. THE BASILICA OF THE HOLY SEPULCHER
Jerusalem

The Basilica of the Holy Sepulcher, which has retained its 12th century appearance despite many nineteenth century alterations, is made up of a series of buildings from the Constantinian age contained within an ordered sequential space in which the sites of the Passion of Christ are juxtaposed. There is the crypt of Saint Helena, the mother of Constantine to whom legend attributes the 'rediscovery' of the holy places, the ditch of the finding of the cross, the cloister of Calvary on the site of the crucifixion and the Rotunda of the Anastasis (Resurrection) built above the sepulcher of Christ

V

THE REVIVAL OF SCULPTURAL DECORATION IN EUROPEAN CHURCHES

The influence of the architectural and decorative forms adopted in the third reconstruction of the monastery of Cluny is particularly noticeable in Bourgogne, where the movement of the same craftsmen from one site to another resulted in the development of a local school. Many ecclesiastical buildings are scaled down or adapted versions of the Cluny III architectural model and always lacking in the most conspicuous element of the double transept. Rich and articulated sculptural decoration was part and parcel of the complex plan and was probably inspired by that of the mother house. Its purpose was to illustrate an edifying theme of relevance to worship and meditation, which was displayed on capitals and portals and in cloisters. The cloisters were crucial to the economy of the Cluniac monastic life and became an integral part of the liturgical itinerary with specific stopping places. In the cloister of Moissac for instance the capitals contained relics, exactly like altars. The purpose of the portals, in their eloquent and at times awe-inspiring way, was to represent the threshold the faithful had to cross from the mundane to the 'sacred' life. This was symbolized by the church, which through its architectural forms and rich liturgical decoration reflected the heavenly Jerusalem. The tympana and the fanlights usually contained scenes of theophany, in which the universal character of the Christian message was condensed.

16

17

18

16. *Encyclopedia of Maurus Hrabanus, De Universo, De linguis gentilum aedificati,* 1028. Montecassino, Abbey Library.

17. Abbey of Saint-Pierre, view of cloister with St Peter, about 1100. Moissac.

18. Bernardo Gilduin, altar, detail of angel, about 1090. Toulouse, Saint-Sernin.

THE ABBEY OF MOISSAC

Founded in the first half of the 7th century in the south of France, the abbey was rebuilt in the following century by Ludovic the Pious, after the devastation caused by muslim troops. After being looted and damaged again during the invasions of the Normans and Hungarians it was given a new lease of life thanks to the support of the Abbey of Cluny to which it had been affiliated in 1048. The abbot Durand de Bredons started up the important *scriptorium* again and commissioned the construction of a new church with three aisles ending in an ambulatory with radial chapels. The works were drawn out to the end of the following century when the cloister was built, in 1100 as the inscription records, and the imposing two-floored tower-portico was attached to the southern flank of the building between 1110 and 1115. There were further alterations to the structure of the church itself, the basilical blueprint being replaced with a single aisle covered by domes on pendentives.

During the fourteenth century, groin-vaulting was used instead of this type of roofing, as can be seen in the present day abbey. The cloister, which was completed in about 1100 is one of the very rare examples of cloisters decorated in the Romanesque period which have survived intact. Its structure is complex, with polychrome marble, coupled or simple columns supporting a system of pointed arches. On the piers, which are placed at the corners and in the middle of the rows of columns, the apostles are portrayed. Despite the lack of foreshortening

19

20

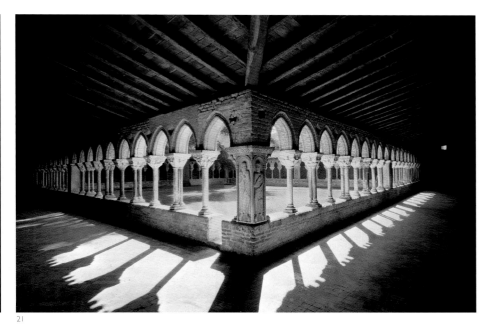

21

19. Abbey of Saint-Pierre, tombstone of Abbot Durand, about 1100. Moissac.

20. Abbey of Saint-Pierre, capital with souls of three martyrs of Tarragona, about 1100. Moissac.

21. Abbey of Saint-Pierre, cloister, about 1100. Moissac.

in the bass-relief, their faces, bodies and clothes are clearly defined. The surfaces of the sixty-six capitals, which are of the truncated pyramid kind, are completely covered in minute and precious reliefs in which scenes from the Old Testament are juxtaposed with animals, monsters, and geometric and plant motifs. The stylistic characteristics of these sculptures, where soft bass-relief is used within symmetrical compositions, bear witness to the influence of miniatures and objects of embossed ivory and goldwork which probably belonged to the Treasury of the monastery.

The tour de force of this impressive decorative scheme is the portal of the tower-portico attached to the southern flank of the church in about 1110. This is covered with rich and complex sculptural decoration enlivened by the animated movement of the figures, the soft, pictorial modeling and the dynamic subtlety of the lines. On the side walls of the

22

23

24

22. Abbey of Saint-Pierre, tower-portico, 1110-15. Moissac.

23. Abbey of Saint-Pierre, jamb of tower-portico with Scenes of Infancy of Christ, 1110-15. Moissac.

24. Abbey of Saint-Pierre, jamb of tower-portico with Death scenes, 1110-15. Moissac.

portico in front of this there is a series of reliefs illustrating the Gospel of Christian salvation – the *Annunciation*, *Visitation*, *Adoration of the Magi*, *Presentation in the Temple* and *Flight into Egypt* – together with other scenes in which the fate of the wicked and the good can be compared with the parable of Lazarus and the rich man, and some scenes of Hell. The figures of Saint Peter and Isaac are carved on the door jambs and that of Saint Paul and a prophet on the *trumeau*. The latter figures are

very elongated and have a rhythmic quality which makes them highly expressive. Higher up, the sculptures of the tympanum count among the most famous examples of representations of the apocalypse. They had a direct influence on Romanesque sculpture in the Languedoc. Christ is portrayed on the Day of Judgment, seated on a throne and surrounded by symbols of the four evangelists, angels and twenty-four venerable elders of the Apocalypse.

25

**25. Abbey of Saint-Pierre,
portal of tower-portico,
1110-15. Moissac.**

Fear of sin, evil, the devil and eternal damnation seemed to haunt the lives of medieval men, although in the Early Christian era such fears are less evident. In the catacombs, for example, the deceased is portrayed in the garden of Paradise, in an attitude of prayer or as a participant in the feast of the Eucharist, with surrounding images relating to the resurrection. Later on, the end of the first millenium reawakened deep anxieties and atavistic fears, which were stirred up by the availability of apocalyptic texts. The visionary content of the apocalypse evoked fantastic and potent images, which became part of the medieval figurative repertory. The Church admonished the faithful with descriptions of the punishments of Hell, where tongues of fire and fierce monsters devoured the bodies of the damned. Set against this was the charm of Paradise, illuminated by divine light and the presence of saints. It was sometimes represented as a garden, sometimes as the heavenly Jerusalem. The priest acted as an intermediary, pointing out the way to salvation and the paths of reward or eternal damnation.

I. Abbey of Sainte-Madeleine, capitel 107, *Two devils fighting*, 1120-50. Vézelay.

II. ORANTE
Rome, Catacombs of San Callisto

In the catacombs there are numerous depictions of the afterlife as a place of serene happiness, despite the new believers' knowledge of anguish and the punishment of sins. Sometimes the deceased are depicted partaking of a heavenly banquet or luxuriating in the peace of a garden full of flowers, doves and peacocks, while others have their arms raised in an attitude of prayer. In the cubiculum of the five saints in the catacomb of Callisto, five praying figures are depicted in the middle of a garden, between fruit and flower-laden plants. Each bears their name and the invocation "*In pace*".

III. THE MOSAIC OF THE TRIUMPHAL ARCH
Rome, Santa Prassede

The mosaic, which dates back to the 9th century, is one of the first examples of Paradise being represented as the heavenly Jerusalem. Its many-towered walls, covered with gems and precious stones contain the figures of Christ, the Madonna, Saint Prassede and the apostles, flanked by the ranks of the elect whom the angels welcome at the two doors.

IV. THE WEIGHING OF THE SOULS, A DETAIL FROM THE FAÇADE
Spoleto, San Pietro

The image of the scales weighing the sins and merits of the deceased is often used to represent human destiny after death, as a warning to the observer. On the façade of the church of San Pietro in Spoleto there are reliefs which, although they may not be of the highest quality, are displayed in an elaborate iconographic pattern. As is customary in Umbria they are arranged in panels in the lower part of the façade . Set beside the *Washing of the Feet* and *Vocation of Saint Peter and Saint Andrew*, and episodes taken from the bestiaries (the presumptuous wolf and the fox who feigned death), are scenes exalting God's mercy towards the penitent and the righteous. In the *Death of the Just*, the scale is leaning towards the archangel Michael although a devil is holding on to one of the scales. In the panel below, the bound body of a sinner is torn to pieces by two demons towards whom the weighing scales are tilted. At the sides, the body of a deceased person is thrown into a cauldron while a disconsolate angel withdraws from the scene.

IV

V. PORTAL OF UNIVERSAL JUSTICE
Conques, Abbey of Sainte-Foy

The usual descriptive iconographic scheme for the *Divine Justice* here assumes a didactic quality as revealed by the wealth of inscriptions intended to clarify the meaning of each of the episodes, which date back to about 1130. The visionary tension of the whole is split between all the different anecdotes: among the blessed the figures of the mythical founder of the abbey, the hermit Dadon, and its benefactor, Charlemagne can be made out, and in the section on Hell, those of some of the monastery's enemies, a fierce feudatory and a simoniac bishop.

V

VI. ANDREA BONAIUTI, THE CHURCH MILITANT
Florence, Santa Maria Novella, Cappellone degli Spagnoli

In the fourteenth century fresco, Paradise is portrayed as the heavenly Jerusalem to which only the elect are admitted. The heavenly building is represented by the image of an isolated door without any architectural setting, which acts as a symbol of the kingdom of Heaven and is guarded by Saint Peter.

VI

SAINT-LAZARE IN AUTUN

The church has an atrium in front of it and three aisles ending in three apses, which are approached through a vast transept and two-bay choir.

The choir and the nave are articulated on three levels with large pointed arches in the lower level, blind arcading in the middle and a clerestory.

The aisles are groin-vaulted and the nave has pointed barrel-vaulting with transverse arches and pilaster strips where they join the walls. The cathedral, which was consecrated in 1132 by Pope Innocent III, was clearly influenced by the architecture of Cluny III, undoubtedly owing to the strong links between Etienne de Baugé, the bishop who commissioned it, and the Abbey of Cluny where he resumed the monastic life in 1132.

The architect of Autun, however, chose a simpler and less elaborate solution to Cluny with its ambulatory with radial chapels.

Light plays a fundamental role, shining through the double row of windows to flood the presbytery, where the relics of Saint Lazarus were kept.

26

28

27

26. Abbey of Saint-Lazare, capital with floral motifs, 12th century. Autun.

27. Abbey of Saint-Lazare, detail of façade, 12th century. Autun.

28. Abbey of Saint-Lazare, nave towards altar, 12th century. Autun.

Saint-Lazare is famed for the splendid sculptures, which adorn its façade and interior and constitute one of the major sculptural cycles of Romanesque art and the Bourgogne school in particular. The tympanum of the portal also bears one of the earliest surviving signatures of a medieval artist. In the lunette there is a *Divine Judgment* which was intended to frighten the sinner into mending his ways. In the center of the composition the image of Christ in Judgment stands out, solemn and impassive, within a mandorla and surrounded by four angels. In two medallions are the sun and moon, which were believed in medieval times to preside over all the most important events of humanity. To the sides of Christ in the top layer, on the left, the Virgin appears seated beside a trumpeting angel and, on the right, another angel is flanked by two apostles. Lower down there are depictions of Paradise and Hell. In the former, an enthroned Saint Peter is surrounded by the blessed while, on the opposite side, Saint Michael is weighing souls in front of a large devil who is engaged in the same activity and surrounded by demoniacal figures.

29

30

203

29. Gislebertus, *trumeau*, central portal, 1125-45. Autun, Saint-Lazare.

30-31. Gislebertus, central portal, façade; following pages, detail of lunette, 1125-45. Autun, Saint-Lazare.

In the lintel the scene of the *Resurrection of the Dead* is depicted: at the center, under Christ's feet, an angel turns away the damned and welcomes the elect amongst whom there are two pilgrims.

The internal archivolt bears a plant motif decoration while the external one depicts the signs of the zodiac together with the tasks associated with the months. Gislebertus endows his sculptures with an unmistakable style, making the bodies elongated and slender and the folds of their garments palpable, luxuriating in realistic and expressive details in such a way as to imbue the marble with the desperation of the damned and the sweet serenity of the blessed. Scholars also attribute the decoration of most of the capitals in the church to him. In an apparently haphazard iconographic scheme, exuberant plant compositions are to be found beside scenes based on the Old and New Testament, chosen on the basis of their didactic moral value. There are episodes from Genesis (the *Sacrifice of Isaac*, *Crime of Cain* and *Noah's Ark*), as well as from the infancy and Passion

32

32. Gislebertus, capital
with *Judas hanged*,
1125-45. Autun, Musée
de Saint-Lazare.

of Christ and the mission of Saint Peter. The most beautiful pieces are now in the museum annexed to the abbey, having been replaced recently by copies. They were placed near the main altar in homage to the most noble part of the presbytery where Christ is present every day in the bread and wine of the Eucharist

At times the treatment becomes vivacious, richly detailed and capable of infusing episodes from the holy story with a light tone. The chisel portrays the awe of the Magi before Jesus: one kneels, not daring to approach, the other lifts the crown from his head as a mark of respect, the third unveils the casket he is holding, almost as if to amuse and surprise the baby.

Another capital movingly portrays the dream of the oriental kings who, worn out by their journey, are sleeping with their crowned heads on the same cushion. An angel reminds them of their mission, waking up the nearest one with the touch of a finger, while the next one half-opens an eye and the third carries on sleeping.

33

33. Gislebertus, capital with *Dream of the three magi*, 1125-45. Autun, Musée de Saint-Lazare.

EVE
Gislebertus, about 1130
Autun, Musée Rolin

SUBJECT

A shapely Eve is portrayed as she stretches an arm to pick the apple in the Garden of Paradise.

One hand plucks the forbidden fruit as the other supports her head, which is turned pensively in the opposite direction. She seems unconscious of her sin and the consequences of her action, distracted by faraway thoughts.

The chisel luxuriates in the portrayal of the perturbing beauty of her body, the softness of the curves and the pulsing life, which makes the skin seem palpable.

The pose recalls the serpent who has led Eve to sin.

The refined treatment of the surfaces is rich in pictorial values particularly in the treatment of the hair, which is formed by fine parallel incisions, and of the trees which are laden with flowers and fleshy fruits.

COMPOSITION

The relief, which served as the lintel of a side portal, is now damaged on one side, probably where the figure of Adam was.

The artist was adept at exploiting the small amount of available space, enclosing the lower part within a heavy rectilinear frame, which acts as a support for the body of Eve, and distancing the background.

He thus creates a deep, adaptable space within which there are three planes: in the foreground the body of Eve stretching an arm sensuously towards the tree, the space behind her and the smooth background.

Within this coherent spatial arrangement Gislebertus creates an interplay of rhythmic and linear correspondences in which Eve's willowy figure and the curving trunks of the trees are interwoven to form a precious tapestry.

SAINTE-MADELEINE IN VÉZELAY

The church belonging to the monastery of Vézelay was an important stopping point for pilgrims along the road to Compostela. The relics of Saint Mary Magdalene were thought to be kept there, and the influence of Cluny III, under whose jurisdiction it was, is evident. It was rebuilt in about 1100 and heavily restored by the architect Viollet-le-Duc between 1840 and 1859, after it had been reduced to a ruin during the French Revolution. Although the imposing façade, with the big window and tower has been almost completely rebuilt and the apse, which is at the end of an extremely long nave, was changed into Gothic style between 1171 and 1198, the rest of the church has retained its Romanesque form.

The influence of Cluny is first of all recognizable in the narthex, which was built between 1120 and 1140 and has three bays supported by powerful piers with columns joined to them.

34

34. Abbey of Sainte-Madeleine, narthex, 1120-40. Vézelay.

35. Abbey of Sainte-
Madeleine, capital 4,
Jacob blessing Isaac,
1120-50. Vézelay.

36. Following pages:
Abbey of Sainte-
Madeleine, lunette,
central portal,
1120-40. Vézelay.

37

However in Vézelay there is a minor vertical development in the architectural structure: the walls of the nave are divided into only two storeys; there are round arches between the naves and the aisles and groin-vaulting, divided by large transverse arches covers the bays.

It is evident that the sculptural decoration, which was carried out between 1120 and 1150, was the work of various workshops, so it does not have the stylistic unity of Saint-Lazare at Autun. In the lunette of the portal between the narthex and the central nave of the church there is a rather rare iconographic theme, which does not appear in other churches. In the center Christ is portrayed sending his apostles out to evangelize the world, which is represented by the figures in the lintel and the radial sections of the archivolt. The sculptor portrays people from faraway and exotic countries such as pygmies from central Africa and cinocephali from India with a certain amount of naturalism. In the archivolts themselves there are depictions of the signs of the zodiac and the working tasks of the months and on the outside there are some plant motifs.

38

214

37. Abbey of Sainte-Madeleine, nave, 1120-50. Vézelay.

38. Abbey of Sainte-Madeleine, detail lunette, south portal, 1120-32. Vézelay.

**39. Abbey of Sainte-
Madeleine, capital 80,
*Personification of four
rivers of Paradise*,
1120-50. Vézelay.**

The work is in the style of the Bourgogne sculpture and not unlike the work of Gislebertus in Autun. The Pentecost motif is given a tragic and visionary interpretation: the Holy Spirit is represented in the shafts of light, which extend from Christ's hands to the heads of the apostles. The strong emotional impact of the miraculous event is felt in the disruption of the composition with the elongation of the figures and their awkward stances and fluttering garments.

Inside the church, the decorative scheme is resumed in the ornamentation, which underpins the essential components of the architectural structure and in the capitals in the nave. They are sculpted with gusto and decorative flair and depict a variety of subjects, which don't seem to belong to a single iconographic scheme.

Among many, two episodes based on pagan mythology stand out: the Education of Achilles and the Rape of Ganimede, but the Biblical subjects are more numerous: the Rivers of Paradise, Fall of Adam and Eve, Sacrifice of Cain and Abel, David and Goliath and Daniel in the Lions' Den. None of the capitals is dedicated to the life of Christ nor to the patron of the church, Saint Mary Magdalen. In their place are episodes from the life of Saint Peter, Saint Anthony, Saint Martin, Saint Benedict and Saint Eugenia.

40

41

40. Abbey of Sainte-Madeleine, capital 93, *Adam and Eve*, 1120-50. Vézelay.

41. Abbey of Sainte-Madeleine, capital 28, *St Anthony and St Paul receiving the miraculous bread*, 1120-50. Vézelay.

SAINT-GILLES DU GARD

In the South of France (Provence, Languedoc) the architectural solutions for the portals and façade s of some of the churches are derived from models related to antiquity, in an area which is so rich in Roman remains (bridges, arches and amphitheatres).

The sculptural decoration is also imbued with the presence and influence of the antique. In the abbey church of Saint-Gilles, in the Gard, there are three large statues of the apostles between the three portals.

The bases of the smooth-shafted columns of the central portal are supported by lions wrestling with human and animal prey. Among the elegant circle motifs which make the door so precious, there are hunting scenes such as that of the centaur and the deer. Friezes of historical scenes feature high-reliefs with biblical scenes (*Cain and Abel, King David playing the Zither*) and stories from the Passion of Christ (the *Washing of the Feet, Last Supper, Kiss of Judas, Christ before Pilate, Flagellation*).

The complex iconographic scheme culminates in three tympana with fundamental scenes connected to Christ – the Epiphany, Cru-

42

42. Façade, second half of 12th century, Saint-Gilles du Gard.

43. In the following pages: *Offerings of Cain and Abel*, detail, central portal. Saint-Gilles du Gard.

44

cifixion and Theophany, where the *Maiestas Domini* is accompanied, as is customary, by the symbols of the four evangelists. In the walls of the building there are numerous clearly decipherable records in stone relating to the craftsmen and installation of the works.

One of the sculptors of the portal of the church of Saint-Gilles even left his own name near one of the apostles in an inscription which is validated by a legible 'signature': *Brunus me fecit* (Brunus made me). The craftsman has been identified as a master stone sculptor and wood carver who appears as a witness in some deeds drawn up between 1171 and 1186.

45

220

44. *Crucifixion*, **Lunette, side portal. Saint-Gilles du Gard.**

45. Pont du Gard.

SAINT-TROPHIME IN ARLES

On the façade of the Provencal church of Saint-Trophime the Christian interpretation of models dating back to antiquity even embraces the Roman triumphal arch. A context such as this lent itself to the re-introduction of statues or figures in the round, which were an integral part of the dialectical relationship between sculpture and architecture at that time. The area boasts some famous examples including that of the not too distant Saint-Gilles du Gard.

The application of different kinds of stone materials within a strictly symmetrical scheme adds to the richness of the façade . Apart from olithic limestone which is the most commonly used kind of stone, Carrara marble, granite, black limestone and other materials, many of which have been very skillfully reused, are all present in the façade .

On raised bases there are lions holding prey and with historical scenes underneath them. They serve as supports for columns and capitals with plant motifs.

Rectangular niches framed by pilasters contain statues of apostles and two archangels. Above them is a frieze of historical scenes which ends in corbel capitals decorated with scenes from the life of Mary (the *Annunciation and Nativity*).

The upper frieze is close-packed with three-dimensional human figures: the blessed on the right and the damned engulfed in flames on the left.

The use of a single column in the middle of the portal gives it elegance and the lintel above contains the twelve apostles, with a crowning tympanum of Christ in Judgment in the Mandorla, surrounded by the symbols of the four evangelists. Friezes with stylized plant motifs, imitation denticulated cornices and corbels with animal sculptures further enrich the sculptural array.

46

47

46. Saint-Gilles du Gard, lunette, portal, end 12th century. Arles.

47. Saint-Gilles du Gard, portal sculpture, end 12th century. Arles.

48

48. Samson fighting the lion, detail, portal, second half 12th century. Arles, Saint-Trophime.

49. Facing page: Detail of portal with apostles, second half 12th century. Arles, Saint-Trophime.

THE MONASTERY OF SANTO DOMINGO DE SILOS

The Benedictine Abbey of Silos, founded at the beginning of the 10th century, was one of the first Iberian centers to be subject to Cluniac revision. Its church was altered from 1041 onwards when San Domenico came to Silos to take charge of the monastery, and enlarged after his death in 1073 due to the influx of pilgrims who flocked to pay homage to the abbot's remains. Since then the monastery of Santo Domingo has been a famous national pilgrimage destination. The cloister is all that is left of the original building and is one of Spain's masterpieces of Romanesque architecture. The sides feature two tiers of round arcading supported by coupled columns, whose capitals are sculpted with plant motifs and fantastic animals of the most refined craftsmanship which is enhanced by the ever-changing interplay of light. Each corner pier is embellished with two sections of sculpted high-relief like those in the cloister of Moissac. There is a *Deposition of Christ*, *Ascension*, *Pentecost* and *Incredulity of Thomas*.

Given the limits of the depth of the relief, the modeling has a surprising energy and rhythmic quality.

50

51

52

50. Monastery of Santo Domingo, view of cloister, second half 11th century. Silos.

51. Cloister, capitals, second half 11th century. Silos, Monastery of Santo Domingo.

52. Cloister, pier with *Crucifixion*, second half 11th century. Silos, Monastery of Santo Domingo.

THE ABBEY OF SANT'ANTIMO

The large abbey church, which was built in the 12th century on the outskirts of Montalcino (Siena) beside the Via Francigena, has a basilical blueprint ending in a large ambulatory with radial chapels which has been recognized as having been influenced by the blueprint adopted in many of the French pilgrimage churches. Columns alternating with piers separate the nave from the aisles, which are covered by groin-vaulting and surmounted by matronea. The aisles form a contrast with the effortless loftiness of the nave, which is flooded by light from the apse. The capitals are richly decorated and usually Corinthian, with a double circle of smooth leaves surmounted by volutes, which provide a satisfactory transition to the quadrangular form of the abacus. This is decorated with interwoven ribbons and geometric motifs. Some are distinguished by a more refined and original decorative sculptural style. The capitals of the apse are decorated with elaborate leaf motifs, animals viewed from the front

53

54

53. Abbey of Sant'Antimo, apse, 12th century. Montalcino.

54. Abbey of Sant'Antimo, façade and bell tower, 12th century. Montalcino.

and a human figure holding a monkey on a lead and bent by the weight of an abacus. In the nave the capital portraying *Daniel in the Lions' Den* stands out. The modeling is soft and sensitive and the figures elongated. The heightened chiaroscuro created by the folds of the disheveled drapery and the elaborate lions' manes infuses the surfaces with vibrancy. While construction started with the apse and refined decorative techniques and more valuable materials were used (the blocks of local travertine stone have a similar transparency and veining to alabaster), the façade was the last part to be built when the monastery's coffers were probably nearly empty. Provision has been made in the walls for the construction of a portico. This would have framed a double portal which has apparently never existed. A compromise was adopted in the form of a single portal preceded by an avant-corps, where the material which had already been sculpted was arranged in the best way possible.

56

57

58

55. Facing page: Abbey of Sant'Antimo, nave, 12th century. Montalcino.

56. Abbey of Sant'Antimo, detail, façade capital, 12th century. Montalcino.

57. Abbey of Sant'Antimo, side portal, 12th century. Montalcino.

58. Abbey of Sant'Antimo, ambulatory, 12th century. Montalcino.

ART OF THE MIDDLE AGES

THE CAPITAL OF DANIEL IN THE LIONS' DEN
**The Master of Cabestany, second half of the 12th century
Montalcino, Sant'Antimo**

SUBJECT
The prophet Daniel is placed in the center of the composition, which contains the ditch where he was thrown for having disobeyed the religious decree issued by the Persian king Dario.

The body is elongated, the hands raised to the sky in an attitude of prayer and the head turned towards an angel who pulls him by a fold of his garment towards a bearded character who is kneeling in front of this miraculous event.

Instead of devouring him, the lions are tamely lowering themselves at his feet, stretching their long muscular bodies across the edges of the capital.

The figures have an extraordinary vigor, which is heightened by very intense chisel-work in which the surfaces are finely cut and the sculptor revels in the intricacies of the manes, beards and folds of the garments.

COMPOSITION

The figure of the prophet Daniel is the focal point of the side of the capital facing the nave. Lions and some small human figures are crammed into a confused tangle of bodies and manes which converges on him.

The architectural structure of the capital is so engulfed by the exuberance of the decoration that even the abacus above is covered by it and the corner volutes can hardly be seen they are so reduced in size. On one of the sides, which are less crowded, and facing the front, a rosette contains the head of Daniel, which extends beyond the architectural borders of the capital.

The abacus itself is covered by vigorous reliefs featuring a succession of roses, bunches of grapes and flowers together with lion heads, birds, griffons, snakes and fighting lions.

THE NORMAN ROMANESQUE STYLE

The Romanesque buildings in Normandy present particular characteristics, which have enabled scholars to distinguish the architectural production in this geographical area from the rest of France. The cruciform piers of the choir and the wall's breadth passage in the southern arm of the transept, together with the two-towered façade, the lofty naves complete with matronea and the choir ambulatory all contribute to the experimental quality of the Norman style. They foreshadow the architectural solutions which will come into force in the Gothic age and which will spread from Normandy to influence contemporary English architecture.

Historical events facilitated this, in that Normandy was given to Rollo the Viking leader in 911 and, as being in favor with the French court gave him a degree of independence, he became more closely connected to England.

59

60

61

59-60. *The banquet*, detail of tapestry of Countess Matilde, about 1077. Bayeux, Centre Guillaume-le-Conquerant.

61. Durham Cathedral, detail, nave walls, 1093-1130.

THE ABBEY CHURCH OF BERNAY

The Abbey of Bernay was founded at the beginning of the 11th century by Countess Judith, wife of Richard II of Normandy, and then entrusted to Guillaume de Volpiano, Abbot of Dijon and Fécamp. Longitudinally the church of Notre-Dame has three aisles, two of which were destroyed in the 17th century, ending in a transept and a graduated crossing in the Cluniac manner. The architectural structure is enriched by a treasure trove of sculpture in the grand style involving three different workshops. The first sculpted the panels and capitals of the choir and transept, producing refined works based on motifs in the Byzantine style; the second favored interlacement motifs of the late medieval type and the third reverted to the traditional type of Corinthian capital for the nave. The church has examples of architectural solutions which were widely used in Normandy such as cruciform piers, the façade flanked by towers and the ambulatory.

62

63

62. Abbey of Notre-Dame, detail, nave, 1017-55. Bernay.

63. Abbey of Notre-Dame, nave pier, 1017-55. Bernay.

64

NOTRE-DAME IN JUMIÈGES

Founded by Saint Philibert in the second half of the 7th century and badly damaged during the Norman invasions, the Benedictine Abbey of Jumièges was only occupied by monks again from the year 928 onwards. With the intention of bringing life back into the monastery, in 1027 they commissioned the rebuilding of the church of Notre-Dame of which only the nave walls with alternating supports and the west side survive. Here high octagonal towers flank the portico, which is surmounted by a tribune. The building stands out due to the vertical emphasis of its components, an emphasis which is attenuated in the tall narrow nave enclosed by slender walls, which have three levels. Above the arcading are the three-mullioned windows of the matroneum, which are in turn surmounted by the clerestory windows. Between the windows, the slender half-columns set in pilaster strips rising from the floor upwards accentuate the verticality of the building. Transverse arches probably sprang from these half-columns and served to support the timber truss roof. Thanks to archeological excavations it has also been possible to trace the plan of the Romanesque single apse with ambulatory, which was rebuilt in the Gothic period and is now in ruins after being destroyed in the eighteenth century.

65

64. Abbey of Notre-Dame, detail, nave, 11th century. Jumièges.

65. Abbey of Notre-Dame, external view, 12th century. Jumièges.

66. Facing page: Abbey of Notre-Dame, view of Westwerk, 11th century. Jumièges.

SAINT-ETIENNE IN CAEN

The church of Saint-Etienne was built in as little as twenty years, between 1064 and 1087, on the initiative of the duke, William, known as the Conqueror. It enabled the king to obtain a pardon from the Pope, who had excommunicated him when he married Matilde de Flandres in 1050. The church is one of the most important monuments of Norman architecture and displays the structural and planimetric characteristics which are typical of this architectural school. Many of the elements present in Jumièges are used, but they are coordinated in a more compact way with better results. The towers are aligned with the main part of the façade, so that they seem part of it, and this creates an effect of heightened power and vertical impetus. The same characteristics are found inside where there is the usual tripartite division, but the articulation is more forceful as the walls are thicker. The church originally had a ceiling, which was replaced with sexpartite groin-vaulting in the middle of the 12th century, while the choir is a valuable example of Norman Gothic.

67

68

67. Abbey of Saint-Etienne, nave, 1064-87. Caen.

68. Abbey of Saint-Etienne, apse, early 13th century. Caen.

DURHAM CATHEDRAL

During the Norman period England underwent a period of intense building activity, during which the most important English Romanesque monuments were built.

Durham Cathedral, which was begun in 1093 and finished in 1133, is one of the archetypes of Anglo-Norman architecture of the 12th century.

In fact it has similar characteristics to the churches of Normandy on which it was probably modeled. It has three aisles, which extend through a pronounced transept, with two aisles to the choir which ends in three apses. The components of the building have a strong vertical impetus: the façade is flanked by two towers while the walls of the nave are divided into three tiers with arches, matronea and windows above a wall passage.

Here the quest for decorative and spectacular effects is intensified as in many English cathedrals.

The choir and nave are also covered with rib vaults, which were inserted in the first decades of the 12th century and replaced the original timber truss roof.

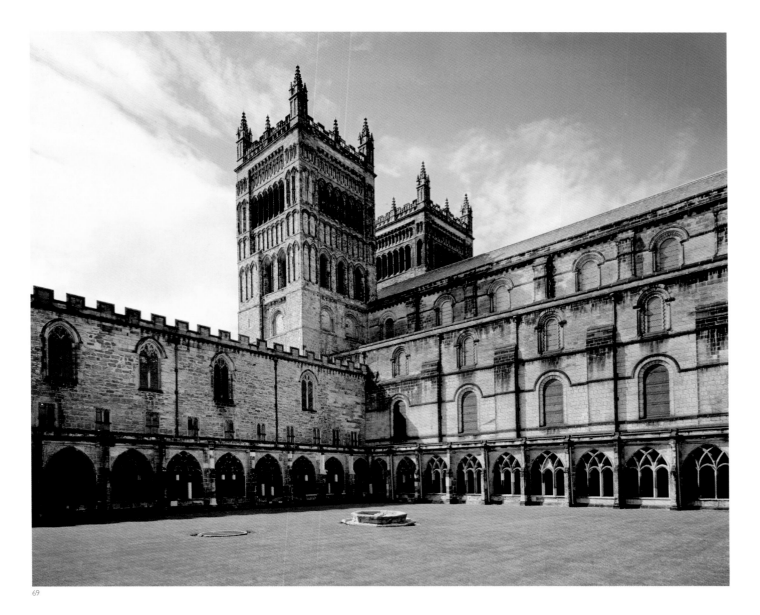

69

**69. Durham Cathedral,
view of southern flank
with cloister, 1093-1133.**

71

72

73

237

70. Facing page: Durham Cathedral, detail, aisle, 1093-1133.

71. Durham Cathedral, nave walls, 1093-1133.

72. Durham Cathedral, decorated portal, cloister, 1093-1133.

73. Durham Cathedral, door-knocker, north portal, 12th century.

THE BAYEUX TAPESTRY

The famous 77 yard long linen tapestry was made in Canterbury between 1066 and 1082, after the Norman conquest of England. It was commissioned by Odo, the Bishop of Bayeux, a relative of William the Conqueror, to celebrate the event. Presumably, after being kept in the palaces of the bishop for a considerable period, the work of art was donated to Bayeux Cathedral where it was kept for centuries before being transferred to the special museum.

The narrative technique is derived from an epic literary tradition. The scenes are all on one level, with ornamental stylized and animal motifs at the top and bottom and integrated explanatory titles.

The tale of the island begins with prior events and continues up to the Battle of Hastings (1066) to which a substantial part is dedicated. William the Conqueror, who was the architect of a model feudal state in Normandy, had been designated successor to Edward the Confessor, Anglo-Saxon king of England, who had no heirs. On Edward's death, however, the English nobles nominated Harold, Count of Sussex, as the new sovereign. This led to William's expedition, the defeat of Harold and the conquest of England.

In the first part there is a series of events set in Normandy and preceding the death of Edward the Confessor, with scenes associated with the customs of court life such as hunting with falcons and banquets. Next there is the funeral of Edward himself and William the Conqueror's decision to attack England. The tale then focuses on preparations for the venture, yielding important details related to the ships, from construction of the fleet to setting sail. This culminates in the embarkation, preparation for battle, depiction of the two armies, appearance of the bishop Odo and final engagement. The clash between the Normans and the Anglo-Saxons is effectively portrayed, with many lively and realistic battle scenes.

The defeat of the Anglo-Saxons is obviously seen from the point of view of the Norman conquerors, but the depiction of numerous details, customs, objects, arms and means of transport makes the work of art a unique historical source which offers valuable insights into daily life of the period.

I-II. *Battle of Hastings,*
detail of the tapestry of
Countess Matilde, about
1066-82. Bayeux, Centre
Guillaume-le-Conquerant.

III

IV

ART OF THE MIDDLE AGES

III. *The banquet,* detail of the tapestry of Countess Matilde, about 1066-82. Bayeux, Centre Guillaume-le-Conquerant.

IV. *The fleet of William Duke of Normandy crossing the Channel,* detail, tapestry of Countess Matilde, about 1066-82. Bayeux, Centre Guillaume-le-Conquerant.

ROMANESQUE CATALAN PAINTING

The illuminated pages produced in the Pyrenean monasteries in the late Middle Ages represent the prelude to the flowering of Romanesque Catalan painting. The famous commentary on the Apocalypse created between 776 and 784 by Beato de Liébana in the Asturias was a turning point. There are 24 known examples produced between the 9th and 13th centuries. At the end of the 10th century a *scriptorium* appeared in the monastery of Ripoll where many miniators from Catalonia and other regions were at work. Their activity, which is distinguished by balanced composition, elegant style and chromatic range, would give rise to cycles of paintings on walls and panels. In time, painting on plasterwork would replace the costly mosaics of the Byzantine tradition, while retaining their stylistic standards. The first examples of this type of wall painting are to be found in the val-leys of the Eastern Pyrenees. One of the oldest is the cycle in the church of San Clemente in Taüll in the Pyrenean valley of Boì. The artist is one of the most important and the cycle is finer than any previous work. The paintings were discovered at the beginning of the twentieth century, then removed and transferred to Barcelona between 1919 and 1923. Further fragments were to follow in the 1970s. The Taüll paintings are the best known among the Catalan Romanesque cycles. The master introduces innovative schemes, fining down the forms of Byzantine origin. In the central apse the figure of Christ the Pantocrator emerges from the mandorla, becoming a being capable of movement rather than the hierarchical divinity of Byzantine mosaics. In terms of traditional features, apart from the mandorla itself, the basic conventions are retained: the right hand raised in benediction, the left hand holding a book, and alpha and omega signs alluding to the beginning and the end beside the face. There is an angel in flight

74

74. *Christ Pantocrator and figures,* San Clemente in Taüll. Barcelona, Museum of Catalan Art.

75

76

and paired symbols of the four evangelists on either side of the mandorla. At the bottom, inserted between the painted arcading, are virgins and saints together with painted names. The fresco dates back to about 1123, the date, once legible on a pier, of the building's consecration. It reveals a consummate harmony of spatial solutions and chromatic development with rich pigments and iconographic detail. Stylistic relationships have been drawn with the monastery of Revello in Piedmont as well as the sculpture of Provence and Toulouse. The day after this consecration the same bishop consecrated the church of Santa Maria, which also has three aisles ending in three semi-circular apses and defined by robust columns supporting arcades, and vaulted roofing. Under a layer of painted plaster one of the crosses drawn for the consecration in 1123 was discovered. This led to the identification of the work of the first group of artists. The main apse, and possibly the side apses, were decorated by them. Artists were also at work in the churches and monastic centers of the center of the Iberian peninsula, creating a different artistic language. In the former Benedictine cenobium of Ripoll, throughout the 12th century, the ancient tradition of illumination was kept up. The area is rich in paintings on panels. These are reminiscent of the work of miniators who imitated the Byzantine style in terms of the chosen colors, structure and rhythm, while the black borders

reveal a knowledge of wall painting. The oldest of these panel paintings is the mid 12th century altar frontal from Vich dedicated to Santa Margerita, in which the relationship with illumination is evident. The work is attributed to an artist trained in the renowned cenobium. In the center the Virgin is seated with the child in benediction. The pose is extremely symmetrical, but curved and spiral lines give weight to the volumes and bodies and a sense of movement to the drapery. Bass-relief paste used as imitation glass mosaic and precious stones makes its first appearance here in the halo of the Madonna and the reliefs in which the scene is set. The side panels contain the story of the martyrdom of the saint who is portrayed completely naked, an innovative technique given only Adam and Eve were usually represented in this way. The relationship between the artists who painted on panels and those who painted on walls is evident in the master who worked in the church of Enguillor. In the middle of the side panel of the altar frontal is the story of the Archangel Michael and the Heavenly Host, with four sections of alternating colors depicting Michael and the weighing of the souls, the fight with the dragon, Raphael and Gabriel, the whole reflecting the monumental scale of the plan. Near the Northern frontier of Catalonia, the work of the master of Soriguerola reveals a revival of interest in ornamental elements and the definitive transition to Gothic art.

75. *Adoration of the Magi*, Santa Maria of Taüll. Barcelona, Museum of Catalan Art.

76. Altar frontal, *Martyrdom of St Margaret*, detail. Vich, Bishop's Palace Museum.

The wall paintings of the Pantéon de los Reyes in the collegiate church of Sant'Isidoro in León, a city which is situated in the north of Spain at the foot of the Montes de Léon, are owed to royal patronage.

León, which was an autonomous kingdom between the 10th and 13th centuries, was also part of the pilgrim network connected to the Santiago Route. This lay behind King Ferdinand II's decision to move to the church, which in the 11th century he had selected as the royal family's burial place, the relics of Isidoro of Seville, the saint who reformed the Visigoth church. At the time, the sovereigns donated a treasure, which dates back to the year of consecration, 1063, to the church. It contained important relics, including those of the titular saint, and is a masterpiece connected stylistically to Ottonian goldwork. The primitive building did not survive but the Pantéon erected by Urrica, the daughter of King Ferdinand and Queen Sancha, remains. It is the first building in the area in the Romanesque style, which also extends to the architectural decoration. Even in the 12th century, Urraca embellished the Pantéon with wall paintings whose iconographic variety and chromatic richness stand out against the uniform white background. The iconographic scheme of the cycle is perfectly attuned to the architectural surfaces, following a virtual spiral line, which begins at the side door, crosses five compartments and ends in a sixth opposite the main entrance. It contains evangelical scenes and the Apocalypse as well as images taken from daily life based on the way time regulates human activities (the cycle of the Months). A wealth of elegant paint-

77

78

242

77. *Scene of the Apocalypse,* 12th century. Sant'Isidoro, León.

78. *Crucifixion,* 12th century. Sant'Isidoro, León.

ed inscriptions is incorporated in the paintings, aiding a fuller understanding. The first episode is that of the *Annunciation*, with the figures of the Archangel Gabriel and Mary and the customary inscriptions. Lower down is the *Nativity* and the *Annunciation to the Shepherds*. The latter is particularly effective in the rendering of details in the objects and animals of the village. Next, in the second and third compartments are *Slaughter of the Innocents* and *Last Supper*. The fourth one contains the scenes of the *Passion* with the *Capture of Christ, Denial by Peter* and *Cyrenian with the Cross*. Between the fourth and fifth compartments the archangels Gabriel and Raphael hold a medallion containing the dove, which symbolizes the Holy Spirit. There is an obvious connection with the next scene, which is dominated by the *Crucifixion* with the Sun and Moon at the sides, the grieving Virgin and

Saint John and the depiction of Golgotha. Scenes and symbols associated with the Apocalypse come next, with different cities implied by various painted architectural styles. The cycle of the Months is placed between the fifth and sixth compartments, with the relevant seasonal tasks depicted in medallions. The cycle is completed by the vision of the Maiestas Domini, with Christ in the mandorla surrounded by the anthropomorphic symbols of the Zodiac in the last arch.

The decoration of the vaulted portico in front of the building's façade is the most extensive and well preserved along the important pilgrimage route. The complex iconographic scheme, as well as some of the stylistic choices, recall the ambience and conventions of contemporary artistic production in western France.

79

79. Vault with
Annunciation to the
***Shepherds*, 12th century.**
Sant'Isidoro, León.

ROMANESQUE PAINTING IN MARIENBERG AND THE ALPINE ARC

The Benedictine monastery of Marienberg is situated in the Upper Val Venosta, along the route which leads to Engadine via the Resia Pass. The crypt, which was consecrated as early as 1156, contains important frescoes. The elongated figures are distinguished by their calligraphic style and luminous, contrasting colors; the blues, greens, yellows and browns are particularly striking.

In the center of the bowl-shaped apse there is a Christ in Benediction in the Mandorla, surrounded by the hierarchy of angels, the symbols of the evangelists and Saint Peter and Saint Paul. The four vaulting cells representing the starry sky in front of it contain more angels with elaborate hair and elegant movements. The cell opposite the apse has a background of monochrome drapery and is outlined with a geometric motif. Within a simple architectural framework are more angels and the figures of two bishops carrying a scroll. Amongst the floor-level curtain motif the single figure

81

80. Facing page: *Christ Pantocrator*, 12th century. León, Sant'Isidoro.

81. *Redeemer in Benediction*, 12th century. Burgusio, Abbey of Montemaria.

of a monk can also be made out. The extensive culture of the master of Marienberg shows that he must have trained outside the limited geographical ambience of the Val Venosta. The influence of the finest Byzantine painting merges with a marked interest in the chromatic innovations particular to the northern *scriptoria*.

The presence of such a significant cycle influenced subsequent painting production in the surrounding areas as far as Val Müstair, where the Carolingian frescoes in the cenobium of Saint John of Müstair were partly covered by new wall paintings.

This influence is even reflected in the thirteenth century decoration of the church of Saint John in Tübre, which was an important stopping place for pilgrims.

82

82. Apse frescoes, detail
with the *Martyrdom
of St Stephen,*
mid-12th century,
Saint John of Müstair.

83. Facing page: *Angel,*
12th century. Burgusio,
Abbey of Montemaria.

4. The Romanesque Period in Northern Italy

From the 11th century onwards a new architectural language spread through the West. It was called "Romanesque" to indicate continuity of the building practices and methods of Roman antiquity and, at the same time, draw an analogy with the maturing Romance languages. This was a period of intense building activity, which led to the construction and rebuilding of many places of worship. As Raoul Glaber wrote, Europe donned "a white mantle of churches", the visible proof of a new architectural style. The adoption of brick roofs entailed the strengthening of support structures: piers replaced columns while the external walls grew thicker and a rigorous system of buttresses and ribbing served to counterbalance the weight and forces of the vaults. New solutions in architectural decoration and sculptural production were an organic part of the buildings. The portals were designated to accommodate narrative sculpture, which at times also appeared in capitals decorated with figures and cloisters. Creatures drawn from the medieval imagination were mixed with scenes from the Old and New Testaments.

2

3

1. Facing page: Six stories of Genesis to left of portal. Verona, San Zeno.

2. Wiligelmo, *Stories of Genesis, Death of Cain at the hand of Lanach*, 1099-1106. Modena, Cathedral.

3. View of façade, 11th to 12th century. Pavia, San Michele.

THE BASILICA OF SANT'AMBROGIO BETWEEN THE 6TH AND 11TH CENTURIES

The story of the basilica began with the bishopric of Ambrose, who occupied the episcopal seat in Milan from the year 374. In fact Ambrose commissioned the building of a church which would house the remains of the martyrs *Gervaso and Protaso*, hence the name *basilica martyrum*. The church, which had a basilical blueprint with three aisles separated by piers ending in an apse, would later house the remains of the canonized bishop. At the end of the 8th century, when the archbishop

Pietro founded a Benedictine cenobium in the ancient basilica, the church had to be adapted to meet the liturgical needs of the growing community and the Eastern end was expanded. The apses were moved back and vaulting placed in front of them while the presbytery was raised and the golden altar was placed in it. The changes upset the spatial unity of the previous building, creating a complex which was in many ways unique and presented an articulated series of distinct volumes, as opposed to the central planning of the Early Christian basilica. A similar geometric precision is reflected in the external decoration of the apse. This is crowned by a long row of deeply recessed arches filled with dense shadows, which serve to break up the expanse

4

4. Basilica of Sant'Ambrogio, quadriportico and façade, 11th to 12th century. Milan.

5. Facing page: Basilica of Sant'Ambrogio, nave towards altar, 11th to 12th century. Milan.

6 7

8 9

6. Basilica of Sant'Ambrogio, capital with animals, 11th to 12th century. Milan.

7. Basilica of Sant'Ambrogio, capital with hunting scene, 11th to 12th century. Milan.

8. Basilica of Sant'Ambrogio, capital with animals and plants, 11th to 12th century. Milan.

9. Basilica of Sant'Ambrogio, capital with lions, 11th to 12th century. Milan.

of brick walling. Three large windows are inserted between a series of slender pilaster strips extending to the roof cornice, which has three filets. In the Romanesque era the whole complex underwent radical changes based on completely new aesthetic and construction criteria, making it one of the most significant examples of the building fervor of the new millenium. It has a quadriportico and a gabled façade with a double tier of deep arcading. The three-aisle plan, which is typical of Early Christian basilicas is present, but transformed by new solutions which will reach maturity during the following century. The new complex is conditioned by the vaulted ceiling with its dynamic interplay of forces and counter-forces. The walls are thicker and compound piers have replaced the columns, while pilaster strips, cornices and transverse arches serve to distribute the weight of the vaults. The shafts of light

alternating with the shadow of the interior create an impression of fragmentation. The rhythmic articulation caused by the accumulation of diverse spaces of differing heights culminates in the octagonal lantern, which covers the exterior of the dome.

The sculptural decoration is linked to the building's phases of construction and is afforded a somewhat subordinate place within the architectural structure. The oldest capitals are situated in the nave; those of the narthex and atrium follow, with the decoration gradually increasing in complexity and refinement so that animals and human figures are juxtaposed with the earlier plant and geometric motifs. There is a surprising variety of interlacement motifs on the capitals, arch lintels, portals and in the narthex arcading, showing what a central role the late medieval decorative repertoire played in the Romanesque era.

10

10. Basilica of Sant'Ambrogio, 11th to 12th century. Milan.

THE SPREAD OF THE LOMBARD ROMANESQUE STYLE

The architectural solutions adopted in the Basilica of Sant'Ambrogio were widely applied within the Lombard area. At the time every city-state had a new cathedral which boasted vaulting and was arranged according to the new spatial canons. In each area the craftsmen adapted different materials and techniques, whilst remaining faithful to local traditions, and original variants were produced. In Pavia, the churches of San Michele and San Pietro in Ciel d'Oro have massive clustered piers separating the three aisles and each is crowned

12

11. San Michele, detail of decoration of portal, 11th to 12th century. Pavia.

12. San Pietro in Ciel d'Oro, façade, about 1132. Pavia.

**13. Sant'Abbondio,
façade, 11th century.
Como.**

with a high octagonal lantern. The internal divisions are reflected in the gabled façade where buttresses form vertical partitions. At the top there is an aerial gallery following the line of the sloping roofs. The presence of single and two-light windows and oculi intensify the chiaroscuro of the brick walls and endow them with a sculptural quality. The reliefs are drawn from a vast and imaginative decorative repertoire which was still early medieval in taste. The lack of awareness of new trends in sculpture in the Emilian area restricts their role to ornamentation of the architectural features. They are concentrated around the portals and windows and sometimes arranged in horizontal bands. Scholars claim that it was often due to the work of itinerant craftsmen that the influence of the solutions adopted in the Basilica of Sant'Ambrogio extended beyond the borders of Lombardy and into other regions of Italy and Europe. They are responsible for the spread of pensile arches, pilaster strips, blind arcading and pretense or real loggias, which breathe life into the walls of the churches. The pilaster strips relieve the monotony of rows of columns, defining distinct spaces and absorbing the forces of the vaulting. In the church of Sant'Abbondio in Como, particularly in the presbyterial area, this architectural language merges with influences from the architecture beyond the Alps. The apse and choir give the impression of being framed within the two bell towers, giving the building an animated, clean-cut profile, which was unusual for Italy, although common at the end of the Carolingian age in areas North of the Alps.

Lombard craftsmen also worked in Tuscany and upper Lazio and arrived as far as Apulia. The Cathedral of San Nicola in Bari is proof of this. Although built during the 12th century, it ends in a presbytery with an iconostasis in the Byzantine tradition. Finally the church of San Vincente of Cardona is an archetypal example of the diffusion of the Lombard Romanesque style in Catalonia. The building was begun in 1018 on the initiative of the Viscount Bermon and has three aisles separated by piers and a transept. The arches at the edges of the crossing support a dome set on squinches with an external octagonal lantern. The nave has barrel-vaulting with transverse arches beneath it and groin vaults at the sides. The presence of a three-aisled groin-vaulted crypt results in a raised presbytery, above which is the broad curve of the central apse, with its external crowning of recessed arches.

15

16

14. Facing page: San Vincent, apse, 11th century. Cardona.

15. Cathedral of San Nicola, view right side, 1087-1197. Bari.

16. Cathedral of Trani, façade, 1097-1200.

THE COLLEGIATE CHURCH OF SANT'ORSO IN AOSTA

The collegiate church of Sant'Orso is the result of a series of modifications effected from the Early Christian and early medieval eras onwards. Most of the existing structures date back to the beginning of the 11th century, when the building was renovated during the bishopric of Anselmo (994-1025). The work began with the crypt and finished in 1014.

The church consists of a hall divided into three aisles by rectangular piers and ending in semi-circular apses. Beneath the roof there is an important cycle of wall paintings, which were also commissioned by the bishop Anselmo. Some of these are still covered over. They are the work of a group of Lombard artists who were also active in the Cathedral of Aosta. In the choir there is a mosaic floor in the centre of which is a portrayal of Sampson fighting the lions with interlacement motif borders. The scene is surrounded by a very famous inscription, whose meaning is elusive: *Rotas Opera Tenet Arepo Sator*.

In the Middle Ages it was thought to have the power to ward off evil. There are also monstrous and fantastic creatures (a dragon, triton and eagle with a single head and two bodies) and another metrically designed inscription. The mosaic is thought to be

17

**17. Collegiate Church
of Sant'Orso, courtyard,
12th century. Aosta.**

from about the fifth decade of the 12th century, like the cloister capitals, judging by their inscriptions.

The cloister is situated on the southern side of the complex. Colonettes and piers with bases and capitals border an open rectangular space. Originally, before there was a roof to cast shadows, the capitals and sculptures must have been polychrome in appearance, owing to the use of different marbles and pigments. One of the legible capital inscriptions refers to this overall effect. Another records the moment when the rule of Saint Augustine was introduced into Sant'Orso in 1132.

There is a wide range of iconographic themes with scenes taken from the Old and New Testaments, together with hagiographical ones and

18

19

18. *Flight into Egypt,* capital in cloister of Sant'Orso, 12th century. Aosta.

19. *Life and miracles of Sant'Orso,* capital of cloister of Sant'Orso, 12th century. Aosta.

20

those connected to the story of Ursula. These are punctuated with plants, animals and the fantastic, drawn from the vast figurative repertoire of the age. Fuller, more rounded forms, enhanced expressions and gestures of the characters, as well as focus on detail, are the distinguishing marks of this significant body of sculpture. It was an isolated case within the

Valle d'Aosta and linked to Lombard sculpture produced between the end of the 11th and the middle of the 12th centuries.

Other cultural features are worthy of attention, given the passage through this area of men and goods, and therefore of knowledge and techniques, in medieval times.

20. *The wolves and the swan*, capital in cloister of Sant'Orso, 12th century.

THE CATHEDRAL OF SAN PIETRO IN SOVANA AND THE PARISH CHURCH OF SAN BRUZIO IN MAGLIANO

Architectural forms derived from the Lombard style found their way into scarcely populated areas, due to the presence of powerful noble families and monastic institutions. Maremma in the South of Tuscany is a case in point. Between the 10th and 11th centuries, Sovana, near the Via Cassia, enjoyed a period of intense development under the patronage of the counts of Aldobrandeschi. At the time they built both their own residence and the city walls.

In the second half of the 11th century, during the pontificate of Pope Gregory VIIth, who was a native of Sovano, building was started on the Cathedral of San Pietro. The works appear to have been suspended in 1085, when the Pope died in Salerno. They were only resumed in the second half of the 12th century. An epigraph in the portal lunette refers to this phase in the construction, which paved the way for the definitive version of the cathedral, complete with the bishop's residence.

The work would be further interrupted and resumed in the thirteenth century. The present building has three aisles, a single apse and dome and a raised presbytery above a crypt with six monolithic columns. Cruciform piers with groin-vaulting rising from their capitals divide the aisles into four bays. There are formal differences in the capitals and dosserets. The capitals with Old Testament stories (*Adam and Eve, Abraham and the wives*) are more reminiscent of the Lombard style, like other solutions adopted in the building, than contemporary Southern Tuscan sculpture. In some cases, the biblical subjects are mixed with

21

21. Cathedral of Sovana (Grosseto), apse, 12th century.

decorative motifs in the early Medieval style, like the ones in the portal lunette. This sort of repertoire was widely used in the region between the 11th and 12th centuries.

In the portal jambs *clipei* contain fine stylized plant motifs and others drawn from the world of fantasy and chivalry, like the siren and the horseman brandishing a sword. At the top there are also two small column-bearing lions fighting two rams, which had negative connotations. Traditional Lombard elements are also to be found in the parish church of San Bruzio near Magliano in Tuscany. All that remains is the apse, which is animated by pilaster strips and pensile arches, and part of the transept and octagonal lantern.

The building dates back to the 12th century and originally had a single aisle and a dome with heavy corner pendentives over the crossing. This was a device which was often used in monastic churches and then spread to the buildings of the secular clergy, especially the priests' houses, but also to numerous parish churches. The floor is made up of regular square stones set in mortar. The interior semi-piers have unusual, deftly-carved capitals. Some have cows' heads, acrobats and human figures and others large flowers in clipei set in octagons. The importance of the building is confirmed by the community statutes of 1356, which give instructions regarding its maintenance.

22

23

24

22. Cathedral, nave,
11th to 12th century.
Sovana.

23. Cathedral, portal left
side. Sovana.

24. San Bruzio, capital.
Magliano in Toscana
(Grosseto).

25. Ruins of the Church of San Bruzio. Magliano in Toscana (Grosseto).

THE CATHEDRAL OF MODENA: TWO PERSONALITIES IN PARTNERSHIP

In the Cathedral of Modena, which had a considerable influence on the architectural production in the Po area, the Lombard Romanesque style is infused with a new spirit and rare compositional harmony. The architect Lanfranco conceived the project and presided over the works from 1099 onwards, as recorded on a stone in the apse and in a 12th century codex in the Modena Chapter Library. He created a centrally-planned complex in which the interior and exterior were profoundly interrelated.

A series of blind arcading, with three-light windows in loggias at the top of each arch, covers the external walls of the cathedral, heightening the chiaroscuro and the animation provided by the various sculptural elements. This is mirrored in the articulation of the aisles. Round arches are surmounted by pretense matronei and self-contained spaces are created by a series of alternating piers and columns. The latter were not however designed for the vaults, which were added in the 15th century.

During the years in which Lanfranco was actively involved, Wiligelmo started on the sculptural decoration of the cathedral, which was integral to the architectural plan. It would be completed in the course of the 12th century by craftsmen of various origins. Some of the façade reliefs, which were originally in other locations, have

26

26. Cathedral of Modena, South side, end 11th to 12th century.

27. Facing page: Cathedral of Modena, view of façade, end 11th to 12th century.

28

29

28. Wiligelmo, *Stories of Genesis, Expulsion from Paradise and Punishment of working the earth*, 1099-1106. Modena, Cathedral.

29. Wiligelmo, *Stories of Genesis, Noah's Ark and Exit from the Ark*, 1099-1106. Modena, Cathedral.

also been attributed to Wiligelmo. Luxuriant plant motifs cover the door jambs of the main portal and some capitals. Robustly carved figures which stand out against a smooth background distinguish the stories from Genesis, the relief with two funerary genii, the foundation stone with the prophets Enoch and Elia and the panel of Sampson killing the lions. Wiligelmo in fact made an active contribution to the development of contemporary sculpture, abandoning the decorative repertoire and bas-reliefs of early medieval sculpture and turning to the sarcophagi and reliefs of Roman sculpture for iconographic methods and inspiration. With Wiligelmo the use of sculpture to narrate events and an enhancement of the gestures and expressiveness of the figures once again come to the fore.

30

31

30. Wiligelmo, main portal, detail with Zacharius, 1099-1106. Modena, Cathedral.

31. Cathedral of Modena, main portal, 12th century.

THE CREATION OF ADAM AND EVE AND ORIGINAL SI

Wiligelmo, 1099-1106
Modena, Cathedral

SUBJECT

The panel depicts three moments from *Genesis* in chronological order. From left to right these are: *The Creation of Adam*, *Creation of Eve* and *Original Sin*. The narrative is in the form of a continuous frieze with no divisions or gaps, in which the characters recur every time they feature in the story.

In the first section on the left, God the Father is portrayed in an ogive held by two angels. The Lord is holding the book of the origin of the world in which there is an inscription beginning with the words "EGO SUM LUX MUNDI". The scene therefore alludes to the creation of light in the universe.

In the section portraying the creation of man, God is depicted standing, in the act of transmitting life to Adam by touching him with his hand. Adam is still unconscious and inanimate, although standing.

In the scene where woman is created, Adam is semi-supine and asleep, while the Lord takes Eve by the hand, thereby rousing her to life. A rushing stream with close-packed curly waves flows under the rock against which Adam is leaning.

COMPOSITION

There is no background scenery and the figures stand out against the neutral backgrounds, which act as a foil to their intense plasticity.

The only plant feature, which is crucial to the understanding of the scene, is the apple tree round which the serpent is wound.

The scene of the *Original Sin* depicts the moment in which Adam and Eve, having eaten the apple, become conscious of their differences and shamefully cover their nudity.

Despite the unconvincing and improbable position of the sleeping Adam in the *Creation of Eve*, the knowledge on the part of Wiligelmo of the guiding principles of classical statuary is plain to see. The similar positions of the right arm and left leg are conspicuous; both are bent according to the correct application of Polyclitan "opposition".

The noticeable physical weight of the naked bodies contrasts with the garment of God the Father, the outline of which is traced with a delicate, flowing line.

As in the basilica of Sant'Ambrogio in Milan, the architectural solutions adopted in the cathedral of Modena exerted a degree of influence on surrounding sites. A case in point is San Zeno in Verona, which was built between 1120 and 1138 and later elongated. The gabled façade, which was endowed with a rose window at the end of the 12th century, is divided by vertical pillars into three sections of differing heights corresponding to the internal aisles. Each section is then divided up by narrow pilaster strips, between which two-light windows are inserted to form a

32

33

272

32. Nicolò, portal of the Zodiac, detail of jamb with symbols of constellations, about 1120. Sacra of San Michele.

33. San Zeno, façade. Verona.

continuous small loggia. The design of the façade shows how the characteristics of the Cathedral of Modena assume a pictorial, rather than plastic value in San Zeno, endowing the surface with subtle chromatic variation. This is heightened by the combination of the warm colour of the tufa with the pink marble of the columns and mullioned windows.

The bulk of the porch, which projects into the square, is attenuated by the slender columns borne by lions and by its triangular crowning. In the rose window there is an image of San Zeno flanked by knights and pages. Either side of the portal there are themes from the religious tradition mixed with images associated with contemporary events.

34

**34. Sacra of San Michele,
12th century.**

Reliefs of scenes taken from the Old and New Testament and some prophets with scrolls are juxtaposed with the paladins Orlando and Oliviero. The master Nicolò worked on the sculptural decoration from 1138 to 1139; it is possible to reconstruct his activity from a series of inscriptions bearing his name. He was trained in the Modena workshop under Wiligelmo and his figures are more realistic. There is a softness about the carving and a focus on naturalistic detail and the definition of the clothing and contemporary accoutrements. Nicolò was active in the Ferrara and Piacenza workshop as well as in the complex known as Sacra di San Michele or Abbazia della Chiusa on the summit of Monte Pirchiriano, a rocky peak at the mouth of the Val di Susa. The complex of buildings is the result of two distinct phases of construction, as can be inferred from the architectural forms which change from Romanesque to Gothic. It is distinguished by the vertical impetus of the structures and the chromatic contrast between the grey stone of the base and the green serpentine of the encircling walls.

The church, with three aisles and apses, dominates the summit of the mountain. Two flights of steps in the lee of the rock lead up to the apse, which is perched high up amongst vaulting and piers. At the top of the steps is the Zodiac portal, a masterpiece of twelfth century sculpture attributable, through an inscription, to Nicolò.

36

35. Facing page: Nicolò, portal of the Zodiac, about 1120. Sacra of San Michele.

36. Nicolò, *Creation of Adam*, detail of façade reliefs, 1138-39. Verona.

THE CATHEDRAL OF PARMA AND THE SCULPTURE OF BENEDETTO ANTELAMI

The Cathedral of Parma, which was rebuilt from 1076 after a serious fire, is particularly complex structurally due to the protraction of the building works. The grandiose proportions of the presbyterial area make it conspicuous: the exterior has an accumulation of cubic and semi-cylindrical volumes decorated with a procession of blind arcades and pilaster strips. The useable loggias at the top add a lighter touch.

The vertical impetus of the structures is emphasized by the raised presbytery above the crypt, culminating in the lantern over which a dome was placed in the seventeenth century. The height of the longitudinal part of the church is also emphasized. It is divided into three aisles by composite piers, which support the very high, pointed ribbed vaulting of the roof. There are matronei, which, unlike the ones in the Cathedral of Modena, are intended for use. The motif of rows of superimposed loggias found in the apse is repeated in the façade decoration. This gives it a strong sculptural quality and creates contrasts through chiaroscuro, which are reciprocated in the porch of the central portal. The Parma site made a fundamental contribution to the development of Italian Romanesque sculpture in the form of Benedetto Antelami. He was active in Parma in 1178, the year in which he produced the pulpit of which only the *Deposition of Christ* survives. Initially he was influenced by the vivid realism of Wiligelmo, but he soon brought a fresh approach to it, producing very elegant sculptures.

He was modern in the way he used models from beyond the Alps, possibly acquired during a stay in Provence, within schemes of greater balance and proportion. A new distribution of space looks forward to the volumetric style and perspective of Gothic sculpture. In about 1200, after he had finished the cathedral pulpit, the artist undertook the sculptural decoration of the Baptistery in Parma, of which he was also the architect. He worked on the lunettes of the three portals and the cycle of the *Months*. During these works he attained a greater artistic awareness. This was expressed through an even more modern language combining realism and monumentality, formal synthesis and narrative immediacy.

37

38

37. Baptistery, Parma, about 1200.

38. Benedetto Antelami, *Legend of Barlaam and Josaphat,* about 1200. Parma, Baptistery.

39

**39. Cathedral of Parma,
interior, from 1076.**

40

41

40. Benedetto Antelami,
Month of February, about
1200. Parma, Baptistery.

41. Benedetto Antelami,
Month of June, about
1200. Parma, Baptistery.

42. Benedetto Antelami,
Month of November,
about 1200. Parma,
Baptistery.

43. Benedetto Antelami,
Month of September,
about 1200. Parma,
Baptistery.

DEPOSITION OF CHRIST
Benedetto Antelami, 1178
Parma, Cathedral

The relief depicting the *Deposition of Christ* formed part of a pulpit which was destroyed.

To the right of Christ are the believers, that is to say the pious women, the apostle John, the Virgin and the personification of the Church.

The bloodless body of Christ is taken down from the cross by Nicodemus and Joseph of Arimathea.

The work is signed at the top on the right by the sculptor, Benedetto Antelami, who completed the work in 1178.

On the other side are the pagans, who are portrayed by soldiers intent on dividing Christ's garment between them, centurions and the synagogue.

The divide between the Jewish and pagan worlds is emphasized by the presence of the sun and moon as symbols of good and evil, from the left to the right respectively.

COMPOSITION

The cross is placed in the middle of the scene, dividing it into two perfectly equal parts.

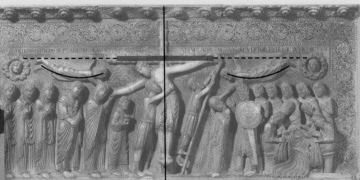

The short arm of the cross forms the edge of the space dedicated to the bas-relief. The flying angels are on the same level, forming a kind of extension of the cross itself.

The figures are placed squarely on the lower border in an orderly line, one beside the other. The drapery is treated in a strictly geometric fashion; the folds fall heavily in such a way as to form contrasts of light and shade.

The scene is framed by a wide band of vine-shoot motifs in niello-work.

The group of soldiers on the right is arranged on parallel planes in an attempt on the part of the sculptor to portray spatial depth.

Like the page of an illuminated codex, the relief is embellished with inscriptions of the names of characters.

EL

S. MA
RIA

ECCL̄A
EXAL
TVR

O

PIETRO DI ALBERICO AND THE SCULPTURE OF THE CATHEDRAL OF BOLOGNA

In about the middle of the 12th century, Bologna was already renowned throughout Europe as a *studium* for the activities of the schools of law. In this cultural context the cathedral had the important role of being the place where the Archdeacon conferred the title of doctor on students. Some years after the fire of 1141, the building underwent a program of restoration. It was then that the sculptural treasures of the portal were produced. Some of the door jamb panels have been preserved. These contain the vine-shoot motif held up by a kneeling telamon. The device is reminiscent of Wiligelmo and other external door jambs in Romanesque portals. The shoots, which fill the relief, seem to grow out of the telamon's hands.

Creatures drawn from the bestiary repertoire, and from encyclopedias which privileged the animal kingdom, 'inhabit' or 'populate' the vine-shoots. There are softly-carved winged and aquatic creatures, fish and amphibians.

In another fragment, in the spaces beneath arches supported by tiny capitals and stylized towers, are stories from the life and infancy of Jesus. The composition is symmetrical, with Christ in the centre while the other characters draw near him, in diminishing order. Like the telamons holding up the plant volutes, the figures' clothes have compact curved folds. Particular iconographic choices are evident, as in the case of the scene of Christ with the doctors, or the crowns on the heads of Jesus and his parents. The panels also have explanatory inscriptions with elegant capital letters and punctuation marks, which reveal a sophisticated graphic culture. The device of placing scenes within an architectural framework is reminiscent of the work of Wiligelmo, while the striking three-dimensional quality of the simple animal figures in the 'inhabited' vine motif recall some of the zodiac symbols by Nicolò in the porch of Ferrara Cathedral. On the other hand there are similar solutions in the drapery of some of the characters of the Porta Ravegnana cross which is now in San Petronio. This was produced by the craftsman Pietro di Alberico in 1159.

The years during which the portal sculptures were produced were crucial for Bologna. In fact in 1159 the city submitted to the Empire and the cross was commissioned during that difficult time. Evidently the cross was invested with a strong symbolic value: almost as if it might ward off the descent of Barbarossa.

Pietro di Alberico, a well-known craftsman, was chosen for the work. In terms of his training, there are links with the sculptor Niccolò and the Piacenza site.

There are records in Bologna of this master, who was the son of a sculptor, having been active in the following decade. In 1164 he signed a memorial tablet attributed to Nonacrina and kept in the complex of San Stefano. The master's workshop must have reached a high technical level to be noticed by the patrons and entrusted with the task of providing the sculptural decoration for the cathedral portal. Work on the building continued in to the 13th century, with the involvement of masters from Campione.

44

44. Workshop of Pietro of Alberico, fragment of jamb with Telamon. Bologna, Cathedral of San Pietro.

45

46

285

45. Workshop of Pietro of Alberico, fragment of jamb with Stories of Christ. Bologna, Cathedral of San Pietro.

46. Workshop of Pietro of Alberico, fragment of jamb with vine motif filled with fantastic animals. Bologna, Cathedral of San Pietro.

LIONS AND DRAGONS:
A FORTUNATE ICONOGRAPHIC THEME

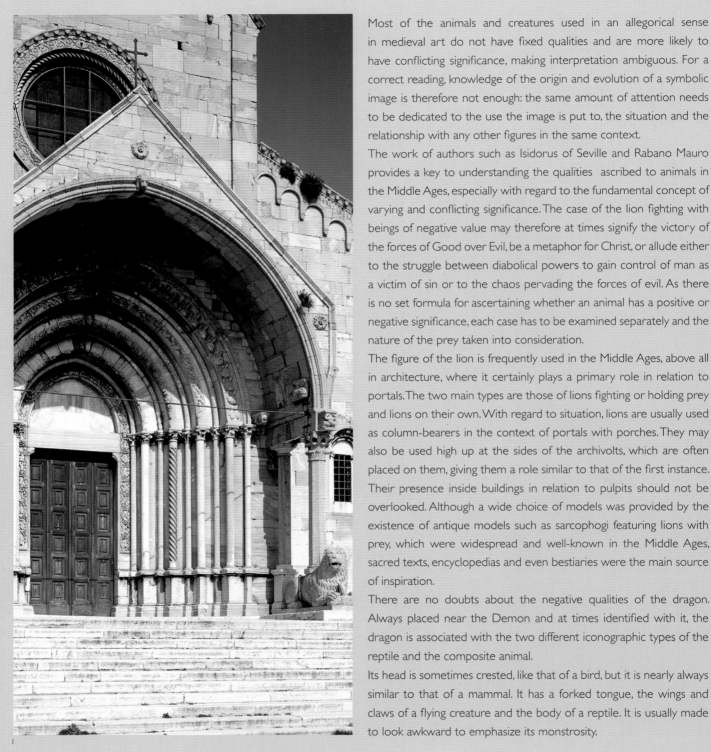

I. Porch, second half 13th
century. Ancona, San
Ciriaco.

Most of the animals and creatures used in an allegorical sense in medieval art do not have fixed qualities and are more likely to have conflicting significance, making interpretation ambiguous. For a correct reading, knowledge of the origin and evolution of a symbolic image is therefore not enough: the same amount of attention needs to be dedicated to the use the image is put to, the situation and the relationship with any other figures in the same context.

The work of authors such as Isidorus of Seville and Rabano Mauro provides a key to understanding the qualities ascribed to animals in the Middle Ages, especially with regard to the fundamental concept of varying and conflicting significance. The case of the lion fighting with beings of negative value may therefore at times signify the victory of the forces of Good over Evil, be a metaphor for Christ, or allude either to the struggle between diabolical powers to gain control of man as a victim of sin or to the chaos pervading the forces of evil. As there is no set formula for ascertaining whether an animal has a positive or negative significance, each case has to be examined separately and the nature of the prey taken into consideration.

The figure of the lion is frequently used in the Middle Ages, above all in architecture, where it certainly plays a primary role in relation to portals. The two main types are those of lions fighting or holding prey and lions on their own. With regard to situation, lions are usually used as column-bearers in the context of portals with porches. They may also be used high up at the sides of the archivolts, which are often placed on them, giving them a role similar to that of the first instance. Their presence inside buildings in relation to pulpits should not be overlooked. Although a wide choice of models was provided by the existence of antique models such as sarcophogi featuring lions with prey, which were widespread and well-known in the Middle Ages, sacred texts, encyclopedias and even bestiaries were the main source of inspiration.

There are no doubts about the negative qualities of the dragon. Always placed near the Demon and at times identified with it, the dragon is associated with the two different iconographic types of the reptile and the composite animal.

Its head is sometimes crested, like that of a bird, but it is nearly always similar to that of a mammal. It has a forked tongue, the wings and claws of a flying creature and the body of a reptile. It is usually made to look awkward to emphasize its monstrosity.

In the Old Testament, where every animal which crawls along the ground is attributed a negative value, the dragon is associated with the serpent and basilisk which are symbolic of evil. In early Medieval encyclopedias, numerous beings were classed with reptiles, including the dragon and the basilisk. This proves how important these monstrous creatures were and also what a huge number of variants existed. The choice of iconographic schemes of varying complexity is often determined by moralistic motives, the aim being to provide a series of examples to follow or avoid in attaining the salvation of the soul. A mentality which was susceptible to magic beliefs and rituals gave rise to a defensive stance, and, to convey its message, the church would often avail of the creatures of the popular imagination, which were recorded in contemporary bestiaries. Each example was interpreted in the light of the sacred texts.

II

III

II. Saint-Trophime, portal, lion holding prey, 12th century. Arles.

III. Workshop of Guido Bigarelli, ambo, third quarter of 13th century. Barga, Cathedral.

IV

IV. San Pietro all'Orto,
detail of portal
decoration,
12th century. Pisa.

V

**V. Cathedral, lion fighting
dragon, detail
of decoration of portal.
Trani (Bari).**

SAINT MARK'S IN VENICE: ROMANESQUE FORMS BETWEEN EAST AND WEST

The involvement of Byzantine craftsmen endows Saint Mark's Basilica with particular characteristics, which make it very different from contemporary Italian Romanesque buildings. It represents the most consummate expression of the strong links which existed between Venice and the Orient. The latter was also, for obvious geographical reasons, the preferred goal in terms of the traffic and commercial relationships which were integral to the marine republic. Building began on the basilica in 1063 – after a fire had destroyed the church built in the 9th century – to accommodate the remains of Saint Mark, which the Venetians had stolen from Alexandra in Egypt. The blueprint of a Greek cross surmounted by five domes is derived from a model of the Church of the Holy Apostles in Constantinople. The latter was destroyed during the course of the 15th century; like Saint Mark's it housed the remains of a saint and had the status of a palatine chapel. The construction of the basilica was protracted over time and this resulted in changes in the appearance of the building. From the 12th century onwards, in fact, the original walls of undressed bricks, which consisted of two storeys of arcading enlivened by ceramic inserts, began to be faced in precious marbles, mosaics and rich sculptural decoration. Cusped tabernacles, statues and ornamental motifs in the Gothic style were added in the 14th century, when the low hemispherical domes were raised. Despite being centrally-planned with a Greek cross layout the building developed as a basilica. This was due to the wider diameter of the nave domes, the reduced Eastern arm ending in three apses and the extension of the Western one by surrounding it with a portico on all three sides.

47

47. Saint Mark's Basilica, detail, 11th to 13th century. Venice.

48

**48. Saint Mark's Basilica,
façade, 11th to 13th
century. Venice.**

49

50

51

49. Saint Mark's Basilica, view of transept, 11th to 13th century. Venice.

50. Saint Mark's Basilica, first portal, 13th century. Venice.

51. Saint Mark's Basilica, door of the Flowers, end 13th century. Venice.

52. Facing page: Saint Mark's Basilica, interior, 11th to 13th century. Venice.

THE MAIN PORTAL

The sculptural decoration of the portals of Saint Mark's was part of the grandiose restructuring project, which took place in the 13th century, involving the façade . The brick walls of the basilica were embellished with precious marbles, mosaics and bas-reliefs. While the four lateral arcades still emulate the Byzantine style, the main portal is receptive to the new artistic currents which had spread throughout the Po area thanks to Antelami. It is like a big conch in which marble columns surmounted by three large arches covered by dense sculpted decoration are embedded. The impressive iconographic cycle depicts human life in urban and country settings together with the theological and biblical fundamentals of the Christian religion. On the inner surfaces, beside the customary repertoire of vine-shoot motifs containing animals and little human figures, the months, trades and signs of the zodiac are depicted, while on the outer surfaces, and therefore in a salient position, the theological and cardinal virtues, the beatitudes and the prophets are portrayed. The lack of stylistic homogeneity in the sculptures proves that different craftsmen were involved. In some the modeling is Romanesque, concise, rough and robust; in others the relief is flattened but animated by slight effects of chiaroscuro; yet others are lively and graceful and Gothic in appearance. The Antelamic influence is most evident in the relief of the *Months*, where the very essence of human destiny has been caught and distilled in the effort of labor: *December* is portrayed holding down a pig, lifting up its head and slitting its throat; *September* is a peasant bent down by a basket of grapes; *February* is an old man warming himself, holding his stiff leg as near as possible to the fire.

53

54

53. Saint Mark's Basilica, central portal, detail with September, 13th century. Venice.

54. Saint Mark's Basilica, central portal, detail with February, 13th century. Venice.

ART OF THE MIDDLE AGES

**55. Saint Mark's Basilica,
central portal, 13th
century. Venice.**

56

57

56. Saint Mark's Basilica, central portal, detail with animal decorations, 13th century. Venice.

57. Saint Mark's Basilica, central portal, arch of the Months, detail with *Virtue*, 13th century. Venice.

58   59

**58. Saint Mark's Basilica,
central portal, detail with
December, 13th century.
Venice.**

**59. Saint Mark's Basilica,
central portal, detail with
March, 13th century.
Venice.**

THE CYCLE OF THE MONTHS

I. Wiligelmo craftsmen, Portale della Pescheria, detail with Month of *June*, 1120-30 circa. Modena, Cathedral.

This was a very popular iconographic theme in the middle centuries of the Middle Ages and there are numerous examples in Italy, France (the Virgins' Portal, Notre-Dame), Spain (Panteon de los reyes Sant'Isidoro a León), Germany and England. The personifications of the Months are based, in particular, on the different tasks involved in work in the fields, focusing on agricultural and related activities. Alongside these, at intervals, there are scenes associated with mythological, biblical and cosmological themes. The images which are considered prototypical, and which were transferred to other figurative media, are to be found in some codices with illuminated calendars. In fact the subjects associated with the representation of the Months also appear in mosaic floors, painted plasterwork, architectural decoration and sculpture.

In the floor mosaics of Aosta (Sant'Orso) and Pavia (San Michele Maggiore), both of which are from the first half of the 12th century, the Months are depicted beside the personification of the year (*Annus*). The latter, portrayed in a throne held up by the sun and moon, also appears in the mosaic floor of the presbytery of San Savino in Piacenza, a building which was consecrated in 1107. The iconographic theme recurs in the crypt of this church, where the months are found alongside the Zodiac and the Constellations, as is frequently the case. The months also appear beside the signs of the Zodiac in the large floor mosaic in the crypt of the abbey church in Bobbio. The cycle is also filled with biblical subjects and monstrous and fantastic creatures.

Similar iconographic choices were to be implemented in the numerous mosaic floors which survive in Southern Italy, of which Otranto is the most famous example.

The theme of the Months was equally popular in the setting of the portals of numerous Romanesque buildings. One of the most famous examples is that of the Cathedral of Modena, in the internal door jambs of the Portale della Pescheria. The personified Months are placed within small aedicules and have explanatory inscriptions.

The relationship between sculptures and inscriptions has helped to place the cycle between 1120 and 1130. In the case of Modena, the iconographic scheme favors tasks associated with the rural world, with some variations, which are probably owed to the harsh climactic conditions. These include the preparation of pigs' trotters (January); pruning (March); the awakening of springtime (April); the harvest (July) and threshing with the hand-thresher or "correggiato"; the grape pressing (September) and wine-making (October); sowing (November); firewood cutting (December). In this, as well as other cases, the cycles of production of the wheat and vines, which occupy more months, are given a central place. This choice was probably also influenced by the significance of bread and wine in Christian symbolism. There are some discrepancies in the relation of tasks to months, which can probably be put down to climactic differences. The late 12th century portal of the Baptistery in Pisa is a case in point: the harvest and threshing are portrayed one month earlier than in the Modena portal.

In the portal of the parish church of Arezzo, the rich detail in the illustration of the Months is reminiscent of the famous cycles sculpted by Benedetto Antelami in the Baptistery of Parma and, also in the Po area, those sculpted by the Master of the Months in Ferrara and Cremona.

In the later cycles, such as those in the Cathedral of San Martino in Lucca and the main portal of Saint Mark's in Venice, the role of embellishing the architectural elements is given to the signs of the Zodiac, with the seasonal tasks being placed between them.

In the surviving painted cycles there are more complex examples in the form of actual calendars, like the thirteenth century one in the Oratory of San Pellegrino a Bominaco, in Abruzzo (1263).

II

III

IV

II. Master of the Months of Ferrara, *July,* **13th century. Ferrara, Cathedral Museum.**

III. Months: Taurus, Gemini, Cancer, about 1263. Bominaco, Oratory of San Pellegrino.

IV. Months: Acquarius, Pisces, Aries, about 1263. Bominaco, Oratory of San Pellegrino.

The exponential growth in economic activity from the 11th century onwards gave rise to new forms of commission and new protagonists in the urban field. In cities, the cathedral was a symbol which could be identified with; it was the very emblem of revival in the community and in the trades and crafts which had contributed to its existence.

Modena is a prime example of the changing role of the city. In 1099 the Modenese had already decided to demolish the ancient cathedral, which had been built in 1070 by the schismatic and empire-loving Eriberto. They built another in its place and the craftsmanship was much praised by contemporaries.

A particularly significant case is that of the reliefs of the trades, which were sculpted in the middle of the 12th century on the piers of the Cathedral of Piacenza, and which portray the merchants and craftsmen who financed the construction. The activities relevant to the crafts are represented with a wealth of detail. Besides the traditional crafts such as cobblers, weavers and knife-grinders, there are even herdsmen (*bubulci*). Evidently these were also affected by the phenomenon of economic growth and the desire for self-representation, which was becoming part of Italian city-state life.

However the main feature of city life is not so much economic power as sociopolitical organization and the concept of civitas.. An epigraph built into the façade of the Cathedral of Ferrara in 1173 actually contains the citizens' statutes. It was during these years that the new social structure of the commune was emerging. It necessitated a

60

**60. Cathedral of Ferrara,
façade, 12th to 14th century.**

**61. Soprana Gate, about
1155-58. Genoa.**

62

63

64

62. Anselmo and Girardo, bas-relief from Roman Gate: *Soldiers in city,* **12th century. Milan, Castello Sforzesco.**

63. Anselmo and Girardo, bas-relief from Roman Gate: *Milanese troups return,* **12th century. Milan, Castello Sforzesco.**

64. Anselmo and Girardo, bas-relief from Roman Gate: *Return of Milanese to City,* **12th century. Milan, Castello Sforzesco.**

reworking of the archetypal *palatium communis*, the town hall, which was to become a constant in the urban spaces of the late Middle Ages. To this new collective client are owed the new building enterprises and artistic production, which are not exclusively connected to religious architecture. In the second half of the 12th century the walls surrounding many cities were extended due to demographic growth, economic activity and civic self-government.

Some monumental urban gates also date back to this period, like the Porta Soprana in Genoa and the destroyed Porta Romana in Milan. The latter was connected to the new city wall built between 1171 and 1172. The bas-relief of the Milanese gate sculpted by Anselmo and now in the Castello Sforzesco contains an example of a lay tale.

Beside the *Expulsion of the Arians by Saint Ambrose* there is, in fact, a premature demonstration of communal pride before the victory of the Lombard League in 1176, in the portrayal of the *Return to the city of the communal army and the Bishop*, which features the city banner, after the defeat suffered at the hands of the imperial troops of Frederick Barbarossa. The urban gate fulfils an important symbolic role, in terms of affirmation of identity, which was to last down successive centuries. This is demonstrated by the numerous inscriptions addressed to foreigners, the function of which was to boast the wonders of the city, as well as to extend a warning to those whose intentions might not be peaceful.

Equal significance was to be attributed by the marine cities to maritime and harbor structures, to the extent of depicting them in areas of "public" importance. An example can be found in the external wall of the Leaning Tower.

65

65. Relief with *Pisan Port*, 12th century. Pisa, Bell tower.

5. The Romanesque Period in Central and Southern Italy

I n these areas of the peninsula the rapport with antiquity is even more noticeable in a wide variety of contexts. It ranges from the authentic restructuring of entire structures to the purely utilitarian reuse of materials, not to speak of direct imitation. Pisa is an example of how regional styles could be transcended. A project such as this had been long planned in the Mediterranean. The ideological choice behind the city's claim to recognition as an heir to Rome was to be extremely influential. Many cities were to follow suit in the architectural renovation of buildings and in fact the phenomenon was so widespread that numerous extraurban sites were also involved. Some monastic centers made a point of bringing together craftsmen from heterogeneous backgrounds, as in the case of Montecassini at the time of the Abbot Desiderio. Many of the workshops which sprang up between the 11th and 12th centuries were ahead of their time in the ways in which they sought to supersede existing liturgical decorations; in many cases their innovative methods were to contribute to a revival in marble sculpture. The particularly fertile cultural ambience which developed in Sicily was owed to the Norman kings, in whose courts local, Byzantine and Islamic craftsmen would work side by side.

2

3

1. Facing page: Baptistery of San Giovanni, detail of marble wall facing, 11th to 13th century. Florence.

2. Façade and left side, 11th to 12th century. Cathedral, Pisa.

3. Cosmatesque floor, detail, 12th to 13th century. Ferentino (Frosinone), Cathedral.

THE ENDURANCE OF CLASSICAL MODELS IN CENTRAL ITALIAN ART.

The central Italian churches afforded the Lombard Romanesque style a very guarded welcome: the use of vaults was limited to crypts and presbyteries and composite pillars were only used sporadically. On the other hand the daily contact with the ruins of Roman buildings was inspiring architects to reclaim antique forms. The results were often imbued with ideological implications, but they did bear witness to a breadth of taste and a greater allegiance to tradition. The prime example of this is to be found in Florence where Lombard structural elements, spatial dialectics and plastic values resulted in extensive clean-cut planes and a reasoned harmony achieved through geometric relationships. The influence of the tradition of antiquity is apparent in the internal layout of churches, where space is demarcated by columns with reused capitals and the decoration reflects a perfect balance between marble carvings and their architectural settings. The way in which the characteristics of Christian architecture persisted is as noticeable in the city of Rome, both in the internal layout of basilicas and in structures with colonnades and roofs. There is, however, a marked departure from the Florentine manner in the decorative work, where antique forms are retained and embellished with highly-colored marble inlay giving extremely original results.

4

5

4. Collegiate Church of Sant'Andrea, detail of portal and marble facing, façade. 12th century. Empoli (Florence).

5. Collegiate Church of Sant'Andrea, façade, 12th century. Empoli (Florence).

6. Facing page: Baptistery of San Giovanni, façade with South door, 11th to 13th century. Florence.

The Baptistery of Saint John is imbued with the classical spirit of Florentine artistic civilization, which had always looked to the great models of antiquity for inspiration. It was constructed on the foundations of an Christian building and is octagonal in shape. The outside is faced with a precious veneer of white Carrara and green Prato marble with the design being based on geometrical criteria. Slight an-

gular buttresses define the sides, which are adorned with a tier of small architraved pillars and a series of blind arcades. Set within these are windows surmounted by triangular or curvilinear pediments. The tambour, decorated with geometric panels, covers a large eight-gored dome. The dome does not rest directly on the outer walls of the building but on an internal shell, which is formed by a lower tier of architraved columns surmounted by a gallery with pretense two-light windows, in undisguised emulation of the Pantheon.

7

7. Baptistery of San Giovanni, matroneum two-light window, 11th to 13th century. Florence.

8. Baptistery of San Giovanni,
interior, towards rectangular
apse, 11th to 13th century.
Florence.

SAN MINIATO AL MONTE IN FLORENCE

Rebuilt between 1018 and 1063, the church of San Miniato reflects a reluctance to yield to the new trends in Romanesque architectural language and remains, on the whole, faithful to the classical and Christian tradition on which the design of the basilica is based. The columns, with their Corinthian capitals, and the roof, with its wooden trusses, blend with the Lombard idiom. This appears in the cruciform pillars, the transversal arches above them and the raised crypt. The marble paneling, which is applied with such symmetry and harmony within the architectural lines of the facade, is also modeled on antiquity. The lower tier of marble veneer facing takes the form of five arches over columns which frame the main portals and false ones between them. This pattern seems to foreshadow the division of the interior by colonnades and is echoed in the decoration of the apse, where the arch motif is repeated. The upper part of the façade, which stems from the 13th century, is less coherent and conformist. It frames a window in the Classicizing style similar to those in the Baptistery in Florence.

10

11

9. Facing page: San Miniato al Monte, façade, 11th to 13th century. Florence.

10. San Miniato al Monte, pulpit, 13th century. Florence.

11. San Miniato al Monte, nave, 11th to 13th century. Florence.

THE CHURCH OF SAN CLEMENTE IN ROME

In the area of the San Clemente Church, the superimposed buildings of varying periods provide a precious source for insights into the history of town planning in this part of the city. In fact, at the end of the 4th Century, a Christian basilica was built on top of two public buildings of the Roman era, beside which there was a mithraeum. The Basilica was severely damaged during the invasion of Robert Guiscard in 1094 and material from it was later used for the foundations of the new church. This was built during the first half of the 12th century at the behest of Pope Paschal II.

Despite eighteenth century modifications, when the walls were covered with stucco-work and frescoes and a coffered ceiling was added, the medieval structure is intact. Preceded by a porch and four-sided portico, where columns with ionic capitals support a rectilinear architrave, the church is divided into three aisles, each having two tiers of seven reused columns on to which ionic capitals and a series of arches have been grafted. Here and there compound piers break up the line of columns, revealing the Lombard Romanesque influence, but, on the whole, the church adheres to the pattern of the Christian basilicas in Rome in which large, centrally-planned, internal spaces are flooded with light.

12

13

14

12. San Clemente, nave towards the apse, 12th century. Rome.

13. San Clemente, façade. Rome.

14. San Clemente, view of the apse, 12th century. Rome.

THE ART OF THE ROMAN MARBLE CRAFTSMEN

The Roman church of San Clemente boasts extraordinarily intact, well-preserved and sumptuous liturgical decoration, which still enriches the simple pattern of the basilica with light and color, apart from providing a valuable record of the activity of the "Cosmati" workshops. This term is used to refer to the marble craftsmen employed in Rome and the surroundings between the 12th and 13th centuries. They were the guardians of a decorative tradition which was passed down through family workshops and tinged by the influence of the Muslim East, through Campania and Montecassino. The floor of San Clemente stretches like a multi-colored carpet from the entrance to the choir, with a narrow central panel formed by medallions of green serpentine and porphyry, at the sides of which are panels decorated with geometric shapes. A balustrade separates off the area of the presbytery. This is reserved for the clergy and its focal point is the altar which is surmounted by a ciborium. Beyond, round the apse, there is a marble bench in whose center stands the Episcopal throne which is adorned with a curved back. In the middle of the nave is the schola cantorum, for the singers who accompanied the liturgical celebrations as ordained in the dictates of the liturgical reform introduced by Urban II in 1095. At the sides stand two ambos, one for the reading of the Epistles and one for that of the Gospels, and the candelabrum for the Easter candle. Each component has an articulated ornate geometric decoration. This is juxtaposed with large neutral areas of white marble with dense polychrome motifs. These are formed by inlay of marble and precious stones and by tesserae of glass mosaic and gold.

15

16

15. Santa Maria in Cosmedin, *schola cantorum*, 11th to 12th century. Rome.

16. Saint Paul outside the walls, cloister, 12th to 13th century. Rome.

18

19

ART OF THE MIDDLE AGES

**17. Facing page:
San Clemente, *schola
cantorum*, 12th century.
Rome.**

**18-19. Cosmatesque altar
and detail of the marble
encrustations. Grotte
Vaticane, San Pietro,
Rome.**

LITURGICAL DECORATION

The grandiosity which marked religious ceremonies was most fully expressed during the Middle Ages in the liturgical decorations which today still adorn the churches. The exuberance of form and the richness of the materials used worked on the imagination of the faithful, underpinning the salient moments of the ceremony. The enclosure surrounding the presbytery separated the space reserved for the clergy from that occupied by the community of the faithful, while the priests read the Gospel, prayed and intoned the liturgical chants from the raised platform of the pulpit. The ambo was used for the same purpose, but unlike the pulpit with its single staircase it had two: the minister would ascend by one and descend by the other. Particular care was taken in the decoration of the altar as the symbolic sine qua non of the Christian ritual and the visual focal point of the whole church. Surmounted by a ciborium and embellished with altar frontals, it took the form of a mensa, on which Christ's sacrifice was renewed from day to day, and through which reference could be made to the relics of a saint preserved in the crypt beneath. The Cathedrals contained the bishop's throne or *cattedra*, from which their name is derived, while the baptismal fonts were kept in parish churches and baptisteries. Sculpted basins gradually replaced the *piscinas* of the Christian era. In the late Middle Ages baptism was extended to include babies, while in the 13th and 14th centuries the sacrament was administered by the sprinkling of water rather than by immersion.

I. *Apparition of the remains of the body of Saint Mark,* detail, 10th to 12th century. Venice, Basilica of Saint Mark.

II. THE CIBORIUM
Anagni, The Cathedral

The term "ciborium" is used for the quadrangular structure above the altar. It is usually open at the sides and is made up of four supports which hold up a roof. It acted as a foil to the altar and perhaps also as a means of hiding the celebration of the Eucharist from the eyes of the faithful by means of curtains.

The Anagni Ciborium is of a sort that was commonly found in 11th Century Romanesque settings, where two tiers of small architraved columns provide a link between the quadrangular form of the base and the octangular form of the covering.

II

III. THE LEFT-HAND PULPIT
Salerno, The Cathedral

The term "pulpit" usually refers to a raised platform which is reached by a flight of stairs. It was used for readings which included the Gospel and the Epistle and for the intonation of liturgical chants. The Salerno examplar reflects the changing artistic styles in Campania in the middle of the 12th century, due firstly to the effect of new influences from Sicily and secondly to a greater interest in the art of antiquity.

Classical influences are apparent in the high quality of the materials used, the sculptures, the capitals and the architectural frames, whose multifarious polychrome decoration is made up of mosaic tesserae and marble encrustations.

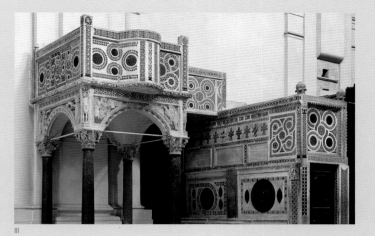
III

IV. GUIDO DA COMO, BAPTISMAL FONT
Pisa, The Baptistery

The octagonal font in Pisa shows how widespread this type of font was in Italy: the proportions were vast and the imposing structure was reminiscent of the Christian piscinas. The finest of materials would generally be arranged within simple aniconic panels. The four corner cavities made it possible for community celebrations to be carried out by more than one minister at the same time. The date 1246 is engraved on the work and this makes it possible to identify its creator as Guido Bigarelli, known as Guido da Como, who was one of a family of sculptors who came from the Canton of Ticino and who were active in Tuscany and Trentino in the 13th Century.

IV

V. THE EASTER CANDELABRUM
Rome, Basilica of Saint Paul outside the walls

References in ancient plain chant to the ceremony of the blessing of the wax, which was an integral part of the Holy Saturday liturgy, prove that Easter Candelabra have existed since the first centuries of Christianity. The Roman exemplar, signed by the sculptors Nicolò and Pietro Vassalletto and probably dating from the beginning of the pontificate of Innocent III (1198-1216), bears the unmistakable hallmark of antiquity. The scenes from the New Testament, placed in bands one above the other, constitute an undisguised emulation of Roman columns with their decoration of historical scenes.

V

20

THE MONUMENTAL COMPLEX OF THE CATHEDRAL OF PISA

The marble slabs on the façade show that construction of the Cathedral began in 1064 under the architect Buscheto, after the victory over the Muslims of Palermo gave fresh impetus to the Republic of Pisa's municipal pride, as well as providing the financial resources for a building project on such a grand scale. Ancient marbles were brought from Rome and gigantic monolithic columns from Elba. The architectural forms of the building alone are fitting testimony to the dynamism of the city, and the original ways in which cultural exchanges and influences were exploited. The Cathedral has five aisles, like the most imposing Christian basilicas in Rome, but it is enhanced by a transept with three aisles, a matroneum and an octagonal dome. The interior, which is extremely light, is animated by the play of chiaroscuro generated by the complex distribution of

21

20. Cathedral of Pisa, façade, 11th to 12th century.

21. Cathedral of Pisa, view with Leaning Tower.

volumes, the vigorous plasticity of the Corinthian and composite capitals and the polychrome decoration. The external walls are made up of a succession of three superimposed structures. In the lower tier there is an expanse of blind arcading on colonnettes, with windows, circles and recessed lozenges. Higher up, narrower pilaster strips with architraves support a moulded cornice, with a crowning of smaller blind arcading on colonnettes. During the following century, when the aisles were extended, the architect Rainaldo completed the facade. This is also divided into three parts but it is so animated in plastic and chromatic terms that a gentle and continuous movement seems to play across the surface. The walls of the round bell tower have the same decoration. There is a lower tier of blind arcading on half-columns and on the upper floors each gallery is separated from the one above by a moulded cornice. Thanks to the urn which was found at the base of the bell tower in 1840, it was possible to identify the first architect as Bonanno. He was succeeded by

22

23

22. Cathedral of Pisa, interior towards entrance, 11th to 12th century.

23. Cathedral of Pisa, view of aisles, 11th to 12th century.

Giovanni di Simone and Tommaso Pisano. On numerous occasions the work had to be suspended due to the alluvial nature of the terrain and the alarming inclination of the tower. The original plan, which was for a tower at least 230 feet high, had to be modified.

In 1152, as recorded in an inscription, Diotisalvi embarked on the construction of the baptistery, which was decorated by Giovanni Pisano and endowed with a dome at the end of the 13th century. It is circular in form with a ring-shaped nave and matroneum on the inside. On the outside the decoration of the lower tier matches that of the buildings nearby, while the "crowning" over the loggia belongs to the Gothic period with its circle of pointed aediculae intercalated with pinnacles and the tympani which decorate the mullioned windows.

24

25

24. Cathedral of Pisa, detail of tambour and dome, 11th to 12th century.

25. Leaning tower, 12th to 13th century. Pisa.

26. Facing page: Baptistery of Pisa, 12th to 13th century.

SCULPTURAL DECORATION: THE BONANNO PORTALS AND THE GUGLIELMO PULPIT

The pulpit sculpted by Guglielmo for the Cathedral of Pisa between 1159 and 1162 was subsequently moved to Cagliari to make way for the new pulpit by Giovanni Pisano. It had marked a turning point in Romanesque sculpture in Tuscany, setting in motion new developments which would foreshadow the style of Giovanni Pisano. It was taken apart and rearranged arbitrarily into two ambos. Originally it was made up of a rectangular casket on four columns borne by lions on top of which were two groups of figures which formed lecterns. In one Saint Paul is flanked by two apostles and in the other there is a tetramorph beside an angel holding a scroll. The high-relief of the parapet, which is set within a frame containing inscriptions and foliage motifs, illustrates the life of Christ, beginning with the *Annunciation* and ending with the *Ascension*. The episodes are arranged in two layers, some are crowded into a single panel while others are developed on two separate levels. For instance the *Annunciation* is set beside that of the *Visitation*, so that the figure of Mary appears twice in the same space, whereas in the *Resurrection* the two Marys at the sepulcher fill the top panel while the one underneath contains the sleeping soldiers. One of the soldiers, who falls from a height and is seized by a naked devil, acts as a link between the two scenes. The figures are thickset and wrapped in heavy garments and there is a sense of solidity of volume in the way in which they emerge powerfully from the background. This attests to a revival of interest in the sculpture of antiquity, fused with experimentation with light and color. Here and there the odd architectural or landscape detail evokes the spatial setting, but in

27

**27. Guglielmo, pulpit,
lion and bull, 1159-62.
Cagliari, Cathedral.**

general this is dealt with by the use of niello-work for the backgrounds. In fact Guglielmo adapts a technique used in goldsmithery, filling the incisions made in the marble with black paste and covering the surfaces with floral and decorative motifs. In addition to being the architect of the bell tower in the Pisan complex, Bonanno designed the bronze portal of the main entrance to the Cathedral which was destroyed by a fire in 1595 and the portal of the so-called "Saint Ranieri" transept. The latter, which dates back to about 1190, is partitioned by frames made up of ornamental classical roses set off by an elegant rope-work border. Different-sized panels are fitted into this grid. The upper and lower long rectangular panels contain, respectively, the *Virgin in Majesty* and a sequence of *Prophets* interspersed with palms, and the middle is taken up by *Stories from the Infancy* and *Passion of Christ* arranged in five bands. The way in which the episodes are arranged entails reading from the bottom to the top, horizontally, and from left to right across the two portals. Each panel contains an assembly of parts produced with different techniques so that the background, the figures and the texts seem to have been modeled separately and subsequently reworked when cold. The figures jut out from the smooth background where the spatial setting is conveyed by a few architectural and naturalistic elements. They stand on a kind of foot-board and the heavy folds of their garments emphasize their thickset bodies which culminate in fully-rounded heads. The compositions, which are balanced and harmonious, are often designed symmetrically, but sometimes the main event is placed at the edge of the scene. This shows how Bonanno transformed the influences which shaped his training, whether classical, Byzantine or from beyond the mountains, to create a style all of his own.

28

28. Guglielmo, pulpit, lion and dragon, 1159-62. Cagliari, Cathedral.

29

30

29. Guglielmo, left ambo,
1159-62. Cagliari,
Cathedral.

30. Guglielmo, right ambo,
1159-62. Cagliari,
Cathedral.

31

32

31. Bonanno Pisano, Door of San Ranieri, detail with prophets, about 1190. Pisa, Cathedral.

32. Bonanno Pisano, Door of San Ranieri, detail from right door, about 1190. Pisa, Cathedral.

33. Bonanno Pisano, Door of San Ranieri, detail with four scenes from right door, about 1190. Pisa, Cathedral.

34

34. Bonanno Pisano, Door of San Ranieri, *Flight into Egypt*, about 1190. Pisa, Cathedral.

**35. Bonanno Pisano, Door
of San Ranieri, *Visitation*,
about 1190. Pisa,
Cathedral.**

SCULPTURE IN TUSCANY IN THE 12TH CENTURY: THE SCHOOL OF GUGLIELMO

The pulpit of Guglielmo had such a profound influence on sculpture production in Tuscany that scholars acknowledge the existence of a "school of Guglielmo" in its own right, which was influenced by the style of Roman sarcophagi. Classical stylistic elements are particularly prevalent in the lunettes and lintels of church portals, which bear the sculptor's signature. One such is the lintel of the main portal of Sant'Andrea a Pistoia, which can be dated 1166 and attributed to Gruamonte, thanks to the inscription beside that of his brother Adeodato (or Deodato). The scene is evoked by means of parataxis, the *Procession of the Magi* merging with the *Adoration*. On the left the

36

37

328

36. Façade of Parish Church, 12th century. San Casciano a Settimo (Pisa).

37. Biduino, central portal, detail with lintel, 1180. Parish Church of San Casciano a Settimo (Pisa).

three kings advance on horseback; there is a vain attempt at conveying movement through the flapping of the hems of their robes. In the center Herod is seated in front of a kneeling servant, possibly commanding the massacre of the innocents. Behind him the Magi present their gifts to the baby Jesus, who is held by the Madonna, while Saint Joseph, wrapped in a large cloak and leaning wearily on his staff, seems to withdraw from the scene. An extraordinary sense of immobility pervades the scene, freezing the protagonists' facial expressions and movements. Biduino, who sculpted the lintel of the portal in the parish church of San Casciano in Settimo, was also trained in the Guglielmo ambience in Pisa. This work is filled with figures, some of which are on two levels, and which portray, from left to right, the *Healing of the Two Blind Men of Jericho*, the *Resurrection of Lazarus* and *Christ's Entry into Jerusalem*. The evangelical episodes are contained, in sequential form, within a single narrative space. This is differentiated by the insertion of a few architectural or naturalistic elements. While the city of Jericho is implied by a two-storey building, an open sarcophogus dominates the second scene, and the movement of the procession towards Jerusalem is punctuated by the outline of a few trees, the city being represented on the far left by a crowded doorway. The last scene fills two thirds of the lintel, with Jesus seated on an ass, preceded by Saint Peter and accompanied by the apostles who, with military precision, hold long palm branches on their shoulders. The tale unfolds amidst the vivacious reactions of the onlookers whose indignation is conveyed by the narrowing of eyes, open mouths and agile movements of their elongated bodies.

38

40

39

329

38. Parish Church of San Casciano a Settimo (Pisa), facade, detail with sculpted head, 12th century.

40. Sant'Andrea, facade, 12th century. Pistoia.

39-41. Gruamonte and Adeodato, main portal; following pages, detail of lintel with *Adoration of the Magi*, 1166. Sant'Andrea, Pistoia.

AGS STE... ... LAMON ET PVERO TRIA MVLERA DON...

ER EIVS

...AG... STEHENRIGVS MEFECIT...

THE INFLUENCE OF THE PISAN ROMANESQUE STYLE

The original project conceived by Buscheto for the Cathedral of Pisa had such a wide-reaching effect on contemporary architecture that it generated a style of architecture in its own right, which was exported by the marine republic to all the territories subjected to its economic and political rule. As a result, the influence of the "Pisan Style" is found not only in the surrounding countryside, but in the Lucchesia, Volterra, Pistoia, Massa Marittima and even as far as Sardinia and Corsica. This style prefers the elegant colonnades of the Christian tradition surmounted by Classicizing capitals to the rustic pillars of the Romanesque language. It covers external walls with blind arcading, recessed lozenges and ceramic bowls. These contribute, together with the dichromatic facing, to the decorative quality of the architectural forms.

42

44

43

42. Cathedral of Cagliari, view of façade, 13th to 14th century.

43. Cathedral of Volterra, view of façade, 12th to 13th century.

44. San Pietro in Torres, façade, 12th century. Borutta.

SAN PAOLO A RIPA D'ARNO IN PISA

The church is a faithful copy of the blueprint of the Pisan cathedral, with its Latin cross crowned by a dome above the crossing of the aisles and transept. Strong analogies to the architectural prototype are also evident in the external walls. These are distinguished by their facing of strips of bichromatic marble, except on the right side, which faces away from the Arno and is therefore less visible. The strips run through the blind arcad-ing which is supported by pilaster strips in the lower tier and columns in the top one. This elegant pattern animates the façade in plastic and chromatic terms, frames the equally elegant portals and is fined down in the little loggias above. The latter technique had already been used by Rainaldo in the cathedral, where they are filled with sculptures, marble inlay and small twisted columns. By contrast the interior seems extremely bare: the walls have regular ashlars, there is a timber truss roof and the aisles are separated by rough pillars surmounted by Corinthian capitals.

45

46

45. San Paolo a Ripa d'Arno, 12th century. Pisa.

46. San Paolo a Ripa d'Arno, façade, detail of portal, 12th century. Pisa.

COLOR IN ARCHITECTURE:
THE CERAMIC BOWLS

The term ceramic bowls refers to monochrome or polychrome vessels of various forms and sizes. Embellished with decorative motifs, they were intended for daily use and were often used to decorate buildings, especially religious ones. They are inserted in the fabric of the building, of which they form an integral part, from the outset, with either bricks or stone being used. The obvious significant relationship between ceramic bowls and architecture enables conclusions to be drawn between the contemporaneous use of artefacts which may have been made in different places, and, conversely, between bowls which are identical in terms of manufacture but appear in different buildings. This is obviously a useful factor when it comes to dating buildings with related bowls, even though in some cases bowls may have been used previously. The phenomenon, which dates back to the 10th century, occurs in a fairly wide area, but in no other place were there so many instances as in the city of Pisa. Here, and in the environs, its use continued right up to the 14th and the beginning of the 15th centuries, as proven by as many as twenty-six buildings and, impressively, by nearly two thousand examples. The ceramic bowls were probably used for their decorative value, which was enhanced by their provenance from other countries, like the other artefacts which were displayed in buildings or which became an integral part of them. In the case of Pisa, up until the end of the 12th century, the ceramic products used were almost exclusively imported, especially from Tunisia and Morocco, from the Valencia area in Spain and Majorca, but also from Sardinia and Sicily. In the 12th century, the increasing recourse to locally-made products accounted for a third of cases, and was to become exclusive by the end of the century and throughout the next one.

I. View of apse,
12th century.
San Piero a Grado.

II

III

IV

II. Islamic Art, ceramic
bowl with green dragon.
Pisa, Museo Nazionale di
San Matteo.

III. Bowl, facade, 13th
century. Santi Prospero
e Tommaso, Certaldo.

IV. Islamic Art, ceramic
bowl with fish. Pisa,
Museo Nazionale
di San Matteo.

THE CATHEDRAL OF SAN MARTINO IN LUCCA

The church, which, as tradition has it, was founded in 1060 by San Frediano, owes its present form to renovations carried out by the bishop Anselmo of Baggio in 1060. The facade, however, was begun by Guidetto in 1204, as recorded in an inscription on the first colonnette on the right. The architect of San Martino copies the Pisan Romanesque stylistic language, with its series of superimposed galleries, but he transforms it by increasing the effect of chiaroscuro. He replaces the lower arcade with a deep portico, removes the row of colonnettes from the walls and inserts sculpted decorative and narrative episodes within the architectural structure almost to the point of overdoing it. The interior, which is divided into three aisles by piers and has a protruding transept, is the result of radical renovation carried out in the second half of the 14th century.

48

47. Facing page: Cathedral of San Martino, façade, 13th century. Lucca.

48. Cathedral of San Martino, apse, 11th to 13th century. Lucca.

A common feature of 12th to 13th century architectural decoration is that of animals which chase each other – the repertoire almost amounts to a contemporary bestiary – and are in their turn pursued by hunters armed with weapons and oliphants. The use in these contexts of animals which represent negative or ambiguous qualities, like the hunters, may allude either to the disorder or chaos pervading the forces of Evil, or to the vices and sins of which the animals are personifications. At the same time there are many examples of the theme of animals and hunters being given a preeminently decorative role. The string-course cornice of the first loggia in the Cathedral of Pisa is a famous example of cases where the evident decorative purpose is imbued with allegorical and moral significance. Both real and fantastic animals chase and attack each other among plants. Directly related to this cornice is the lintel which was produced in the Biduino workshop at San Casciano a Settimo near Pisa. Generic descendents of these worth noting in Lucca are the later reliefs of San Martino and San Michele in Foro, where the theme recurs in the marble inlay of the facades. Out of all the hunting scenes selected for architectural decoration, mosaic flooring and marble sculpture, the wild boar hunts were particularly popular. The significance in

I. Marble inlay with hunters and animals. San Michele in Foro, Lucca.

II. Matteo, lintel with wild boar hunt, 12th century. Parish Church of San Giovanni, Campiglia Marittima (Livorno).

classical mythology of this iconographic theme, which was so widely used in antiquity, was triumph over death and the forces of darkness. This explains why it was used above all in the Roman sarcophagi, in those inspired by them in the Christian era and in revivals in successive centuries. The design of the famous relief of a medieval wild boar hunt sculpted by Girauldus for the tympanum of Saint-Ursin in Bourges can even be directly traced to a sarcophogus in Déols (Indre). The latter was conserved in the crypt of the abbey and reused as a tomb for Saint Ludre, who is referred to in the hagiographic tradition as a disciple of Saint Ursin. In the Middle Ages symbolic use of the hunting scene escalated. The hunter would represent either an image of Christ or the Devil, just as the animals, and therefore the wild boar as well, stood for vices and sins as well as sinners. Its implicit moral content accounts for the popularity of the theme, which was revived and imitated on numerous occasions. One of the best known is from the late Middle Ages in the Cathedral of Civita Castellana (Viterbo). There are also numerous examples in and near Lucca. One of the most effective in visual and narrative terms is the one sculpted by craftsmen working with the sculptor Guidetto on a capital of the Baptistery in Pisa.

III

IV

III. Roman Sarcophagus, detail with wild boar hunt. Cathedral Crypt, Osimo.

IV. Biduino workshop, lintel of side door, 12th century. San Casciano a Settimo, Pisa.

ART OF THE MIDDLE AGES

49

**49. Master Roberto,
baptismal font, 12th
century. San Frediano,
Lucca.**

THE FONT OF SAN FREDIANO IN LUCCA

The font situated within the first bay of the Basilica of San Frediano in Lucca was reassembled in 1952 after having been dismantled in the 13th century, part of it then being kept for a long time in the Bargello Museum in Florence. A document from 1173 mentions a font in San Frediano, but it might refer to another artefact. The present one was probably a holy water fountain originally used in the context of the former monastery here and, only at a later date, as a baptismal font. This would account for the twelve animal heads from which water spurts and the circular form of the lower bowl. The bowl is formed by six marble staves, four with stories of Moses and two with symbolic figures within a series of arcades. Apart from the animal heads, the upper part is made up of two superimposed registers, the lower one with the months and the upper one, which may originally have been surmounted with an acroterium, with the Apostles. The high-reliefs on the font are based on the Holy Scriptures and the cycle of life. Different episodes from the life of Moses are shown, from the *Exile of the Jews in Egypt* and the *Miracle of the Transformation of the Staff into a Snake*, represented here as a dragon. The tale continues with the *Crossing of the Red Sea*, depicting the moment in which the waves overwhelm the Egyptian horsemen. Here a means of making the narrative more effective has been adopted: in fact, in trying to make an opening in the waves, the army moves in the opposite direction to that of the reliefs. The *Delivery of the Tablets of the Law* concludes the sequence, with God in a clipeus held up by a sapling. On another two staves seven characters in togas are portrayed. Their symbolic significance is uncertain, but they may represent the Planets, which are associated with the gifts of the Holy Spirit. A pier, with stylized flowing water decoration and anthropomorphic faces at the top, supports the goblet with the twelve animal heads from which water spurts, while six red marble colonnettes with composite capitals hold up the top which is decorated with the Apostles and Months. The cycle of the year begins with Ianu-January and presents the customary iconography of the working tasks of men associated with the seasons, and the personification of the months. The animals are portrayed in a detailed, naturalistic fashion and with attention to anatomical detail, as in the case of the hog and the oxen. The same methods were used in the workshop of the sculptor Biduino, who was active at the same time and well-known for his interest in the animal repertoire. The work of at least three different hands is usually recognizable: Roberto, the craftsman who signs the work, the Master of the Moses stories, and the Master of the Months and Apostles. In the staves of the fountain Roberto copies from an Early Christian sarcophogus, just as the Master of the Moses stories has in mind reliefs from late antiquity. In his turn, the Master of the Months and Apostles looks for inspiration to models taken from antique sculpture. Reused Roman remains are to be found in the basilica; the practice was widespread between the 11th and 12th centuries, but is particularly prevalent in Lucca and Pisa. Roman sarcophagi were reused for the burial of San Frediano himself. The choice of the architectural and iconographic structure of the font is probably attributable to the Master Roberto. The words he inscribes on the lower basin of the font, *Me Fecit Robertus in Arte Peritus*, express the self-consciousness which is often found in works of the time in this cultural milieu and elsewhere.

50

**50. Master Roberto,
baptismal font, detail,
12th century.
San Frediano, Lucca.**

SAN GIOVANNI FUORCIVITAS IN PISTOIA

The church, built in the Lombard period, was completely rebuilt in the 12th century. Today all that remains of the rectangular hall and apse in the Romanesque plan is the Northern side, which was incorporated in the fourteenth century enlargement of the church. This is distinguished by the violent polychrome effect of the facing obtained by alternating rows of white marble and green serpentine. The chromatic impact negates the architecturally harmonious and elegant partitioning of the walls where blind arches on pilaster strips support two tiers of false galleries. The influence of the Cathedral of Pisa is revealed in the use of recessed lozenges, cornices and geometric inlay, but the sculptural decoration is overdone and the bichromatic facing is so forced that the graceful balance of the prototype is completely lost.

51

52

342

51. Church of San Giovanni Fuorcivitas, detail, 12th century. Pistoia.

52. Church of San Giovanni Fuorcivitas, Northern side, 12th century. Pistoia.

THE CATHEDRAL OF MASSA MARITTIMA

There is a theatricality in the way the Cathedral of San Cerbone is placed in the square in front of it. It is raised on a high podium with its corner facing the square while the slant of the façade is accentuated by an optical effect. The entrance portal is decentralized and the light in the blind arches diminishes gradually towards the right. The influence of the Pisan Romanesque style is evident firstly in the external decoration, where a system of blind arcading covers the bulk of the building, secondly in the partitioning of the aisles by columns alternating with piers and surmounted with Classicizing capitals and thirdly in the bichromatic wall facing, which is most noticeable in the upper part of the nave. The building of the church was completed in the Gothic period, when a loggia crowned with cusped elements was added to the façade and the area of the presbytery was enlarged.

53

54

53. Cathedral of San Cerbone, 12th to 13th century. Massa Marittima.

54. Cathedral of San Cerbone, detail, 12th to 13th century. Massa Marittima.

THE CAPITALS OF THE CATHEDRAL
OF SAN CERBONE IN MASSA MARITTIMA

The first building phase of the Cathedral of San Cerbone must have begun during the years in which stronger links were being forged between the city of Pisa and the diocesan seat in Massa Marittima (Grosseto). Therefore the first tier of blind arcading in the Pisan style must have been completed by the end of the 12th century. This hypothesis is borne out by the architectural decoration and sculptures on the sides and facade, and the way in which the columns inside are interspersed with piers and imitation capitals, some of which are the work of the master sculptor Enricus. The name of the craftsman is well-known as it is inscribed on one of the capitals in the nave in oncial script and capital letters. It reads "*Enricus hoc / opus fecit*" (Enrico made this work). The fact that the master was probably trained on the site of the Pisan cathedral would account for the high quality of workmanship and the preference for styles which imitate the Corinthian and composite capitals of antiquity.

On the other hand, notable differences in workmanship point to the likelihood of the presence of other craftsmen alongside Enrico.

On one of the capitals in the nave, four eagles grasp their respective prey: a dragon, a ram, a wild boar and a fourth quadruped whose association with the others has evident negative connotations.

The eagle often appears in Romanesque architecture, particularly in single-windowed archivolts, although there is no shortage of examples in the decoration of lintels and friezes.

Although in many cases the winged creature is only used for decorative purposes, there are just as many examples where its presence has a symbolic meaning. Albeit the role of psychopomp bird assigned to the

55

55. Cathedral, nave.
Massa Marittima.

56

eagle in antiquity endured for a long time, and as king of the birds it was compared to Christ, the image of the destructive soul-plundering predator prevailed.

As with other animals, in each case the personified meaning can only be correctly deduced by close attention to the type of prey caught and the qualities attributed to the latter.

56. View of façade, capitals, 12th to 13th century. Cathedral of San Cerbone, Massa Marittima.

THE SAN CERBONE LINTEL
12th century
Massa Marittima, Cathedral

SUBJECT

The lintel is placed in the entrance portal and dates back to the Romanesque period of construction. It is divided into panels and illustrates in a simple manner the life of San Cerbone, after whom the church, like the former Cathedral of Populonia, is named. The same story is further illustrated in the Arch of Goro di Gregorio, which can be seen in the apse of the cathedral today.

The saint played a fundamental role in the ecclesiastical history of the diocese. When he arrived on the Tyrrhenian coast of Africa he was among the first to spread the Gospel in the area and he was cruelly persecuted by the Goths and Lombards. After he became Bishop of Populonia he was forced to take refuge on Elba. He died on the island in 575, but in accordance with his explicit wish his remains were removed to Populonia and from there, when the seat of the bishop was transferred, to Massa Marittima.

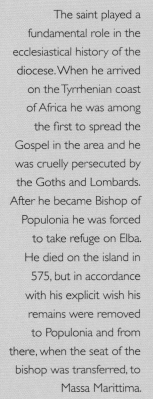

Goro di Gregorio, Arch of San Cerbone, detail with *Death of the Saint*, 1324. Massa Marittima, Cathedral.

COMPOSITION

The primary purpose of the relief was therefore to narrate the principal events of the saint's life, which, as they were well-known to them, the people of Massa would easily recognize in the lintel. However this purpose is complemented by remarkable compositional skill applied in a different way to each panel. The refined workmanship transforms the surfaces into the vibrant movement of the sea, the feathers of geese and the lightness of garments, while the branches of the trees and the antlars of the deer stand out from the background and glass mosaics decorate the altar.

In the first panel, the journey of the saint towards the port of Baratti is portrayed.

In the second the king Totila, with his sceptre and crown, condemns him to be torn to pieces by bears, but the wild beasts bow down at his feet.

The following panels illustrate one of the principal miracles of San Cerbone. When he is summoned to Rome, after being accused of celebrating mass before dawn when no-one could attend, he quenches the thirst of the papal envoys who accompany him with the milk of two does who docilely allow themselves to be milked, and persuades a flock of geese to accompany him to the Pope.

In the last panel he celebrates mass before the Pope while a choir of angels above the clouds chants the Gloria.

THE CHURCH OF THE SANTISSIMA TRINITÀ IN SACCARGIA

Outside Tuscany, the church of the Santissima Trinità in Saccargia, in Sardegna, is a paradigm of the spread of the Pisan style. Its structure bears the impress of the traces of two distinct building phases. Scholars date the back part of the building, where the apse, the transept and the tribune are like bare geometric blocks, as 11th century. They note the influence of the Pisan Cathedral in the front part and put forward the hypothesis that it was built in about 1150. With the portico in front of it, this part is distinguished by the striking polychromy of the black and white facing, which is regular in the front and the bell-tower and freer at the sides. At the front, the chromatic effect is enriched by a pretense gallery of blind arches, which contain oculi and recessed lozenges decorated with minute marble inlay. Below, the massive structure of the portico stands out. It is roofed with groin-vaults and has three open arched sides, with white marble columns and piers at the edges and a sculpted cornice at the front.

57

58

59

57. Church of Santissima Trinità, about 1150. Saccargia.

58. Church of Santissima Trinità, detail of façade decoration, about 1150. Saccargia.

59. Church of Santissima Trinità, apse and bell tower, about 1150. Saccargia.

60

61

RELIGIOUS ARCHITECTURE IN DALMATIA: ZARA

Some of the most interesting examples of pre-Romanesque buildings and ornamental elements in the area are preserved in Zara, a city on the Dalmation coast The first phase of the church of San Donato dates back to the 9th century. It was rebuilt in the Roman forum in a circular form with a ring-shaped nave, gallery and three radial apses, and has a considerable number of reused elements such as columns.

In the second half of the 12th century, in the area of the late antique basilica, the cathedral dedicated to the martyr Sant'Anastasia was built. She came from Sirmio and was patron of the city and her remains are preserved in a small stone sarcophagus with a dedicatory inscription.

At the time, the building, which has a crypt, incorporated part of the pre-existent structures. It was made up of three aisles separated by piers and columns, a matroneum and a single apse. The four tiers of blind arcades, which divide up the façade of the cathedral, are the result of a later enlargement at the beginning of the next century.

They are reminiscent of Pisan architecture and in fact relations between the Dalmation city and the marine republic are documented. In 1188 an anti-Venetian treaty was signed and a diplomatic delegation from Pisa remained in Dalmatia for some time.

The rebuilding of the cathedral, however, belongs to a period of upsurge in construction which affected the whole area and also included other buildings in the city of Zara, such as the Abbey of San Crisogono which was consecrated in 1175.

A great deal of Roman sculpture preserved in Dalmatia was also produced in Zara in the 12th century.

60. Church of San Donato, 9th century. Zara.

61. Church of Sant'Anastasia, façade, 12th to 13th century. Zara.

THE REUSE OF ANTIQUE MATERIALS
IN THE MEDIEVAL PERIOD

In the medieval world the reuse of antique materials in a new context was widespread. It affected all the arts from sculpture to minor arts and, above all, architecture. The end of paganism and the demographic decline due to the fall of the Roman Empire led to a greater availability of finished materials, which could be salvaged from ruined buildings and reused in the construction of new ones. While in the early Middle Ages the material was sometimes used in a haphazard way and the original function of the reused item was often misinterpreted or ignored on purpose, Romanesque architecture developed selective criteria and used the remains in a more informed fashion. The antique item might be valued for its aesthetic appeal in which case it would be placed in a prominent position, but sometimes it acquired political significance from its connection with the grandeur of ancient Rome. On the other hand, in the context of the Gothic building, remains no longer had a value per se, which led to their being unrecognizable once absorbed into the fabric of a new building.

62

63

62. Cathedral of Siracusa, interior. The building was erected in the 7th century on the ruins of a 5th century BC Greek temple, whose columns it includes.

63. Casa dei Crescenzi, detail of lintel inscription, 11th century. Rome.

64

65

UTILITARIAN REUSE

The phenomenon of reuse is particularly prevalent in the Middle Ages, when, due to the severe demographic decline, the ancient Roman cities were only partly occupied and turned into landscapes full of ruins. Daily contact with these ruins resulted in the widespread practice of reuse of materials. Both time and work could be saved by using finished pieces or buildings which were still standing. Ancient buildings turned into veritable treasure troves of material or, with a few adaptations, were modified to perform a new function. The case of the Pantheon in Rome is emblematic. At the beginning of the 7th century it was changed into a church dedicated to the Madonna and all the martyrs. The passing of time had probably helped eradicate the aversion towards the pagan places of worship of the first Christian era, when the Fathers of the Church incited the destruction of all the temples. As far as reuse of antique materials is concerned, we know from imperial decrees that the phenomenon was so widespread as to require regulation by special legislation; for instance, in 458, a law authorized reuse of material, provided that it was taken from buildings which were past the point of restoration or no longer in public use. Reuse often revealed a complete indifference towards the original function of the antique piece. This was demoted to mere building material, the decorated or engraved parts being hidden by the brickwork. In such cases the antiquity of the piece wasn't so important as the opportunity to make use of ready-made building elements. As some materials were not easy to find, and there was a decline in craftsmanship production processes, an antique piece was often used for the material out of which it was made; for instance, in many cases statues were melted down to make arms.

64. Pantheon, exterior, 118-128 AD. Rome.

65. Cathedral of Pisa, detail with fragments of Roman epigraphs inserted in walls.

66

66. Cathedral of Salerno,
quadriportico, detail with
reused columns and
capitals, 12th century.

REUSE FOR "PRESTIGE"

Besides utilitarian reuse, where the antique piece was used to save time and work, scholars have identified a reuse for "prestige". Here the aesthetic qualities of the Roman remains were appreciated and they were consequently afforded a position of prominence within the new construction. Antique fragments were inserted in the most visible places and therefore mainly near doorways, while in churches they were concentrated in the presbyterial area. The production of new exemplars was made superfluous by the wide availability of architectural fragments and ready-made pieces. These were sometimes used in their former role and sometimes for their ornamental qualities. The reuse of columns and capitals was very common. This enabled churches to be adorned with precious marbles and materials of refined workmanship. These would otherwise have been unobtainable in an age when commercial relationships and mining activity were in such decline and the quality of the products of craftsmen's workshops was so poor. While in early Christian churches strict criteria governed the selection of material such as this, the early Middle Ages is marked by a total disregard for rules. In fact, examples of reuse reveal a complete lack, not only of understanding of the canon, but also of sensitivity towards proportions: the diameter of columns does not match that of capitals; shafts are often installed upside-down, or the bases are even used as capitals and viceversa. Afterwards, in Romanesque architecture, the remains were treated with greater selectivity and used for conscious effect, as in the Cathedral of Pisa, the Abbey of Montecassino, the Cathedral of Salerno and the 12th century Romanesque churches.

In the case of the reuse of lintels, these sometimes fulfill their original function inside buildings which manifestly emulate the model of the Constantinian basilica, and sometimes act as doorjambs or portal trabeations in which case they may be turned round or used upside-down. While antique sarcophagi were generally used for important burials without substantial changes, other items were completely altered depending on their new purpose. So it was with capitals: after being hollowed out they were transformed into holy water stoups; altars became baptismal fonts or recipients for alms, and lintels and column shafts were turned into sarcophagi.

67

68

67. San Miniato, view of aisles with reused columns and capitals, 11th century. Florence.

68. Church of San Lorenzo fuori le Mura, capital decorated with trophies and Winged Victories. Rome. In the presbytery of the church antique fragments have been reused: Roman columns and capitals hold up a trabeation composed of pieces of diverse provenance.

The reuse of antique items and monuments is often infused with implications and significance from which we can deduce the purpose of numerous architectural programs and the motives of those who commissioned them. For instance the phenomenon of the transformation of temples into churches was tangible proof of the victory of Christianity over pagan religions, while the horses of the Saint Mark's Basilica, which were removed from Constantinople after the conquest in 1204, were more like war trophies and emblems of the dominion attained by the Republic of Venice. The extensive trade in items of Roman origin also shows how the capital of the Roman Empire represented an enduring model and point of reference. Literary sources recall that items reused at Montecassino, in Durham Cathedral and at Saint-Denis were of Roman origin, while Charlemagne legitimized his own empire with remains brought from Rome and Ravenna to decorate the chapel of Aachen. This was, in fact, how great institutions used the eternal city as a point of reference and proclaimed themselves heirs to its greatness: the phenomenon of reused was a feature of 12th century Papal patronage, Southern Italy during Norman rule and building fostered by Italian city states.

69

69. Bronze horses, 4th century. Saint Mark's Museum, Venice.

70. Facing page: Casa dei Crescenzi, view of facade, mid-11th century. Rome. In the tower-house of Nicola of Crescenzio, erected in the middle of the 11th century, the reuse of antique material becomes a visible expression of the political plans of a private citizen who, as the inscription above the door records, wished to revive the "splendor of Rome".

MEDIEVAL IMITATION OF ANTIQUITY: THE CASE OF PISA

In the field of the phenomenon of reuse a distinction can be made between Roman remains which were moved physically and cases in which reuse applied rather to preceding styles, motifs and themes.

The demand for *spolia* is even more interesting than the supply, in as far as it led not only to reused of what was available, but above and beyond research and importation, even to imitation. The presence of the latter entails a distinction between total imitation and a lexicon of generic antique derivation, given the widespread presence of the antique.

Whereas the antique constitutes a source of technical, formal and iconographic solutions, there is no shortage of cases where the result is scarcely distinguishable from the reproduction. Owing to the neo-antique tendency which was generically widespread in Tuscany in the 11th and the 12th centuries and common in other towns, this particular aspect is very noticeable in Pisa, where the phenomenon assumed significant proportions.

In the Pisan cathedral, the great architrave with leaf motif volutes of the San Ranieri portal is made up partly of reused material and partly of a medieval imitation. It generated no little controversy.

For the burial of the Pisan Giratto, who died in 1176, the sculptor Biduino adopts the same solution and makes a strigilated sarcophagus. The sarcophagus, which is now in the Camposanto Monumentale in Pisa, is an example of the perfect synthesis of the three levels of technique, form and iconography on which the imitation is based. In the same vein

71

71. Biduino, sarcophagus of the judge Giratto, about 1176. Camposanto, Pisa.

72. Facing page: Bonanno Pisano, door of San Ranieri, about 1180. Cathedral, Pisa.

73

74

73. Baptismal font with figure, 12th century. Parish Church of Calci, Pisa.

74. Sarcophagus "of the Muses". Camposanto, Pisa.

and worth noting are works such as the font in the parish church of Calci (Pisa) which has been recognized as copied from the sarcophagus of the Muse, which is kept in the Camposanto at Pisa.

Still in the area of Pisan influence is the lintel with the wild boar hunt in the side portal of the parish church of San Giovanni in Campiglia.

This is surmounted by a cornice of acanthus leaves which is itself an imitation. In the Calci font, apart from some iconographic solutions, the craftsman also copied the architectural plan from the front of a sarcophagus with figures in niches, while at Campiglia the top of a sarcophagus was copied.

75

76

75-76. Matteo, lintel with boar hunt, 12th century. Left side portal, Parish Church of San Giovanni, Campiglia Marittima.

WOOD SCULPTURE

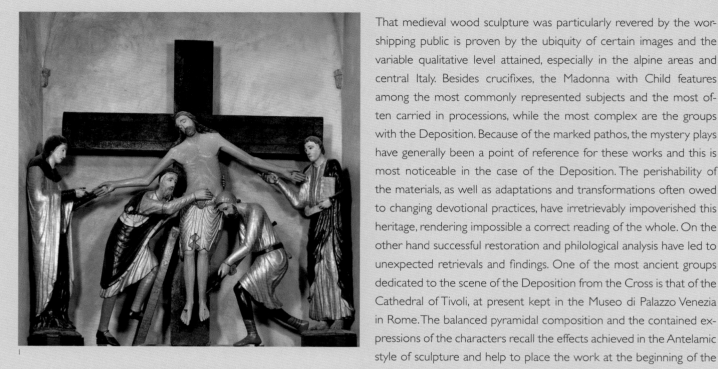

That medieval wood sculpture was particularly revered by the worshipping public is proven by the ubiquity of certain images and the variable qualitative level attained, especially in the alpine areas and central Italy. Besides crucifixes, the Madonna with Child features among the most commonly represented subjects and the most often carried in processions, while the most complex are the groups with the Deposition. Because of the marked pathos, the mystery plays have generally been a point of reference for these works and this is most noticeable in the case of the Deposition. The perishability of the materials, as well as adaptations and transformations often owed to changing devotional practices, have irretrievably impoverished this heritage, rendering impossible a correct reading of the whole. On the other hand successful restoration and philological analysis have led to unexpected retrievals and findings. One of the most ancient groups dedicated to the scene of the Deposition from the Cross is that of the Cathedral of Tivoli, at present kept in the Museo di Palazzo Venezia in Rome. The balanced pyramidal composition and the contained expressions of the characters recall the effects achieved in the Antelamic style of sculpture and help to place the work at the beginning of the 13th century. The group in the Cathedral of Volterra is possibly the best preserved amongst those that are known, replete with all the characters. In fact apart from Christ and the grieving Mary and Saint John, Nicodemus and Joseph of Arimathea can be identified, prizing the nails out and taking the body down from the cross. Compared to the previous case, the group is distinguished by its animated composition and greater expressive power created by the contact of all the characters with Christ. The polychromy of the characters' clothes and bodies is well-preserved while the use of monochrome to pick out certain details of the cross and clothes is reminiscent of contemporary Pisan painting. The main point of reference is the work of the painter Giunta Pisano who was already working in Assisi in 1236. In the Pisan area, in the parish church of Santa Maria a Vicopisano, there is a similar group in terms of the presence of the five main characters, to whom two angels in flight have been added. In this case the polychromy has almost completely disappeared, except for the flesh tones and the loincloth of Christ, where it is partially preserved. Many of the anatomical details were added in the nineteenth century.

The group dates back to the first decades of the 13th century and is thought to be the work of Pisan craftsmen.

I. *Deposition from the Cross,* about 1228. Cathedral, Volterra.

II. *Deposition from the Cross,* ex Tivoli Cathedral, detail, 13th century. Museo di Palazzo Venezia, Rome.

III. *Deposition from the Cross*, ex Tivoli Cathedral, 13th century. Museo di Palazzo Venezia, Rome.

SAN NICOLA IN BARI AND THE ROMANESQUE IN APULIA

In the Middle Ages Apulia had strong links with the Adriatic area: there are many similarities between Apulian and Dalmatian architecture up to the 13th century. The Basilica of San Nicola a Bari was begun in 1087, when the remains of the body San Niccolò di Mira arrived in the city. The Benedictine abbot, Elia, built the basilica-sanctuary on land donated by the duke Ruggero: probably on the site of the former seat of the Byzantine governor. Abbot Elia, who oversaw the works until his death in 1105, had previously been a monk in the prestigious

abbey of Cava dei Tirreni, which was also frequented by Desiderio, the famous abbot of Montecassino. He also had close links with Pope Urban II, a former monk of Cluny. The Basilica of San Nicola was begun in 1087 and finished in 1197 and, like the Cathedral of Salerno, its huge transept containing all the aisles and the three apses was based on the Montecassini model. There are deep matronea in the Lombard style in the central nave and the minor aisles are in the form of deep monumental arcades. The inclusion of the apses in a wall beyond the transept, making them hard to distinguish from the outside, gives the building a civil rather than religious air and has even given rise to the theory that the presumed former palace of the Byzantine governor

77

78

77. Cathedral of San Nicola, façade, 11th to 12th century. Bari.

78. Cathedral of San Nicola, internal view of apse, 11th to 12th century. Bari.

was changed into a church. It is in fact more likely that the Basilica of San Nicola was conceived as an independent entity. It certainly counts as a "one-off" in the context of the Romanesque.

The layout is in the form of a vast rectangle, with two towers placed on the East and West sides. The original plan made provision for two more towers for the other two sides, but they were abandoned, like the dome (or lantern) over the crossing.

The oriental influences in this monument are particularly noticeable in the sculptures, such as those in the main portal with the porch, the side portals, the rear window and the capitals. The *Episcopal throne* of Elia (1098) is reminiscent of Lombard sculpture.

The upper part is divided up by five little pillars. Carved in a series of lozenges in the central section are a winged griffon, a lion, a pelican, a calf and a heraldic eagle.

At the base, three telamons strain to hold up the front part of the seat, while at the back two lionesses with human heads in their mouths appear between three little pillars whose capitals are decorated with leaf motifs. Both structural and decorative motifs from San Nicola are copied in other Apulian churches, including San Gregorio, which is also in Bari and in the cathedrals of Barletta, Bitonto, Trani and Troia. In all these churches columns alternate with piers and sculptural decoration is confined to the corbels and the frames of the apsidal windows.

79

79. Cathedral of San Nicola, interior of presbytery aisle towards façade, 11th to 12th century. Bari.

80

80. Ciborium,
11th to 12th century.
San Nicola, Bari.

81

82

83

**81-83. Throne of Elia
and details, about 1098.
Bari.**

The building is not far from the city of Siponto and the archbishop's seat and has been renowned since 1127. The monastic complex to which it belonged was part of a series of monasteries and hospices in the Monte Sant'Angelo area, which were connected to the pilgrimage itinerary lead-ing to the sanctuary of San Michele. It was a stopping place for crusaders on their way to the Holy Land and this role, as well as the numerous donations it received from Norman feudal vassals and the autonomous Bishop of Siponto, contributed to the centrality and importance of the institution, until, like others, it encountered problems in the thirteenth century.

84

85

84. San Leonardo of
Siponto, portal, mid-12th
century. Manfredonia.

85. San Leonardo
of Siponto, left jamb,
portal, mid-12th century.
Manfredonia.

The main portal is situated on the North side of the building, where pilaster strips and small arches animate the surface. It is generally agreed that the decoration of the portal and the rest of the building dates back to the second half of the 12th century and the beginning of the next century and is associated with the sculpture of the Abbey of San Clemente in Casauria, in Abruzzo, and the architectural decoration of Apulian buildings. There are also more subtle references to the portals in Bourgogne and South-West France.

During the priorate of Riccardo (1152-1167) work was begun on the new church. The chronology can be ascertained from the masonry which is mid 12th century. The building was modeled on a wooden-dome type of church, which was oriental in origin, and adapted to the Benedictine ambience. After a ten year interval the work was resumed in the 1180s by the successors of Riccardo, Pietro II and III, and finished with a few variations to the initial plan.

Among the craftsmen of the first phase was the sculptor responsible for the North portal, who came from San Clemente in Casauria. The column-bearing lions and the griffons above them in the porch of Sipone are based on a design which was frequently used in Apulia, but absent in San Clemente in Casauria and completely unknown in Abruzzo.

The door jambs of the portal have plant volutes with animal and fantastic motifs, such as the archer centaur or the dragon from whose mouth the plant shoot itself issues, a product of highly sophisticated stone intaglio work. San Michele and a pilgrim are figured in the two imposing capitals of the door jambs which are decorated with historical scenes and, in the lunette above, Christ appears in the *mandorla* carried by two angels.

The scheme for the portal, which faces the site where the archangel Michael appeared, includes the theme of pilgrimage as a journey towards salvation. This scheme seems to be reinforced in the interior by the significance inherent in the ray of sunlight which penetrates the building through a gnomonic aperture and, on the day of the summer solstice, traces a circle of light between the pillars in front of the entrance.

86

**86. San Leonardo
of Siponto, view of side,
mid-12th century.
Manfredonia.**

**87-88. San Leonardo
of Siponto, portal,
details, 12th century.
Manfredonia.**

The highest number of bronze doors in the peninsular is concentrated in the South of Italy, and particularly in the buildings of Romanesque Apulia (Monte Sant'Angelo, Canosa, Troia, Trani).

The first noteable exemplar is connected to the Santuario di San Michele Arcangelo in Gargano, a famous place of pilgrimage. It is also significant because the date (1076) and the place where the doors were made, Constantinople, are both known, thanks to an inscription. The latter also throws light on the patron, Pantaleone da Amalfi, who came from an important family of merchants in Bisanzio.

The iconographic scheme, which takes the form of 23 panels and an

89

91

90

89. Bronze door of grotto, with sacrifice of Isaac, about 1076. Monte Sant'Angelo, Sanctuary of the Archangel Michael.

90. Bronze door of grotto, about 1076. Monte Sant'Angelo, Sanctuary of the Archangel Michael.

91. Barisano da Trani, bronze door, second half of 12th century. Trani, Cathedral.

92

93

94

92 and 94. Door of Tomb of Boemondo of Altavilla, before 1120. Canosa di Puglia.

93. Oderisio da Benevento, door, about 1119. Troia, Cathedral.

extra one for the dedicatory inscription, is attributed to a Benedictine monk called Gerardo who came from Montecassino and became archbishop of the diocese of Siponto.

The subjects are taken from the Old and New Testaments and other hagiographic events in which the three appearances of the angel play an important part.

The narrative scenes are portrayed in mixed metals and niello, which were used regularly in metallurgy and goldsmithery. Six lion heads support the doors.

In Canosa, the Mausoleum of Bohemund d'Hauteville, who died in 1111, has two doors with no wooden support. They were cast by Ruggero da Melfi in about 1120 in a single fusion. Here there is also a leonine mask to which the circular handle is attached. The right-hand door has four panels, two central ones with narrative scenes in mixed metal and two with geometric motifs of mainly Islamic origin.

This is an example of significant Norman patronage, preceding the works commissioned by Roger II, but obviously related to Sicily and the Orient, as is often the case after the first Crusade. In fact the two scenes represent the sons of Robert Guiscard in the act of praying to the Virgin and at the bottom there are Norman princes of the new generation.

In Troia, in the Cathedral of Santa Maria Assunta there are, remarkably, two examples of bronze doors with inscriptions bearing the dates of 1119 for the main door and 1127 for the smaller side one. In one of

95

96

95. Barisano da Trani, central door, detail of panel, about 1179. Trani, Cathedral.

96. Barisano da Trani, central door, detail of panel with Saint George and the Dragon, about 1179. Trani, Cathedral.

the latter's frames the name of the craftsman, Oderisionda Benevento, appears, and in the other frame he is portrayed beside Berardo, who may have been the architect.

In the 24 panels of the minor door, 4 have leonine masks and as many as 7 bear an inscription in capital letters conveying the decision of the people of Troia to stand up to Roger II in defense of their liberty, a gesture of civic pride for which they were to pay with the siege of the city.

The detail of the other panels has been executed using the *cire perdue* method, enabling a greater expressive capacity to be attained through the three-dimensional effect, and at the same time fixing the panels to the wooden support.

There are winged dragons of highly sophisticated workmanship holding the door-knockers. In the Cathedral of Trani, at some moment during the last decade of the 12th century, the commission of the main portal was entrusted to the well-known author of two other bronze doors in Ravello and Monreale and native of Trani, Barisano. Here again an impressive number of panels is attached to a wooden support by sturdy frames.

Of the 32 panels, 20 bear single images of saints, similar to icons in the Byzantine tradition, while in the others there are archers and jugglers, like those in Ravello. There is also a tree of life with dragons and lions. Some of the iconographic motifs chosen are therefore profane in nature while others are associated with religious ceremony.

97

**97. Oderisio da Benevento,
detail of door, about 1119.
Troia, Cathedral.**

THE BRONZE DOORS: TECHNIQUES, CRAFTSMEN, COMMISSIONS

The deep symbolic significance of the door in medieval buildings gave rise to greater monumentality and increased expertise in plastic terms, with regard not only to buildings such as abbeys and cathedrals but also to those of more modest dimensions. That the doors were a particularly valued element of the building is proven both by the precious materials with which they were made and by the dedicatory inscriptions to be found on them relating to the names of patrons and craftsmen and yielding precious information regarding their dates. In Southern Italy numerous examples have been preserved, some of which were commissioned by the Normans. Bronze doors were placed at the entrances of the Palatine Chapel in Palermo, and between 1185 and 1186 arguably the two most famous artists, Barisano da Trani and Bonanno Pisano were summoned to Monreale by William II. The bishops of Amalfi and De-

I. Barisano da Trani,
door, detail, about 1186.
Monreale, Cathedral.

II. Barisano da Trani,
door, about 1186.
Monreale, Cathedral.

siderio Abbot of Montecassino himself had already commissioned bronze doors for their own buildings in Consantinople. They received donations from the Pantaleone, the mercantile Amalfi family, who also played a mediatory role. The last bronze door to be cast in Constantinople and installed, in 1099, in Campania, is that of the Cathedral of Salerno. The high value of the metal alloy used, the technical expertise required and the emulation of works of antiquity all bear witness to the demanding expectations of the patrons and entail a similar consciousness on the part of the craftsmen of their role, hence the signatures and portraits so often incorporated in the works. Notes for descendants regarding maintenance are also not uncommon; a prime example is that of the door of the Santuario di San Michele Arcangelo in Gargano which even gives instructions on how to keep the surfaces shiny.

III. Bonanno Pisano, door, scene with Original Sin, about 1186. Monreale, Cathedral.

IV. Door panels, about 1066. Amalfi, Cathedral.

THE ROMANESQUE PERIOD IN CAMPANIA

The political and economic fortune of the cities of the Campania coast Amalfi, Gaeta, Naples and Salerno as well as the subsequent Norman Conquest also fostered the broadening of cultural horizons in Southern Italy. The resumption of maritime trading and the political interests of the new ruling class transcended insularity. Among other consequences, there was a receptiveness not only towards the Arab and Byzantine world but also towards the first Anglo-Norman Gothic influences. Another factor in the broadening of the cultural picture was the revival of the study of Latin classics in the monastic context

98

**98. Cathedral
of San Michele, view
of lantern, 12th century.
Caserta Vecchia.**

owed to the reform of the monastic orders. New influences from the antique world merged with the adventurous and sentimental characteristics of the new profane literature. Within a feudal, Latin context a bid for synthesis was bearing fruit, using only the most perfect and applicable aspects of the most vibrant cultures present in the Mediterranean. In Gaeta, the magnificent and imposing Cathedral

99. Niccolò di Angelo, bell tower, about 1148-1174. Gaeta, Cathedral.

100. Easter candelabrum, end 12th century. Gaeta, Cathedral.

101

bell-tower, which is 187 feet and three storeys high, has the air of a triumphal arch. It is such an exceptional work that it even bears the signature of the Roman marble sculptor, Niccolo` di Angelo (1148-1174). The influence of Islamic architecture is evident in the external decoration, as in the case of the lantern of the Cathedral of Caserta Vecchia. The central arch of the façade of the Cathedral of Sessa Aurunca (12th century), which has a majestic triple-arched portico, contains a classically refined bass-relief of the story of Saint Peter. It is placed beside reused Roman sculptures and is clearly influenced by the Sicilian school. The Easter candelabrum of Gaeta (late 12th century) and the contemporary candelabrum signed by Vassalletto in San Paolo Fuori le Mura in Rome are reminiscent of Roman columns decorated with historical scenes with their superimposed bands of sculpture. They reveal the resilience of the classical heritage even though their stories are taken from the New Testament.

102

101. *Temptation of Jesus*, detail of Easter candelabrum, end 12th century. Gaeta, Cathedral.

102. Detail of lion, base of portal, 12th century. Sessa Aurunca, Cathedral.

THE CATHEDRAL OF SAN MATTEO IN SALERNO

After the conquest of the city on December 13th 1076 by the Norman, Robert the Guiscard, the decision was taken to build the Cathedral of San Matteo. It was constructed at the behest of Guiscard himself, between 1080 and 1084, and is one of the largest buildings of that time.

An ample inscription contains the dedication to the Evangelist saint and other important information, which shows that the work was finished some time before the death of Guiscard.

Once the crypt was finished, the basilica above was built in less than five years, beginning with the large transept. The monumental complex is most readily comparable to the Montecassino church begun by Desiderio in 1066. This saw the revival of elements of Roman origin which included the plan of a basilica with three aisles, a transept with three apses, a four-doored portico and the presence of a significant number of Roman remains.

A considerable number of materials have been reused in different ways, in alignment with common practice. As is frequently the case elsewhere, sarcophagi are reused for prestigious burials, like the one beside the portal with wild-boar hunt decoration, in which the remains of William d'Hauteville, Duke of Salerno between 1111 e 1127 are buried. The lions of the portal represent a precocious examplar, in terms of this area, of large-dimension sculpture, although this is consonant with contemporary artistic production in Southern Italy.

Men and animals can be distinguished amongst the vine shoots on the door jambs, while the lintel is embellished with medieval inscriptions.

The bronze doors of the main entrance to the basilica are made

103

104

103-104. Façade and detail of quadriportico with sarcophagi, 11th century. Salerno, Cathedral.

up of 54 panels placed in 9 horizontal rows. One of these is completely dedicated to the figures of the Virgin, Christ and other saints, including Saint Matthew who is accompanied by two donors and an invocation in capital and oncial letters. The door is probably attributable to craftsmen of Byzantine origin, judging by a feature of technical expertise to be found in similar works. This involves the use of the same metal alloy, which is not pure bronze as it contains copper and tin as well as zinc and lead.

During the first half of the 12th century the construction slowed down. The last parts to be built were the four-doored portico and the bell tower, commissioned by Guglielmo of Ravenna, Bishop of Salerno from 1137 to 1152. The date can be pinpointed as falling within a restricted time-scale thanks to the use of decorative motifs on the superimposed arches on the exterior of the belfry.

105

106

105. Bell tower, mid-12th century. Salerno, Cathedral of San Matteo.

106. Left pulpit, 12th century. Salerno, Cathedral of San Matteo.

107. Facing page: Portal of the Lions, 11th century. Salerno, Cathedral of San Matteo.

THE ROMANESQUE PERIOD IN SICILY: ARAB AND NORMAN INFLUENCES

The Norman conquest of Sicily, which took place in the mid 11th century, marked the beginning of a period of intense artistic fertility in the island. The new sovereigns commissioned the construction of grandiose buildings, in which different styles inherited from previous occupations merged in a highly original culture. The structural and decorative elements of the Arab tradition are now combined with Byzantine blueprints and mosaic decoration. Red domes rise from the compact volumes of the churches, which are centrally-planned or basilical, their external walls covered by a series of polychrome interlaced arches. The exuberant decoration of the interiors is striking: there are stalactite ceilings, marble encrustations, pointed arches and rich mosaic cycles. The craftsmen were Byzantine in origin and capable of adapting experimental iconographic programs to the original structures of the Sicilian churches.

108

108. Church of San Giovanni degli Eremiti, view of cloister, 12th century. Palermo.

109

110

111

109. La Cuba, 12th century. Palermo.

110. Church of San Cataldo, view, 12th century. Palermo.

111. Church of San Cataldo, detail of vaults and dome, 12th century. Palermo.

THE MARTORANA IN PALERMO

The construction of the church of Santa Maria dell'Ammiraglio, commonly known as "La Martorana", was commissioned in the middle of the 12th century by George of Antioch, Grand Admiral of the Kingdom of Sicily, as a way of offering thanks to the Madonna for the protection afforded him during his maritime campaigns. The whole structure is imbued with Byzantine culture. The square, triple-apsed plan is divided, on the inside, into three small aisles by four columns of oriental granite with Corinthian capitals. Four pointed arches spring from these and in their turn support the central dome, which is preceded by an octagonal tambour, while barrel-vaulting covers the arms of the crossing and groin-vaulting the side areas. The façade of the church, together with the atrium which preceded it, was destroyed in 1588, when the aisles were prolonged up to the bell tower, creating the present-day Latin cross plan. A century later a large square chapel was joined to this to form a presbytery. If the external walls seem bare and scarcely enlivened by a series of blind arcades, a magnificent mosaic cycle embellishes the interior. The Byzantine influences are apparent in the arrangement of the subjects, the iconographical choices, the style and even the Greek inscriptions incorporated in each panel. In the very center of the Dome there is a *Cristo Pantocrator* framed within a medallion and seated on a throne, surrounded by adoring angels, prophets and evangelists. The *Annunciation* adorns the triumphal arch, while the figures of Saint James and Saint Anne occupy the minor apses and busts of the saints line the inner surfaces of the arches. The purpose of these images, together with those situated in front of the presbytery and the *Nativity of Christ* and *Death of the Virgin*, is to underline the dedication of the church to the Madonna.

112

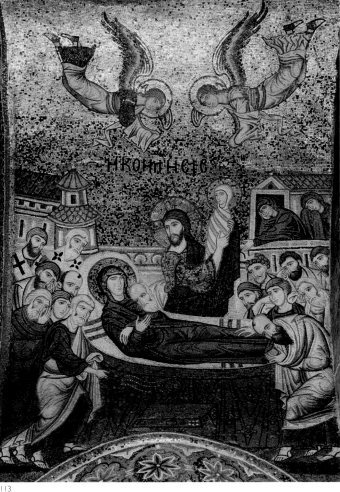

113

384

112. *George of Antioch at the Virgin's Feet,* **12th century. Palermo, La Martorana.**

113. *Death of the Virgin,* **12th century. Palermo, La Martorana.**

114. Facing page: *Incoronation of King Roger,* **12th century. Palermo, La Martorana.**

THE PALATINE CHAPEL IN PALERMO

The royal oratory of the Palazzo dei Normanni, the Cappella Palatina, was built at the behest of Roger II in the first half of the 12th century. It is a combination of the centrally-planned Byzantine church, with its raised dome-topped presbytery, and the basilical form of aisles divided by columns which here support Arab arches with extremely long piers. This perfect fusion of different cultures pervades the whole building. The sumptuous "stalactite" and lacunar wooden ceiling reflects Islamic influences, while the cycle of mosaics which covers the entire wall space with colors and light is the work of Byzantine and local mosaic craftsmen working side by side. The ceiling is decorated with very vibrant paintings depicting the pleasures of court life and the prince's entertainments. They are juxtaposed with the traditional religious themes, which are the subjects of the mosaics, in a scheme which is intended to celebrate the lay prince and the Lord of the Christians alike. The floor mosaic, which completes the sumptuous decoration of the chapel, is in semi-precious stones, gold and enamel.

115

116

115. Palatine chapel,
Cristo Pantocrator,
1132-43. Palermo, Palazzo dei Normanni.

116. Palatine chapel, wooden ceiling, 1132-43. Palermo, Palazzo dei Normanni.

**117. Palatine chapel, view
of dome, 1132-43.
Palermo, Palazzo dei
Normanni.**

The Cathedral stands in the highest part of Cefalù against the background of a rocky massif and with the vast expanse of the sea in front of it. It was founded in 1131 by Roger II to celebrate the colonization of the Arabian part of Sicily at the same time as providing the Hauteville family with a mausoleum. When he died in 1154, however, the construction work was suspended. Consequently the church was only consecrated in 1267 and it bears the marks of the structural changes to which it was subjected. The facade, which was completed in 1240 as recorded in an inscription, is enclosed within two robust four-storey towers of which the last is recessed and crowned with a pyramid-shaped spire. In the 15th century, to protect the richly sculpted entrance portal, a portico with three supporting arches, of which there

118

**118. Cathedral of Cefalù,
interior towards altar,
12th century.**

are two pointed ones either side of a round central one, was placed against it. The upper part of the façade is decorated with two superimposed rows of round blind arcading, resting on colonnettes, which are attached to the wall. In the lower row, the arches are interlaced and join in the middle where there is a big window. Like the uneven decoration of the sides, the apsidal part of the Cathedral bears the signs of its travailed building history. Although it is lower than foreseen in the original plan, the contrasting elements and grandiosity of the transept make it stand out as it emerges from the longitudinal part of the church, which has the layout of a basilica. Eight granite columns divide up the three aisles, their capitals being richly decorated in the classical and Byzantine style. From these spring high piers supporting pointed arches, while the walls are covered with rich mosaic decoration, which was evidently applied in four distinct phases.

119

121

120

119. *Heavenly hierarchies*, 12th century. Cefalù, Cathedral.

120. Cathedral of Cefalù, façade, 12th to 13th century with 15th century portico.

121. Capital, 12th century. Cefalù, Cathedral.

THE PAINTED CEILING

The history of the paintings on the false ceiling in wood runs parallel to that of the construction of the cathedral. It was founded in 1131 and designed by Roger II who was buried there in 1145. As this king provided the funding, the works were probably suspended after his death, as in the case of Salerno Cathedral, which was conceived and financed by another Norman, Robert Guiscard.

The paintings consist of a long series of medallions containing portrayals of richly appareled characters involved in various aspects of court life. Between each clipeus there are animal warriors, horsemen and heraldic animals. The relationship of Roger II with Muslim culture is revealed in the plant and geometric motifs as well as the star motif intaglio, while other features recall the Egypt of the Fatimidi dynasty, Byzantine and Rome. Different groups of craftsmen were allocated to each compartment and the work was done in situ as the paint-covered nails show. The panels were probably in cedar wood, which was widely used for this purpose in Egypt. They are one foot high and the total length is 360 feet. Some of the pastel tones and white lines, which were used to highlight faces, clothes, the bodies of the animals and garlands, have survived, and there are even some remaining traces of goldleaf, used in some figure details. There are no inscriptions of any kind; the painted red monogram on the back of some of the panels is only connected to their transport or assem-

122

123

122. Paintings on ceiling beams, detail with scene of court life, about 1140. Cefalù, Cathedral.

123. Paintings on ceiling beams, detail with drinker in polygonal medallion, about 1140. Cefalù, Cathedral.

bly. There is no narrative theme, the subject of the paintings being symbolic imagery. There are two types of recurrent decoration: real or fantastic animals fighting or working (camels, gazelles, lions, eagles and rabbits, ibis, peacocks, falcons, sphynxes, griffons, antilopes, dogs and elephants), and human and hybrid figures between and outside the clypei (musicians, scribes with scrolls, drum-beaters on elephants, falconiers, cavaliers, drinkers, zither and castanet players, archer sirens and fighting sirens). The clypeus motif is recurrent in contemporary mosaics like those of the Martorana in Palermo. The hunting theme is used to decorate many of the ivory caskets and oliphants produced in Southern Italy. The tree of life, where skill in linking the images is needed, is very common. The Cefalù cycle belongs to the iconogra-

phy of the medieval Muslim world and the iconographic, technical and stylistic choices are owed to the indissoluble ties between Roger II and the Islamic community. Geometry, astronomy, music and hunting were fundamental to a culture which was at that time infiltrating Europe from the Mediterranean. Cefalù is not an isolated case, but an example of those cycles of painting on wood, which had Islamic characteristics and were widespread in Southern Italy. In Sicily itself, for instance, there are the cycles in the Palatine Chapel and the Palazzo Steri in Palermo and the lost ceiling of Messina Cathedral. In Apulia, in Otranto, there is an example of a painting executed between 1253 and 1282, which blends in a remarkable way with the floor mosaic from the previous century.

124

125

124. Paintings on ceiling beams, detail of medallion with characters, about 1140. Cefalù, Cathedral.

125. Paintings on ceiling beams, detail of decoration with animals and haloed character bearing cross, about 1140. Cefalù, Cathedral.

126

THE CATHEDRAL OF MONREALE

Founded by the Norman kings of Sicily to accommodate their tombs, the Cathedral of Monreale is the result of a unique fusion of very different artistic elements.

The characteristic external decoration of interlaced arches is owed to Arabic craftsmen engaged in the construction of the building, while the capitals used for the columns of the aisles have been salvaged from classical buildings. The exquisite mosaics, which decorate the whole of the interior, are the work of teams of artists who were brought from Byzantium for the purpose, while the deep presbytery is typical of Norman churches.

127

126. Apse with *Christ in Benediction,* 1180-90. Monreale, Cathedral.

127. Nave towards apse, 1172-85. Monreale, Cathedral.

**128. Apse, detail of
decoration,
1172-85. Monreale,
Cathedral.**

6. Italian painting between the 11th and 13th centuries

The development of Italian painting between the 11th and 12th centuries was influenced by the diverse civilizations which descended on the country during that period. The varied sociopolitical conditions in vast areas of the peninsula and the presence of places of pilgrimage, not to mention the interweaving of exchanges and relations with Islamic and Byzantine culture, fostered a kaleidoscopic development of pictorial languages. At times the varied pictorial repertoire would be characterized by a quest for naturalism which reflected real life, at others by the endurance of the Byzantine style, or by an Islamic linear decorativeness. Setting aside the differences, painting was used everywhere as a didactic instrument, mainly in the narration of sacred stories to draw the souls of the faithful to piety. The mosaic decoration, which was widely used, particularly in Venice and Palermo, has a predominately hieratical aspect achieved through the static figures and the prevalence of gold and blue and decorative elements, which heighten the ascetic effect of the images. Painted panels are more rare, although they did exist at the time, especially as altar frontals and often dedicated to the figure of Mary, or the saints and their lives. The altar crosses were infused with an even greater sacred value as the ultimate symbol of Christian doctrine.

2

3

1. Facing page: *Jesus on the Mount of Olives*, 13th century. Venice, Saint Mark's.

2. *Tetramorph*, first half 13th century. Anagni, Cathedral.

3. *Abraham and Melchisedec*, first half 13th century. Anagni, Cathedral.

THE CYCLE OF SANT'ELDRADO AND SAN NICOLA AT THE NOVALESA

The fresco cycle in the chapel dedicated to Sant'Eldrado in the Novalese monastic complex forms part of the program of initiatives implemented in the well-known monastery situated in the upper Val di Susa, between the abbacy of Adraldo (1060-1097) and that of Guglielmo of Breme (1097-1129). It is attributed to a Lombard atelier, which was active at the end of the 11th century, and is regarded as being similar to the paintings of Civate. The unusual iconographic choice was prompted by the presence of a relic, in the form of the finger of Saint Nicholas, which was being taken from Apulia to France. The stories of the Bishop of Mira are set beside those of Eldrado, who was Abbot of Novalesa in the 9th century and was canonized. The scenes are presented in specular fashion, with each occupying a compartment, covering four vaulting cells, and with two walls for each saint. The stories of Nicholas are in the aisle near the altar, while those of Saint Eldrado are in the first bay near the entrance.

The scenes from the life of Saint Nicholas feature his election and consecration as Bishop of Mira, the miracle of the dowry and the two poor maidens and that of the saint saving three boys. The details taken from daily life are worth noting: the image of a woman breast-feeding,

4

4. *Saint Nicholas accompanied to the episcopal seat*, end 11th century. Novalesa, Chapel of Saint Eldrado.

5. Facing page: *Arnulfo dresses and consecrates Saint Eldrado*, end 11th century. Novalesa, Chapel of Saint Eldrado.

MARIA

DOMN AMBLULF ABS·

AMB

ELDRADVS

IPE ABITUM S BENEDICTI CORDE BENIGN

6

the wicker basket with the ball of wool, the rumpled bed sheets. In the wall frescoes Nicolas puts to rout the pagan cults, like Eldrado who drives the serpents from the monastery.

There are other noticeable similarities, such as the symbolic images depicted in the middle of the two vaults, the mystic lamb in that of Saint Nicholas and the dove in the other one. The two saints also appear together beside the *Maiestas Domini* in the apse of the little oratory. Next to them are kneeling monks, one of whom has been identified as Abbot Adraldo. The archangels Michael and Gabriel complete the scene, bearing banners with Christological symbols. On the inside of the façade, a *Last Judgment* matches the *Maiestas Domini*, with Christ the Pantocrator seated on a throne. Events from the life of Eldrado, whom some believe to be a native of Provence (Ambillis), fill the cells of the next vault and the two corresponding lateral walls. The four cells meet in a central tondo with a haloed dove symbolizing the Holy Spirit. Eldrado is portrayed in the first cell, in the guise of a youth in a red tunic, intent on tending vines in the Castle of Ambillis. Next come Eldrado firstly receiving the pilgim's knapsack and staff, then arriving exhausted at Novalese, which is conveyed symbolically by a depiction of the

most ancient chapels of Saint Peter and Saint Mary, and, finally, with the tonsure, as he receives the monk's apparel from the Abbot Amblulfo. The specular design is apparent: the labour in the fields mirrors that of the pilgrim and the conferring of the monk's habit matches the pilgrim's garments. The lateral walls feature the miracle of the serpents driven from the monastery grounds and the death of the saint. Here the serenity of the Abbot's face contrasts with the sadness of the monks. Under the Abbot's deathbed the artist has depicted the casket for his sepulcher, in a reference to the hagiographic tradition, according to which Eldrado, in common with many other abbots of the early Middle Ages, prepared for his own burial while alive.

The distinctive features of the cycle are its importance in chromatic terms, the expressiveness of the characters, the use of painted architecture as background scenery and the many details taken from daily life.

Also worth noting is the cross with *Agnus Dei*, which is used to divide one of the compartments into four scenes, corresponding to the four cells. The program, which is divided into sections determined by the symmetry inherent in each cycle, is provided with explanatory inscriptions in white capital letters and with abbreviations.

6. *Saint Eldrado the peasant*, end 11th century. Novalesa, Cappella di Saint Eldrado.

7

THE MOSAIC FLOOR OF THE CATHEDRAL OF OTRANTO

Between the 11th and 12th centuries, the tradition of late-antique and early medieval mosaic floors continued. The work of the floors of Otranto, Trani, Bari and Taranto has been attributed to a homogenous group who specialized in a rich and varied iconographic repertoire.

The Cathedral of Otranto, which is dedicated to the Virgin, was founded after the Norman Conquest, probably in about 1080. During the 12th century the building was subjected to considerable renovations, which culminated in the installation of the famous mosaic floor. This is adapted to the new blueprint, occupying the three aisles and the transept. The

8

7. Pantaleone the priest,
Eve, 1163-65. Otranto,
Cathedral.

8. Pantaleone the priest,
Zodiac with months of
November and December,
1163-65. Otranto,
Cathedral.

10

11

inscriptions play an important part in explaining the images and also provide the name of the person who commissioned them, the Bishop of Otranto, and the artist, the priest Pantaleone, whose workshop was also responsible for the Cathedral of Trani. Two more inscriptions include the dates of 1163 and 1165, between which the work must have been executed, since one is near the main altar and the other near the entrance. Moving backwards it is also possible to trace the development of the work. The rich series of images can be appreciated most fully in the nave, while in the right-hand aisle little of the decoration has remained intact. The overall iconographic scheme consists of two elephants holding up a tree, which stretches from the entrance of the cathedral to the apse. Sixteen clipei containing different characters and creatures are placed symmetrically on the branches. Among the biblical ones are Adam and Eve, King Solomon and the Queen of Sheba, Sampson fighting the lion, and the prophet Jonah. Alongside them are actual narrative scenes such as the Flood and the Construction of the Tower of Babel. Added to these subjects there are real and fantastic monstrous creatures, characters derived from history and tales of chivalry, such as Alexander the Great and King Arthur and, finally, the portrayal of the Months and the Zodiac. The narrative organization is not based on the order of the Bible and, above all, the Holy Scriptures are not the only point of reference. Inspiration is drawn from the whole of medieval knowledge, including encyclopedias and bestiaries. Some scenes actually reveal knowledge of the *Physiologus*, the famous late-antique 'ancestor' of bestiaries available between the 11th and 12th centuries. The elephants are a case in point: they were believed to sleep leaning against trees. Besides the well-known Western sources, there were both sacred and profane Byzantine and Arabian ones, which makes it possible to compare the animals portrayed in the tondi with the ivory oliphants of Islamic origin. The cycle of the Months also provides an interesting repertoire of details taken from daily life, with reference to the seasonal tasks of agricultural labor. From the beginning of the tale told by the huge mosaic carpet, the allegorical significance in terms of Christian morality is clear: from a state of sin it is possible to attain salvation

9. Facing page: Pantaleone the priest, *Tree of Life*, 1163-65. Otranto, Cathedral.

10. Pantaleone the priest, *The Construction of Noah's Ark*, 1163-65. Otranto, Cathedral.

11. Pantaleone the priest, *The Construction of the Tower of Babel*, 1163-65. Otranto, Cathedral.

A bestiary is a scientific and educational collection of writings about animals. Bestiaries were very fashionable in the West in the Middle Ages between the 12th and 13th centuries. Thanks to them, the naturalistic knowledge from antiquity was disseminated; this included the images which provided an inexhaustible source for the symbolic repertoire of medieval culture. The origin of bestiaries is connected to an antecedent, the *Physiologus*. This was an anonymous Greek work, which dates back to the second century AD and was translated into Latin in the fifth century. It is a collection of a series of moralistic, allegorical interpretations of the significance of the animals named in the Greek translation of the Old Testament. The term bestiarium may have originated from a chapter of the *Ethimologiae* of Isidorus Hispalensis of Seville, who lived between the 6th and 7th centuries and was the first author who attempted to gather the whole of human knowledge in to a single encyclopedia, namely the *Ethimologiae*. The use of the term, together with the analogous *erbarium*, only occurs in texts and some library inventories in the second half of the 12th century, in parallel with the definitive emergence of the genre, which was to reach maximum popularity during the following century. The bestiaries were primarily used as collections of exempla, which

I. Master Ermengaut,
November, Acorn Harvest,
f. 59v. Escorial, Monastery
of San Lorenzo, Library.

were referred to during sermons. At the same time they reflect those elements of the fantastic and the supernatural in the early medieval imagination, which had first appeared in the so-called Libri monstruorum during the early Middle Ages. The popularity of the genre is proven by the existence of nearly five hundred surviving manuscripts of bestiaries, almost a fifth of which are embellished with illuminated images with specially designed borders. For each animal, a realistic interpretation was provided alongside an allegorical, moralizing one originating in the Christian tradition. The descriptions of the author of the Physiologus and Isidorus were supplemented by a progeny of creatures whose 'spawning' must have been the result of a new interest aroused by a knowledge of exotic animals, which intensified at the time of the Crusades. Animals which had never previously been seen, such as the giraffe and the rhinoceros, appeared, but it is worth remembering that a body of composite beings already existed, including winged griffons with lions' bodies and eagles' heads. To a medieval mentality attuned to other levels of interpretation, checking the reliability of what was described or portrayed in these compilations was of no interest: it was the symbolic aspect which was important. It is therefore worth focusing on the meaning, or rather meanings, of existing, or completely imaginary, beings. There are a great many of them, and interpretation is further complicated by the qualities attributed to them and the fact that these are often conflicting. The animals which occur so often in medieval art are derived from a variety of sources and traditions – in the Bible alone nearly one hundred and fifty animals are mentioned. These may have derived partly from the bestiaries, but are ultimately all related to the same cultural heritage.

II

III

IV

II. Joseph Asafarti de Cervera, Cervera Bible, illuminated page, about 1299. Lisbon, Library.

III. French School, Bestiary of Saltykowchsh Edring, Griffon, 12th century. Leningrad, State Public Library.

IV. English School, *Dog chasing a Porcupine, Wolf chasing a Rabbit, Cat chasing a Mouse,* early 13th century.

University of Cambridge, Fitzwilliam Museum.

Work on the mosaic decoration of Saint Mark's began in the 12th century, as soon as its construction was completed, and was to continue throughout the following century. This explains the lack of stylistic homogeneity, which serves to alleviate the dominant gold background. It also provides an interesting compendium of the aesthetic tastes of the time in Venice. The successive craftsmen do however stick to the original iconographic scheme, which elaborates the glorification of the Church Of Christ, and begins in the apse

12

12. Dome of the Genesis, 13th century. Venice, Saint Mark's.

13. Facing page: *Alcove with the Forefathers*, 12th to 13th century. Venice, Saint Mark's.

with the figure of the *Pantocrator*. This was renewed in the sixteenth century, and is surrounded by saints and apostles. The scheme continues in the central domes, with the *Annunciation of the Church by the Prophets*, the *Church living in Christ* and the *Church formed by the apostles after Pentecost*. The rest of the decoration is related to this central theme and every surface is covered with allegorical figures, saints, prophets and stories from the life of Christ, the Virgin, Saint Mark and Saint John. The mosaics in the small domes of the narthex were executed by Venetian craftsmen in the thirteenth century. They feature stories of the Old Testament presented in a Western guise. The dome of the Genesis stands out, with its scenes displayed in long concentric bands. The lively colors and freedom of style invest the naturalistic details of the background and the sturdiness of the figures with spontaneity.

14

14. *Jesus on the Mount of Olives*, detail, 13th century. Venice, Saint Mark's.

THE FRESCOES OF THE ANAGNI CRYPT

The cycle of frescoes which decorates the Anagni crypt, practically all of which has survived intact, constitutes one of the major exemplars of pre-Assisi medieval painting. The complex iconographic scheme covers theories on the origin of the cosmos (symbolized by the dialogue of Hippocrates and Galen) and its portrayal, together with the hagiographic cycles on the saints Magno and Secondina, an apocalyptic cycle, and stories from the Ark of the Covenant and from Samuel. The aim was to represent the order which prevails throughout creation and which also governs the distribution of power on the earth. Scholars attribute the whole pictorial cycle to the first half of the thirteenth century, despite the stylistic differences due to the involvement of different artists. The influence of Byzantine painting is present throughout the work, however differently it may have been interpreted or reworked. In the Twenty-four lords of the Apocalypse, for example, the outlines are pronounced, the colors fresh and the figures animated by convulsive movement. In other cases color is depended on to convey a three-dimensional quality, with vivid patches being juxtaposed with splashes of light. The so-called Master of the "translations", on the other hand, uses a decorative repertoire which is early Christian in flavor, and archaic methods, which have led some to advance the hypothesis that the frescoes attributed to him are from the previous century.

15

15. *Twenty-four lords of the Apocalypse,* first half 13th century. Anagni, Cathedral.

16

16. *Hippocrates and Galen,* first half 13th century. Anagni, Cathedral.

17. Facing page: *Enthroned Madonna with Child,* first half 13th century. Anagni, Cathedral.

Unlike the cycles of frescoes on the walls of Romanesque churches, whose purpose was the pictorial narration of the Word of God, the painted cross has a less illustrative, more meditative value.

Whether Christ is painted alive and upright, in the Byzantine iconography of the *Christus triumphans*, alluding to triumph over death, or represented as dead, in the *Christus patiens*, emphasizing the dramatic sacrifice consummated for the whole of humanity, the image of the savior is intended to involve the faithful in a personal dialogue.

The figure of Christ conveys the mystery of death and resurrection through its solemn, fixed expression and by means of the wounds and blood. The area in which the cross is generally situated is also chosen in relation to its symbolic value. It is usually placed on the iconostasis

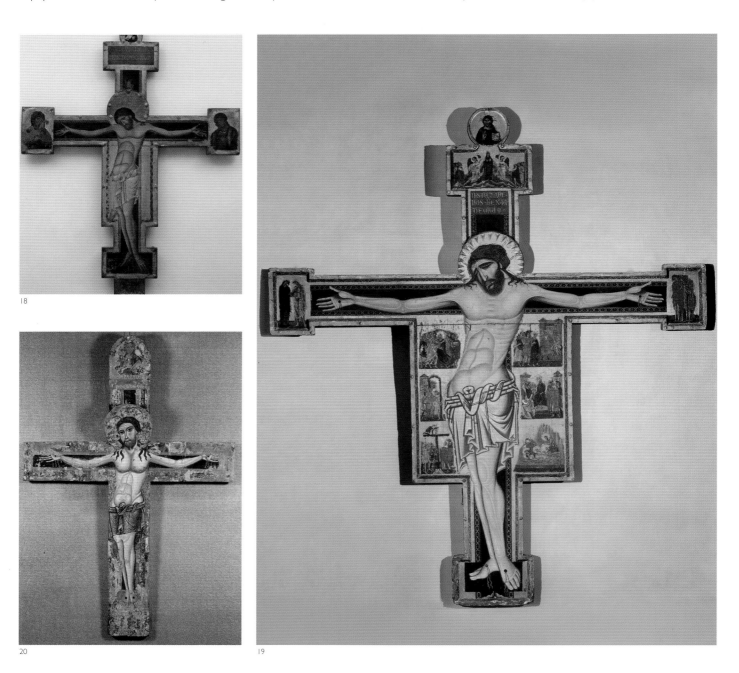

18

20

19

18. Giunta Pisano, *Crucifixion*, first half 13th century. Assisi, Santa Maria degli Angeli.

19. Coppo di Marcovaldo, *Crucifixion with Stories of Passion*, second half 13th century. San Gimignano, Pinacoteca Civica.

20. Margaritone d'Arezzo, *Crucifixion*, second half 13th century. Siena, Chigi Saracini Collection.

or hung from the triumphal arch, above the main altar, the only means through which the believer can attain Paradise. The panels portraying Christ crucified are placed alongside the tablets of the Virgin and Saint John, witnesses of the divine death. It is more rare to find Christ accompanied by episodes from the Passion.

The tradition of painted crosses became widespread from the 12th century onwards, especially in the area of Lucca and Pisa. The paintings were either executed directly on the wood or on sheets of parchment or leather, which were stuck onto the cross-shaped wooden support. After the first painting of this kind, which was signed by a certain Master Guglielmo and dated 1138, the prototype of the cross was developed, in the middle of the 13th century, by Giunta Pisano, who exploited the dramatic and emotional potential through an almost expressionistic emphasis on the graphic element.

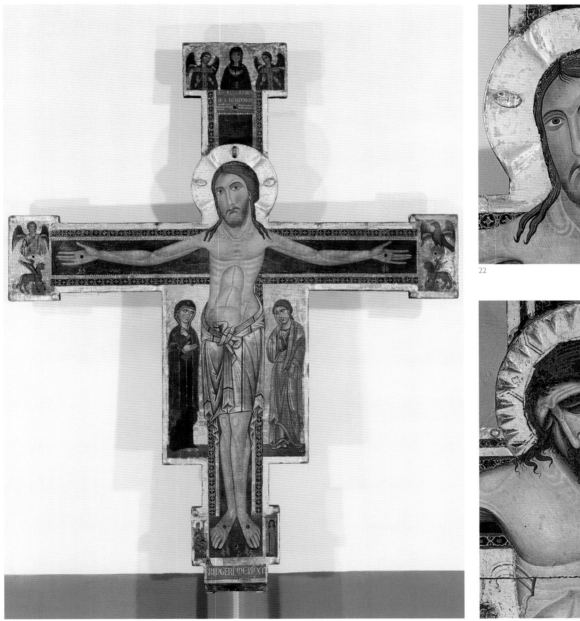

21

23

21. Berlinghiero Berlinghieri, *Crucifixion*, second half 13th century. Lucca, Villa Guinigi Museum.

22. Berlinghiero Berlinghieri, *Crucifixion*, detail, second half 13th century. Lucca, Villa Guinigi Museum.

23. Coppo di Marcovaldo, *Crucifixion with stories of the Passion*, detail, second half 13th century. San Gimignano, Pinacoteca Civica.

CRUCIFIXION
Giunta Pisano, about 1240
Pisa, Museo di San Matteo

The painting was executed in about 1240 by Giunta Pisano, who signed the work at the foot of the cross.

SUBJECT

The large painted cross displays the pale, bloodless body of Christ Crucified in the manner of the Byzantine Christ patiens. This prototype, which is more modern compared to the painted crosses which present the figure of Christ alive and triumphing over death, was very successful in the 13th century and soon replaced the Christ triumphant prototype.

The body of Christ is tense from the pain of death and follows the line of a curve beginning with the inclined position of the head. The anatomy is delineated using graphic conventions, which highlight the abdomen, thorax and the muscles in the arms and legs. The sculptural quality of the figure is achieved through use of intense chiaroscuro, which is heightened at the edges of the figure.

The top of the cross ends in a tondo with the figure of Christ the redeemer, portrayed in the act of benediction.

At the sides of Christ, in panels at either end of the horizontal cross, there are half-length portraits of the Virgin and Saint John the Evangelist. Each figure is leaning their face against their hand in a gesture of grief.

The inscription INRI, which is often present in images of the crucifixion of Christ, is an abbreviation of the Latin phrase "IESUS NAZARENUS REX IUDEORUM", meaning "Jesus of Nazareth, King of the Jews".

COMPOSITION

The crucifix represents a synthesis of the evangelistic episode of the Crucifixion, with the placing in the side panels of the half-length portraits of the grieving Mary and John. The figure of Christ imitates the shape of the cross behind it in, as far as its pale outline stands out against the dark background,

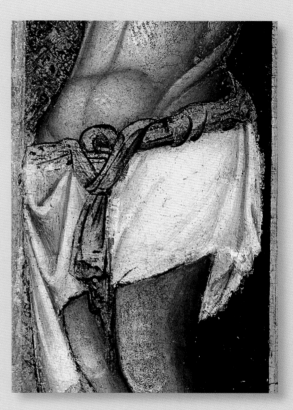

but the painful arching of the body contrasts with this shape where it overlaps its border and rests against the painted background of precious material.

The expressionistic vein of the graphic style emphasizes the dramatic force of the scene, accentuating the sinuous shape of the crucified body and bluntly exposing the physical agony evinced by the contracted muscles of the arms and legs, the divisions in the stomach and the thin torso with protruding ribs.

THE MOSAICS IN THE BAPTISTERY OF FLORENCE

The octagonal dome of the Baptistery in Florence is completely faced with rich mosaic decoration, which was begun in 1225 and finished in the 16th century. Biblical and evangelical episodes are fitted within a framework of columns.

In the three central segments there is a grandiose portrayal of *Universal Judgment*, with the gigantic figure of Christ seated and surrounded by angels, the Virgin, the Baptist (patron saint of Florence), the apostles and the patriarchs.

On either side and on different levels are the episodes of Genesis and the *Stories of Joseph*, *Christ* and the *Baptist*, whose function is to illustrate the story of the salvation of mankind from the Creation to the Judgment.

Some parts of the large mosaic cycle have been attributed during the course of time to artists who were active in Florence during that period. The names of Cimabue, the Master of the Magdalene, Melior, Gaddo Gaddi and Grifo di Tancredi have been cited.

In the depiction of Hell, many scholars have also recognized the vigorous style of Coppo di Marcovaldo, which is distinguished by strong outlines and chromatic contrasts.

It is also thought that Venetian craftsmen specialized in mosaic technique worked alongside the local artists.

24

25

24. *Christ in Judgment*, 12th to14th century. Florence, Baptistery of San Giovanni.

25. Baptistery of San Giovanni, capital of the purse, 12th to 14th century. Florence.

26

26. Baptistery of San Giovanni, view of dome, 12th to 14th century. Florence.

27. Following pages: *Hell*, detail, 12th to 14th century. Florence, Baptistery of San Giovanni.

THE MADONNAS OF COPPO DI MARCOVALDO

The inscription of the *Madonna del bordone*, which is kept in the church of Santa Maria dei Servi in Siena, means it can be attributed to Coppo di Marcovaldo without any doubt, and also enables the methods of the artist to be analyzed. On the basis of comparison, scholars have also attributed to him the *Madonna and child* in Santa Maria dei Servi in Orvieto. Some maintain that Marcovaldo also worked on the so-called *Madonna "del Carmelo"*, which is painted, with sculpted parts, in Santa Maria Maggiore in Florence. In these works the artist uses the motif of the enthroned Madonna, in accordance with the canons of Byzantine tradition, but he transforms it in a quest for

28

29

28. Coppo di Marcovaldo,
Madonna del bordone,
1261. Siena, Santa Maria
dei Servi.

29. Coppo di Marcovaldo,
Madonna with Child,
about 1270. Orvieto, Santa
Maria dei Servi.

more robust modeling. He places the figure partly sideways on, giving a three-quarters view, making the gestures more natural but retaining the enameled coloring and linear pattern of Byzantine painting. He tones down the colors, obtaining a violent chiaroscuro. The garments have a broken-up, angular aspect and appear heavy, despite the conventional obsessive use of linear light effects.

31

30

32

33

421

30. Workshop of Coppo di Marcovaldo, *Madonna del Carmelo,* **second half 13th century. Florence, Santa Maria Maggiore.**

31. Workshop of Coppo di Marcovaldo, *Madonna del Carmelo,* **detail, second half 13th century. Florence, Santa Maria Maggiore.**

32. Coppo di Marcovaldo, *Madonna with Child,* **detail, about 270. Orvieto, Santa Maria dei Servi.**

33. Coppo di Marcovaldo, *Madonna del bordone,* **detail, 1261. Siena, Santa Maria dei Servi.**

ICONOGRAPHY OF THE MADONNA

With regard to New Testament narratives, since its beginning, the Mariological debate has revolved around two fundamental concepts: that of the divine maternity and the virginity of Mary. The first concept was officially recognized in the year 431, during the Council of Ephesus, while the perpetua virginitas of the Madonna was affirmed at the Council of Constantinople in the year 553. While in the first examples of Christian art there is no specific Marian iconography and the Madonna is mainly portrayed praying, or as the mother of God with the child in her arms, later on she becomes a living icon, instilling a respectful fear in the faithful. When portrayed as Theotokos ("mother of God"), as in the setting of the Council of Ephesus, she is seated on a chair decorated with lions' paws, on a high podium, which is reached by two steps, wearing precious vestments, which reveal the influence of Constantinople court ceremony. At the time of the Benedictine reform, on the other hand, there is a departure from the frontal pose of previous iconographic schemes. Now the Madonna assumes the position of the Byzantine *Odighitria* ("one who shows the way"), indicating the baby Jesus with her hand, in a gesture which expresses both devotion and humility. In Northern Italy, Nicolò invested the Madonna with greater humanity, inserting episodes from her life into decorations, as was to happen in the great cycles which decorate the buildings of Île-de-France. Maria occupies a central position to emphasize her role as mother of all the faithful, for whom she intercedes with her son. In the tympana, she is portrayed in scenes from the *Coronation*, or placed beside God in Universal Judgment. The Madonna iconography was radically reformed in the thirteenth and fourteenth centuries, thanks to the initiative of the

34

34. Margaritone d'Arezzo,
Madonna with Child,
second half 13th century.
Monte San Savino, Santa
Maria delle Vertighe.

Cistercians and the mendicant orders, who made a large contribution to the development of Mariology. The stories of the life of the Virgin are rich in episodes from her childhood, derived from the tales of the apocryphal gospels. These were very successful due to their similarity to fables and anecdotal tone. Images influenced by Byzantine icons imported from Constantinople during the crusades were very common, showing that the humanization of the image of the Madonna had finally been attained. The Madonna painted by Coppo di Marcovaldo in 1261 for the Servi constituted a turning point, taking the three-quarter position and affectionate attitude from the icons. After him, other artists would contribute to the evolution of this prototype, while continuing to use the form of Majesty. This was both a symbol of prestige and a vehicle for political propaganda in Italian city-states, where the Madonna is portrayed enthroned and surrounded by angels, saints and prophets.

35

36

423

35. Cimabue, *Madonna with Child*, end 13th century. Castelfiorentino, Santa Verdiana.

36. *Madonna with Child*. Cefalù, Museo Mandralisca.

CHRONOLOGY

284-305 · Rule of Diocletian who reorganizes the empire, instituting the system of tetrarchy: he keeps the East for himself, with the capital at Nicomedia, while he entrusts Italy and Africa to Massimiano, who establishes the capital at Milan.

313 · Edict of Milan: Constantine grants Christians liberty to worship.

326 · Pope Sylvester consecrates the Basilica of Saint Peter in Rome.

330 · The Emperor Constantine transfers the capital of the Roman Empire to Constantinople.

337 · In Rome the building of the Mausoleum of Saint Constance begins. The sarcophagus of Princess Constantina was originally kept here (now in the Vatican Museums).

359 · Defeat of Giunio Basso, Prefect of Rome. The date is recorded in an inscription in the sarcophagus in which he is buried; some scholars believe this was sculpted in the middle of the fourth century, others in the third.

374-97 · Ambrose is Bishop of Milan. During his bishopric he initiates the construction of the Basilica of the Martyrs (Sant'Ambrogio).

379 · Theodosius is proclaimed Emperor in the East.

380 · Theodosius declares Christianity to be the state religion.

394-95 · Theodosius is sole emperor. His death sees the end of the unity of the Empire, which is divided between his three sons: he has appointed Arcadius Emperor of the East, Honorius Emperor of the West.

404 · The Emperor Honorius transfers the capital to Ravenna.

422-32 · The wooden door is sculpted for the Basilica of Saint Sabina in Rome.

425-50 · Galla Placidia, sister of Honorius, rules the Empire in the name of her son Valentinian III. During his rule, The Mausoleum of Galla Placidia is built in Ravenna.

431 · IThe Council of Ephesus affirms the divinity of Christ from his birth and proclaims Mary "Mother of God".

432-40 · Pontificate of Sixtus III who commissions the reconstruction of the Basilica of Saint Mary Major.

476 · End of the Roman Empire in the West: General Odoacer deposes Emperor Romolus "Augustulus".

482-511 · Reign of Clovis, first king of the Franks; he eliminates the remains of Roman domination in Gaul.

493 · Theodoric, King of the Ostrogoths, defeats Odoacer and installs himself in Ravenna. During his reign the church of Sant'Apollinare Nuovo, the Baptistery of the Ariani and the Mausoleum of Theodoric are built.
· The Visigoths invade Spain.

529 · Saint Benedict founds the Monastery of Montecassino and draws up the Benedictine Rule.

532 · Justinian commissions the construction of the Basilica of Hagia Sophia in Constantinople.

535-53 · Greek-Gothic War: the victory of Justinian marks the beginning of Byzantine rule in Italy during which the Basilica of Sant'Apollinare Nuovo in Ravenna is consecrated for Catholic worship. The interior middle tier is redecorated and dedicated to the processions of martyrs.

546-66 · Bishopric of Massimiano in Ravenna. His monogram appear on the ivory cattedra (throne), which bears his name and is now kept in the Archiepiscopal Museum.

547 · Massimiano consecrates the Basilica of San Vitale in Ravenna.

568 · The Lombards cross the Alps and invade Italy.

590-604 · Pontificate of Gregory the Great.

591-616 · Agilulf reigns in Italy: the Lombard king is portrayed on the frontlet of a helmet kept in the Museo del Bargello in Florence.

603 · Pope Gregory the Great gives the Lombard Queen Theodolinda the cover of the missal kept in the Treasury of the Cathedral in Monza.

625-38 · (about) Building of the Early Christian Basilica of Saint Agnes outside the Walls in Rome.

670 · (about) On the initiative of Bishop Angilbert construction of the crypt of Jouarre is begun.

711 · Arabian invasion of Spain.

726 · Issue of the decree prohibiting the worship of images: beginning of iconoclasm, which will last until 787.

737-744 · (about) Sculpture of the altar which the Duke Ratchis gave to the church of San Martino a Cividale, as recorded in the inscription.

751 · End of Merovingian reign in France: Pepin the Short deposes Childeric III and is crowned King of the Franks.

755 · Having conquered most of Southern Spain, the Arab Abd er-Rahman installs himself in Cordova as Emir.

760 · (about) Sculpture of the Ferentillo stone slab bearing the name of Duke Ilderico.

774 · Defeat of the troops of the Lombard king Desiderius by Charlemagne: end of Lombard rule in Italy.
· In Milan, the archbishop Pietro founds a Benedictine cenobium in the Basilica of Sant'Ambrogio; rebuilding of the presbytery.
· (about) Charlemagne founds the Abbey-church of Saint John of Müstair.
· (about) Rebuilding of Abbey of Lorsch, founded in 764; a precious cycle of Carolingian paintings is kept in the Gatehouse.

790-800 · Building of the Palatine Chapel of Aachen.

800 · Charlemagne is crowned Emperor by the Pope.

817-24 · Pontificate of Paschal I who has numerous Roman churches embellished with mosaics and goldwork. In this period the chapels of San Zeno and Santa Prassede are decorated.

824-59 · Angilbert II is Bishop of Milan, he donates the gold altar of Vuolvinio to the Basilica of Sant'Ambrogio.

826-843	· Fresco decoration of the crypt in the monastery of San Vincenzo al Volturno, during the bishopric of Epiphanius.
842-850	· Building begins on the Church of Santa Maria de Naranco, former Royal palace of Ramiro I, in Oviedo.
843	· The treaty of Verdun sanctions the partitioning of the Carolingian empire.
847-855	· During the Pontificate of Leo IV, the lower Basilica of San Clemente in Rome is decorated with frescoes.
860-870	· (about) The Equestrian statuette of Charlemagne, in the classical style, is made.
875	· Charles the Bald is crowned as Emperor in Rome by Pope John VIII, to whom he gives the Bible which is now kept in Saint Paul's outside the Walls in Rome.
910	· Founding of Abbey of Cluny, birthplace of Benedictine reform.
927	· Consecration of the first Cluny church.
948-81	· Construction of the second Cluny church.
962	· Otto I, former King of Germany, is crowned Holy Roman Emperor by Pope John XII.
972	· Marriage of Otto II to the Byzantine princess Theophano.
973-83	· Reign of Otto II.
980	· (about) Placchetta Trivulzio executed in Rome, now kept in Castello Sforzesco.
980-90	· ((about) On the initiative of Abbot Witigow, a cycle of frescoes is painted in the church of Saint George in Oberzell.
983-1002	· Reign of Otto III.
987-96	· Hugh Capet, founder of the Capetian line, crowned King of France.
990	· (about) In the basilica of Sant'Ambrogio the stucco-work ciborium is placed above the altar of Vuolvinio.
996	· Otto III is crowned as Holy Roman Emperor.
996-1022	· During his bishopric Bernward fosters the production of precious manuscripts and founds the church of San Michele, masterpiece of Ottonian architecture.
1002	· Death of Otto III; he is succeeded by his cousin Henry, while in Italy those who hold power in the peninsula elect Arduino d'Ivrea.
1004	· Arduino d'Ivrea is defeated at Chiuse di Valsugana by Henry II. · Venice has dominion over Dalmatia as far as Zara.
1005-30	· The church of Romeinmôtier is rebuilt; one of the first examples of churches based on the Cluniac model.
1008	· Work on rebuilding the cathedral begins in Torcello.
1012	· Saint Romualdo founds the Camaldolensian order in Camaldoli.
1014	· Henry II of Swabia is crowned Holy Roman Emperor.

1015-16	· The Pisans and the Genoese seize Corsica and Sardinia from the Saracens.
1018	· In Cardona in Catalonia, construction begins on the church of Saint Vincent on the initiative of Viscount Bermon.
1018-63	· The church of San Miniato al Monte in Florence is built.
1020-32	· Abbot Oliva, architect and theologian, initiates construction of the Abbey of Santa Maria a Ripoll in Catalonia, consecrated in 1032.
1024	· Death of Henry II and end of the Saxon line of emperors. The imperial crown passes to Franconia with Conrad II the Salian. · Conrad II the Salian orders the rebuilding of the Cathedral of Spira.
1027	· The Norman, Rainulf Drengo, obtains the county of Aversa from the Duke of Naples. · Rebuilding of the Church of Notre-Dame in Jumièges in Normandy begins.
1031	· The Omayyad of Spain cede power to the Almoravidi Berber line.
1035-65	· Ferdinand I of Castile initiates the Reconquest.
1039	· Death of Conrad II; Henry III succeeds him. · The Vallombrosian order is founded in Vallombrosa.
1040	· (about) Arrival of Robert d'Hauteville, known as the Guiscard, in Southern Italy.
1041	· Building of the Basilica of Sainte-Foy in Conques begins.
1043	· Humphrey d'Hauteville takes the county of Melfi from the Duke of Salerno.
1052	· Robert Guiscard begins the Conquest of Calabria.
1053	· Robert Guiscard defeats the Papal troops in Benevento, wins the Battle of Civitate and declares himself vassal of Pope Leo IX.
1054	· Schism of the East: breach between the Eastern Greek Orthodox and Roman Catholic churche.
1056	· Death of Henry III; he is succeeded by the child Henry IV.
1057	· Robert Guiscard becomes Duke of Apulia.
1058	· Desiderio is Abbot of Montecassino.
1058-61	· Pontificate of Niccolò II.
1059	· Treaty of Melfi signed by the Papacy and the Normans. Roberto the Guiscard is invested by Pope Nicholas II as Duke of Calabria and Apulia, the first acknowledgement of Norman dominion in the South. · Lateran Council: the election of the Pontiff is confined to the cardinals and lay authorities are forbidden to hold ecclesiastical posts. · Consecration of the Baptistery in Florence.
1060	· Rebuilding of the Cathedral of San Martino in Lucca begins; completed in 1204 with the Guidetto facade. · On the initiative of William the Conqueror, the Church of

CHRONOLOGY

Saint-Etienne in Caen in Normandy is built.

1061	· The Normans embark on the Conquest of Sicily.
1061-73	· Pontificate of Alexander II.
1063	· Alexander II supports the Reconquest. · The Pisans defeat the Muslim fleet in Palermo. · Work begins on the Basilica of Saint Mark in Venice.
1064	· Buscheto starts construction of the Cathedral in Pisa.
1066	· William the Conqueror invades England. He is elected King of England after the Battle of Hastings.
1067	· Consecration of the church of Notre-Dame in Jumièges.
1070-77	· Canterbury Cathedral is rebuilt.
1071	· Robert Guiscard drives the Byzantines out of Italy. · Desiderio inaugurates the Abbey of Montecassino.
1071-85	· Under the doge Domenico Selvo the mosaic decoration of Saint Mark's in Venice begins and will be protracted until the mid 15th century.
1072	· The Normans, in alliance with the Pisans, wrest Palermo from the Arabs.
1073	· The Normans conquer Amalfi.
1073-1085	· Pontificate of Gregory VII.
1075	· The *Dictatus* Popee of Gregory VII proclaims the superiority of the pontificate over the sovereign leading to the Investiture Contest.
1075-1128	· Rebuilding of the sanctuary at Santiago de Compostela, a pilgrimage destination since the 10th century.
1076	· Henry IV holds the Sinod of Worms against Gregory VII, who excommunicates him. · Rebuilding of the Cathedral of Parma begins, after its destruction by fire.
1077	· Henry IV submits to Gregory at Canossa. · Roberto Guiscard conquers Salerno: apart from Benevento, the whole of the South is in Norman hands.
1080	· Gregory VII excommunicates Henry IV for the second time.
1080-90	· Construction of the Abbey of Notre-Dame in La Charité-sur-Loire begins.
1081	· Institution of consular government in Pisa.
1082	· Alexius Comnenus invests Venice with sovereignty over Southern Dalmatia as far as Ragusa and trading rights throughout the Byzantine empire.
1084	· Henry IV is crowned Emperor by the anti-Pope Clement III.
1085	· Death of Roberto Guiscard. · Death of Gregory VII.
1087	· Death of William the Conqueror.

	· In Bari work begins on construction of the Basilica of Saint Nicholas, consecrated in 1197.
1088	· Construction of the third Abbey of Cluny begins in Bourgogne.
1088-99	· Pontificate of Urban II.
1090	· Alfonso VI, King of Castile, initiates the construction of the walls of Avila.
1091	· The Normans complete their conquest of Sicily: Roger I is named Count of Sicily.
1093	· Bishop William of St. Calais begins construction of Durham Cathedral, which is completed in 1133.
1095	· Alexius I Comnenus invokes the aid of the Pope against the Turks. · At the Council of Clermont Urban II proclaims the First Crusade. · Consuls of the City-State in Asti. · Consecration of the church of Sant'Abbondio in Como.
1096	· The first groups of Crusaders reach Constantinople. · Consecration of the Basilica of Saint Mark in Venice.
1097	· The Crusaders take Nicaea, defeat the Turks in Dorylaeum and conquer Edessa.
1098	· Christian conquest of Antioch, which is enfeoffed to Boemondo di Taranto, Prince of the Norman line. This and religious differences resulting from the Schism of the East lead to a rupture in relations between the Byzantines and the Crusaders. · Consuls of the City-State in Arezzo. · Saint Bernard of Clairville founds the Cistercian Order.
1098-1112	· The Church of Citeaux is built in accordance with the dictates of the new Cistercian Rule.
1099	· Jerusalem is conquered by the Crusaders and the inhabitants ruthlessly massacred. · Godfrey of Bouillon rules over the Kingdom of Jerusalem with the title "Defender of the Holy Sepulcher". · Consuls of the City-State in Genoa. · Christian victory in Ascalona: the whole of the Holy Land is in Western hands. · Lanfranco begins construction of the Cathedral of Modena.
1099-1106	· Sculpture by Wiligelmo of the series of bass-reliefs in the Cathedral of Modena.
1100	· (about) Construction of the Cloister of the Abbey of Moissac completed.
1104	· Deposition of Emperor Henry IV.
1105	· Consuls of the City-State in Pistoia, Lucca, Ferrara.
1106	· Henry V succeeds a Henry IV.
1110	· Sculpture of the reliefs in the tympanum of the South portal of the Abbey-church of Moissac.
1112	· Consuls of the City-State in Cremona.
1115	· Bernard becomes Abbot of Clairvaux.

1117	· Construction of the Basilica of San Michele in Pavia begins.
1118	· Foundation of the Order of Knights Templar. · Consecration of the Cathedral of Pisa.
1119	· Founding of the Abbey of Pontigny.
1119-24	· Pontificate of Calixtus II.
1120-40	· (about) Rebuilding of Abbey of Sainte-Madeleine in Vézelay, Bourgogne. The decoration which is added in successive years is very significant in the context of Romanesque sculpture.
1120-38	· In Verona work begins on the Church of San Zeno.
1120-1150	· Sculptural decoration of the Abbey-church of Sainte-Madeleine in Vézelay, Bourgogne.
1122	· Concordat at Worms between Henry V and Calixtus II ends the Investiture Contest, establishing that the Pope will invest bishops and the emperor assign political positions.
1123	· Consuls of the City-State in Piacenza and Bologna. · (about) Fresco decoration of the apse of the Church of Santa Maria of Taull in Catalonia.
1125	· In Germany the death of Henry V gives rise to dispute over succession.
1125-45	· Gislebertus works on the sculptural decoration of the Church of Saint-Lazare of Autun in Bourgogne.
1128	· Bernard of Clairvaux dictates the rules of the Knight-Monastic Orders. Founding of the Knight-Monastic Order of the Johnites (subsequently Knights of Rhodes and Malta).
1130	· Roger II is acknowledged sole King of the Normans as King of Sicily, Calabria and Apulia. · Consuls of the City-State in Perugia. · (about) Sculpture of tympanum relief in the Church of Sainte-Foy in Conques, portraying *Universal Judgment*.
1131	· Roger II initiates construction of the Cathedral of Cefalù, consecrated in 1267.
1132	· Innocent II consecrates the church of Saint-Lazare in Autun, Bourgogne.
1132-43	· Mosaic decoration of the Palatine Chapel in the Palace of the Normans in Palermo, by group of Byzantine artists in conjunction with local craftsmen.
1135-40	· On the initiative of Abbot Suger construction begun on the Church of Saint-Denis.
1138	· Conrad III of Swabia becomes Emperor. · Institution of the Consulate in Florence. · Guglielmo paints the cross in Sarzana.
1138-39	· Nicolò sculpts the reliefs of the facade of San Zeno in Verona.
1139	· Norman Conquest of Naples. · Roger II defeats Pope Innocent II on Garigliano and is acknowledged King of Sicily.
1139-47	· Construction of the Abbey-church of Fontenay, which be-

	comes a model for monasteries of the Cistercian Order.
1143	· Portugal breaks free of Castile and becomes an autonomous kingdom. · Creation of the City-state of Rome: the Pope is forced to leave the city.
1144	· Muslim Reconquest of Edessa.
1145-70	· Sculpture of the Portal of the Kings in Chartres Cathedral; it luckily escapes the fire of 1194.
1146	· Norman Conquest of Tripoli.
1147	· (ante) The goldsmiths of the school of Saint-Denis make the vase known as *Aquila di Suger*.
1147-49	· Second crusade, proclaimed by Bernard de Clairvaux and led by Conrad III of Swabia and Louis VII of France, who tries in vain to besiege Damascus.
1147-54	· Arnaldo of Brescia is ruler of the City-state of Rome.
1152	· Frederick I Barbarossa is elected King of Germany. · Construction of the Baptistery of Pisa begins under the architect Diotisalvi.
1153	· Pact of Constance between Barbarossa and Pope Eugenius III.
1154	· First expedition of Barbarossa to Italy. · First Diet of Roncaglia, annulling autonomous city-states. · Federick Barbarossa is crowned Emperor by Pope Adrian IV. · Death of Roger II. · Pope Eugenius III recognizes William I 'the Bad' as King of Sicily.
1154-89	· Reign of Henry II, Plantagenet, in England.
1158-62	· Second expedition of Barbarossa to Italy and second Diet of Roncaglia.
1159-62	· In Pisa Guglielmo sculpts the reliefs of the pulpit; in 1312 it is moved to the Cathedral of Cagliari.
1159-81	· Pontificate of Alexander III.
1160	· (about) Construction of Notre-Dame begins in Paris.
1162	· Milan and Crema are razed to the ground by Barbarossa.
1163-64	· Third expedition of Barbarossa to Italy.
1164	· Founding of the League of Verona against Barbarossa.
1165-70	· Sculpting of some of the capital reliefs in the cloister of Saint-Trophime in Arles by Benedetto Antelami (according to certain scholars).
1166	· Lintel reliefs sculpted by Gruamonte and Deodato in the Church of Sant'Andrea in Pistoia.
1166-68	· Fourth expedition of Barbarossa to Italy.
1166-89	· William 'the Good' II is King of Sicily.
1167	· Oath of Pontida and founding of the Lombard League.

CHRONOLOGY

1172-85
· Building of the Cathedral of Monreale, synthesis of Western and Eastern Byzantine forms.

1173
· In Pisa Bonanno begins construction of the bell tower.

1174
· Using the language of the people, Valdo begins preaching about the need for the Church to return to apostolic purity and simplicity.

1174-78
· Fifth expedition of Barbarossa to Italy.

1174-84
· Rebuilding of the choir of Canterbury Cathedral (founded in 1070), after destruction by fire.

1176
· The league of City-States defeats the Emperor in Legnano.
· Building of the Cathedral of Notre-Dame in Strasbourg begins.
· Valdo founds the movement the "Poor of Christ" or "Poor of Lyon" which spreads to Switzerland, Northern Italy, Spain, Germany and Eastern Europe.

1178
· Benedetto Antelami sculpts the *Deposition* in the Cathedral of Parma; this was part of a pulpit which was destroyed.
· Building of the Abbey of Alcobaça begins.

1179
· Pietro Valdo visits Pope Alexander III.

1180
· Biduino sculpts the lintel of San Casciano a Settimo.

1180-90
· (about) Byzantine craftsmen decorate the walls of the Cathedral of Monreale with a cycle of mosaics.

1180-1223
· Philip II Augustus reigns in France.

1182
· Birth of Francis of Assisi.
· Consecration of the Cathedral of Notre-Dame in Paris.

1183
· The Peace of Constance grants freedom to the Lombard City-states.

1184
· The Council of Verona condemns the Waldensians as heretics.

1186
· Sixth expedition of Barbarossa to Italy for the marriage of his son Henry VI to Constance d'Hauteville.
· Henry VI is crowned King of Italy in Milan.

1187
· Saladin wins back Palestine and Jerusalem: the Christians only retain Saint John of Acre and Tyre (the remaining part of the Kingdom of Jerusalem) and, further North, Antioch and Tripoli.
· Construction of the Cistercian Abbey of Fossanova begins.

1189
· Philip II Augustus of France imposes the treaty of Azay-le-Rideau on Henry II of England.
· The crown of Sicily passes to Constance d'Hauteville, wife of the Emperor Henry VI.

1189-92
· Third crusade, proclaimed by Pope Gregory VIII; the major powers of the age participate: Frederick I Barbarossa, Philip Augustus King of France, Richard Coeur de Lyon King of England, William II King of Sicily.

1189-99
· Richard Coeur de Lyon reigns in England.

1190
· Death of Federick Barbarossa during the third crusade.
· Bonanno Pisano casts the bronze door of the Cathedral of Monreale; it portrays stories from the Old and New Testaments.
· (about) Bonanno Pisano casts the San Ranieri bronze door of the Cathedral of Pisa.

1191
· Philip II Augustus and John Coeur de Lyon conquer Saint John of Acre during the third crusade, but they fall out and fail to take back Jerusalem, which remains in Muslim hands along with almost the whole of Palestine.

1194
· Birth of Chiara of Assisi.
· After its destruction by fire the rebuilding of Chartres Cathedral begins.

1196
· Pope Celestine III approves the rule of the new community founded by Gioacchino da Fiore.

1197
· Death of Henry VI, followed by the double election in Germany of the Guelph, Otto IV of Brunswick, and the Ghibelline Philip of Swabia.

1198-1216
· Pontificate of Innocent III.

1199-1216
· Reign of John the Landless in England.

1200
· (about) Benedetto Antelami sculpts the Series of the Months in the Baptistery of Parma.

1202-04
· Fourth crusade initiated by Pope Innocent III and led by Baldwin of Flanders and Bonifacio del Monferrato. The Venetians, who financed the expedition, change the course of the crusaders to Constantinople.

1204
· The crusaders conquer Constantinople. Founding of the Latin Empire of the East.
· Guidetto begins construction of the facade of the Cathedral of San Martino in Lucca, rebuilt in 1060 at the behest of Anselmo da Baggio.

1208
· Consecration of the Abbey-church of Fossanova.

1210
· San Francis draws up the first rules for himself and his followers.
· The marble craftsmen Jacopo di Lorenzo and Cosma sculpt the portal of the Cathedral of Civita Castellana.

1211
· Work begins on construction of Rheims Cathedral.

1212
· Frederick II of Swabia is proclaimed King of Sicily.

1215
· The Dominican Order receives verbal approval from Innocent III.

1215-20
· (about) Birth of Nicola Pisano, probably in Apulia.

1215-32
· Cloister sculptures of San Giovanni in Laterano in Rome by the Vassalletto family of craftsmen.

1216
· Honorius III recognizes the Dominican Order.

1216-27
· Pontificate of Honorius III.

1219-27
· Building of the church of Sant'Andrea a Vercelli, probably the last work of Antelami.

1220
· Frederick II of Swabia is crowned emperor.

1221
· Construction begins on the Cathedral of Bourges, ushering in the Gothic Age.

1223
· Founding of the mendicant order of the Franciscans and minor friars.

1224-25
· Saint Francis composes the *Canticle of the Creatures*.

1225
· Birth of Thomas Aquinas.
· Work begins on the mosaic decoration of the dome of the Baptistery in Florence; it will be completed in the 14th century.
· Construction begins on the Southern arm of Saint John's Chapel in the Cathedral of Strasbourg, in the Gothic style.
· (about) Birth of Coppo di Marcovaldo in Florence.

1226
· Death of Francis of Assisi.

1227-41
· Pontificate of Gregory IX.

1228
· Bonaventura Berlinghieri is active in Lucca and is mentioned in a document of this date.
· Two years after the saint's death, construction begins on the Basilica of Saint Francis of Assisi.

1228-29
· Fifth crusade of Frederick II: the Emperor obtains Jerusalem by diplomatic treaty and is crowned king of the city.

1229
· First mention of Giunta Pisano.

1230
· Benedetto Antelami dies in Parma.
· Berlinghiero Berlinghieri paints the *Crucifix* in the Museum of Villa Guinigi in Lucca.
· The Treaty of San Germano between Frederick II and Gregory IX: Frederick is reconfirmed as ruler of the Empire and the Kingdom of Sicily.
· Gregory IX authorizes the Franciscans to accept the offerings of the faithful.
· (about) Decoration of the tympanum of the Western portal of the Cathedral of Strasbourg with the depiction of the *Death of the Virgin*.

1231
· Sculpture of the *Bust of Frederick II*, kept in the Museo Civico in Barletta.
· Frederick II draws up his code of political-administrative laws in the Constitutions of Melfi, whose main tenets are the formation of a centralized state and the submission of feudalities and the city-states.

1234-39
· Frederick II initiates the construction of the port of Capua, an example of the classicistic tendencies of his court.

1235
· Bonaventura Berlinghieri signs the altar-piece portraying Saint Francis and some episodes from his life, executed for the church of the same name in Pescia (Pistoia).

1237
· In the Battle of Cortenuova (Brescia), Frederick II defeats the Po city-states, which had just joined forces as the Lombarda and San Zenone Leagues.

1239
· Gregory IX excommunicates Frederick II, fearing that the emperor intends to take control of Rome and make it the capital of the Empire.

1240
· The D'Este familyis in power in Ferrara.
· (about) Birth of Cimabue in Florence.
· (about) Giunta Pisano paints the *Crucifix* now kept in the Museo di San Matteo in Pisa.
· (about) Decoration of the portal of the Virgin begins in the Cathedral of Rheims.

1240-50
· Castel del Monte is built near Andria.

1241
· On the Island of Giglio, Frederick II captures the cardinals who were on their way to the Council called by Gregory IX to depose the emperor.

1243-57
· Pontificate of Innocent IV.

1244
· Thomas Aquinas enters the Dominican Order.

1245
· (about) Birth of Arnolfo di Cambio in Colle Val d'Elsa (Siena).
· The General Council at Lyon, called by Innocent IV, deposes and excommunicates Frederick II.
· Seigniory of the Guelph Della Torre family in Milan.

1246-48
· Building of the Sainte-Chapelle, in the courtyard of the Palais Royal (today's Palais de Justice), in Paris; one of the first examples of full-blown Gothic.

1248
· (about) Birth of Giovanni Pisano in Pisa.
· Frederick II is defeated in Parma.

1248-54
· Sixth crusade proclaimed by Louis IX, King of France, against Egypt. The King, taken prisoner during the Battle of al-Mansūra, is released in exchange for a high ransom.

1249
· Enzo, the son of Frederick II, is defeated and taken prisoner by the Bolognese in the Battle of Fossallta, having come to his father's aid. He will die a prisoner in Bologna.

1250
· (about) Giunta Pisano executes the *Crucifix* in the church of San Domenico in Bologna.
· Death of Frederick II in Ferentino in Apulia.

1250-54
· Conrad IV succedes his father Frederick II as Emperor.

INDEX OF ARTISTS

The following is a list of the artists referred to in this volume in alphabetical order. Light numbers refer to pages where the artist is mentioned; italics to the title of an illustration; numbers in bold to a special focus on a masterpiece.